D0558872

International Events
and the Comparative Analysis of Foreign Policy

International Events and the Comparative Analysis of Foreign Policy

Edited by

Charles W. Kegley, Jr.
Gregory A. Raymond
Robert M. Rood
Richard A. Skinner

INTERNATIONAL RELATIONS SERIES NUMBER 4
PUBLISHED FOR THE Institute of International Studies

University of South Carolina

BY THE
UNIVERSITY OF SOUTH CAROLINA PRESS
Columbia, South Carolina

Copyright © University of South Carolina, 1975

FIRST EDITION

Published in Columbia, S.C., by the
University of South Carolina Press, 1975

Manufactured in the United States of America

Library of Congress Cataloging in Publication Data

Main entry under title:

International events and the comparative analysis of
  foreign policy.

  (International relations series ; no. 4)
  Bibliography: p.
  1. International relations—Research—Addresses,
essays, lectures.   I. Kegley, Charles W., ed.
II. South Carolina. University. Institute of International Studies.   III.   Series: International relations
series (Columbia, S. C.) ; no. 4.
JX1291.I47   327′.07′2   74–23206
ISBN 0–87249–333–4

Contents

Part I: State of the Field

Part II: Methodological Issues

Part III: Indicators of Foreign Policy Behavior

Part IV: Analyzing Foreign Policy Behavior

Tables

Figures

Foreword

The academic study of international relations has generated a flood of new ideas during the past decade about questions of theory and methodology. Particularly important has been the work of a group of scholars interested in clarifying the nature of foreign policy acts and the ways by which they might be analyzed with greater precision. In any discipline, of course, intellectual growth does not proceed in a straight line. This has been especially true in the field of international relations, where debates concerning the meaning of basic concepts have been frequent and prolonged. Disagreements have also arisen concerning the most appropriate methods of generating and analyzing data. The very richness of these debates and disagreements has created special difficulties for anyone who seeks to keep abreast of developments within the discipline, whether a beginning student or mature scholar.

This volume of essays is designed to provide a partial remedy for that confusion by presenting a series of papers that introduce the principal theoretical refinements on which the comparative analysis of foreign policy is based and offer some examples of the insights to which such analyses can lead. The editors and compilers of the volume are themselves active participants in the development of the literature in this field. As recent graduates who have come to intellectual maturity while this body of ideas was taking shape, they experienced the need for an overview of the field and they have drawn together a cross-section of writing from some of the leading contemporary contributors to its evolution in order to demonstrate how comparative analysis of events data can increase our understanding of foreign policy.

Charles W. Kegley and Robert M. Rood are faculty research associates of the Institute of International Studies at the University of South Carolina, and Gregory Raymond and Richard Skinner have been graduate research assistants in the Institute. This volume is the fourth in the series of major studies of international relations sponsored by the Institute. Within that series, it breaks new ground by focusing on theoretical dimensions of the study of foreign policy and it reflects the Institute's desire to promote the growth of international relations as an academic discipline by encouraging the timely dissemination of important ideas.

Columbia, S.C.　　　　　　　　D. BRUCE MARSHALL
1 November 1974　　　　　　　　*Associate Director*
　　　　　　　　　　　　　　　　Publications and Research
　　　　　　　　　　　　　　　　Institute of International Studies

Preface

After twenty-five years of bitter antagonism between the United States and mainland China, the world witnessed an American President sightseeing on the Great Wall. In late 1973 yet another war erupted between Arabs and Israelis. These and the countless other events occurring daily between nations form the subject matter of foreign policy analysis. For most of this century such research came under the rubric of diplomatic studies or current affairs and was generally the domain of the historian and the journalist. Their accounts enlightened the reader on the intricacies of a specific historical incident or provided insight into the thoughts of key figures. But no matter how rigorous the historian's method or entertaining the journalist's account, the products of their inquiries failed to provide a type of knowledge which could be applied irrespective of time, place, and observer. Increasingly, many students of foreign policy attributed this failure to the methods of their predecessors and began active appeals for the adoption of scientific methodology.

What began a decade and a half ago as a cry for the application of rigorous scientific investigative procedures to the analysis of foreign policy has now culminated in a vast and rapidly expanding research community dedicated to the empirical study of foreign policy. This transition from what was once a fad in research practice with fantastic hopes to a distinct and reputable field (Rosenau, Burgess, and Hermann 1973) was facilitated by a convergence of views among scholars on a shared analytic perspective—the comparative method—and the emergence of data regarding foreign policy behavior—events data—with which theories of external conduct could be tested. Termed the *comparative study of foreign policy* and *event interaction analysis*, respectively, the two fields developed in a symbiotic fashion: the data provided from events research provoked the need for scientific theory, while the theoretical efforts of nomothetically inclined thinkers such as Rosenau (1971) called for data with which pretheoretical insights might be empirically tested. Consequently, there has been a gradual tendency for the interests, activities, and identities of events researchers and comparativists to merge, so that currently the distinction between them has become blurred. Today, it is not surprising to find that many students of foreign policy are events data consumers; and most events data producers employ their data for the comparative investigation of interstate relations.

As the title of this volume indicates, it is this convergence of international events and the comparative analysis of foreign policy which serves to rationalize the organization of this book and to determine its scope and focus: the nature of scientific methodology, the observation and collection of data, the process of empirical generalization through data analysis, and the refinement of theory through policy prediction. These interrelated components of the scientific enterprise define the basic organizational structure of the volume. Rosenau's introductory essay describes several features of this process and anticipates the feasibility of building theory about external performance from this paradigm; he also introduces some of the major sociological aspects of the academic discipline itself which serve to facilitate or impede the prospects for achievement. Part II focuses upon the objectives of comparative inquiry and the research design problems that arise in the shift from hypothesis to observation. Part III discusses the use of events data in measurement as a means of moving from observation to generalization. Part IV centers upon the testing of generalizations in the attempt to build theory, while Part V both completes the circular process of inquiry and begins another spiral by dealing with theory application as a way of moving from theory to new hypotheses. The student is invited to begin his own foray into this exciting field with the data provided in Part VI. Hence the aim is to compile the necessary material for the advanced undergraduate or beginning graduate student to understand the current status and assumptions of the comparative study of foreign policy and to grasp the role he himself can play in its future development.

An underlying motivation for assembling this volume is that, despite the ever-growing attention being given to this new field, there is a serious communication lag concerning research that has been conducted or is currently under way. As the bibliography indicates, much of the work in this field is still unpublished, with the result that the dissemination of the products of the research movement is slow and scholars eager to learn about this type of analysis lack a handy compilation of current research. Moreover, until recently they had few basic texts at their disposal with which to introduce students to existing research monographs in the field. Consequently, this book is designed to serve as a primer on the current advances, conceptual and empirical, being made in the comparison of the political relations of nations, particularly through the use of events data.

In an effort to present this research in a comprehensive yet understandable manner, several leading scholars in the field were invited to summarize these activities. Five essays were commissioned to complement several previously published papers of particularly enduring quality. The topics presented here reflect our desire for a single volume unified by a conception of scientific research as a dynamic, circular process of inquiry. In this way, we hope to provide the instructor and the student with a text more pedagogically useful than a disjointed collection of essays would be.

None of the authors in this volume would purport to have provided solutions to the many problems confronted by analysts of foreign policy. But the essays presented here do suggest that the necessary building blocks of the effort have been obtained: we have a common research language, agreement on the important questions to be asked, the methods with which to address these questions, and a body of evidence. The challenge to current and future researchers is to advance the field from these first critical steps toward a mature discipline whose findings are cumulative and in which verifiable knowledge has replaced conventional wisdom and folklore.

No book is possible without the help of many individuals, and this volume is no exception. We wish to thank Richard L. Walker, director of the Institute of International Studies at the University of South Carolina; James G. Holland, Jr., associate director of the Institute; and D. Bruce Marshall, chairman of the Publications Committee of the Institute, for their willingness to support this project. For his confidence and cooperation, we dedicate this volume to Professor Walker, and also to the members of the Institute of International Studies. Secondly, we wish to thank the contributors for their generosity in sharing their research through the informal exchange of mimeographed papers. In particular, we appreciate the support of James N. Rosenau and his Inter-University Comparative Foreign Policy study group, and the scholars at over ninety United States and foreign academic institutions who are members of the Foreign Policy and International Events Section of the International Studies Association. Without their research activities there would be no "international events and comparative analysis of foreign policy" field to describe. Third, we thank our students, instructors, and colleagues for stimulating our thinking and providing us with the intellectual feedback necessary for the organization and presentation of the volume. And finally, we are grateful to many people who assisted with the numerous editorial and clerical chores. It goes without saying that our wives and friends deserve untold gratitude for tolerating our eccentricities during the development of this book.

Part I
State of the Field

1

Comparative Foreign Policy: One-Time Fad, Realized Fantasy, and Normal Field

JAMES N. ROSENAU

This chapter was originally written early in 1967, and the invitation to update it for this volume provides a useful opportunity to assess progress in the comparative study of foreign policy. In order to facilitate such an assessment, I have left the original version intact, adding this initial paragraph and a postscript which revises some of the observations made eight years ago and answers some of the questions then posed in the light of subsequent developments. The reader can thus compare the current state of inquiry with that of eight years ago and evaluate whether or not the intervening period has been one of progress. My own evaluation, presented in the postscript, is summarized in the alterations in the original title of the article.

All signs are pointing in the same direction: as a television commercial might describe it, "Comparative Foreign Policy is coming on strong for the 1970's!" A few undergraduate and graduate courses with this title are

This chapter was originally published as "Comparative Foreign Policy: Fad, Fantasy, or Field?" in *International Studies Quarterly* 12 (September 1968) : 296–329. Copyright © 1968 by Sage Publications, Inc., Beverly Hills, Calif. An introductory paragraph and a postscript have been added to the original version. Reprinted by permission of the author and the publisher. The original paper was presented to the Conference Seminar of the Committee on Comparative Politics, The University of Michigan, on 10 March 1967, prior to publication. (Rosenau 1968a) now being taught.[1] Several conferences on allied topics have recently been held, the most recent being the occasion at the University of Michigan for which this paper was written, and a couple of these have even resulted in the appearance of publications on the subject (Farrell 1966; McKay 1966; Rosenau 1967a). Occasionally a paper is delivered[2] or book published (Waltz 1967; Hanrieder 1967a) which is devoted to the subject, and a perusal of recent lists of dissertations in progress reveals that other research findings along this line are soon to become available.[3] Then there is perhaps the surest sign of all: textbook publishers, those astute students of trends in Academe, have discerned a stirring in this direction and are busily drumming up manuscripts that can be adopted as texts when the trend achieves discipline-wide acceptance.

In sum, it seems more than likely that in the coming years something called comparative foreign policy will occupy a prominent place in the teaching of political science and in the research of political scientists. But is such a development desirable? Is the phrase "comparative foreign policy" a contentless symbol to which students of international politics pay lip service in order to remain *au courant* with their colleagues elsewhere in the discipline? Does it stand for a scientific impulse that can never be realized because foreign policy phenomena do not lend themselves to comparative analysis? Or does it designate an important and distinguishable set of empirical phenomena that can usefully be subjected to extended examination? Is comparative foreign policy, in short, a fad, a fantasy, or a field?

In some respects it is all of these, and the purpose of this paper is to identify the fad and fantasy dimensions in order to minimize confusion and contradiction as the field evolves. Although the field is barely in its infancy, an assessment of its inception and an attempt to identify its boundaries and problems can, even at this early stage, lessen the growing pains that lie ahead.

The Sources of Reorientation

That the fad, the fantasy, and the field are all of recent origin can be readily demonstrated. Traditionally, the analysis of foreign policy phe-

---

[1] For example, at Northwestern University during the 1965–66 academic year.

[2] Cf. the papers prepared for the International Relations panels at the Annual Meeting of the American Political Science Association, September 1966.

[3] In the 1966 listing (*American Political Science Review* 60: 786–91), nine dissertations carried titles that suggested research on topics involving the comparative study of foreign policy.

nomena has consisted of a policy-oriented concern with particular situations faced by specific nations. Thus the single case, limited in time by its importance to the relevant actors and in scope by the immediacy of its manifest repercussions, has dominated the literature for decades (Rosenau 1966, pp. 31–37). Attempts to contrast two or more empirical cases have been distinct exceptions and have been narrowly confined to the problem of whether democracies or dictatorships are more likely to conduct themselves effectively in the international arena (Friedrich 1938). Even those political scientists of the early postwar era who explicitly sought to render foreign policy analysis more systematic by focusing on decision-making processes did not move in a comparative direction. The decision-making approach to foreign policy called attention to a host of important variables and greatly diminished the long-standing tendency to posit national actors as abstract entities endowed with human capacities and qualities. But in demanding that foreign policy be analyzed from the perspective of concrete and identifiable decision-makers, the approach also tended to preclude examination of the possibility that the perspectives of decision-makers in different societies might be similar, or at least comparable. Thus, throughout the 1950's and well into the 1960's, the newly discovered decision-making variables served to improve the quality of the case histories rather than to replace them with new modes of analysis (Rosenau 1967d).

To be sure, the immediate postwar period did not lack attempts to generalize about the processes whereby any society formulates and conducts its foreign policy. In addition to Richard C. Snyder and others who pioneered in decision-making analysis (Snyder, Bruck, and Sapin 1954; Deutsch 1957; Frankel 1959; Furniss 1954), several more eclectic observers sought to specify the variables that operate wherever foreign policy phenomena are found (Gross 1954; Halle 1962; London 1949; Marshall 1954; Modelski 1954), and a few textbook editors also undertook to bring together in one volume analyses of how different countries made and sustained their external relations (Macridis 1958; Buck and Travis 1957). In none of the more abstract formulations, however, was the possibility of engaging in comparative analysis seriously considered. Foreign policy variables were identified and discussed as if they operated in identical ways in all societies, and the hypothetical society abstracted therefrom was described in terms of a multiplicity of examples drawn largely from the "lessons" of modern international history.[4] The appease-

[4] London (1949, pp. 99–153) also presented separate descriptions of policymaking in Washington, London, Paris, Berlin, and Moscow, but these were not subjected to comparative analysis.

ment at Munich, the betrayal at Pearl Harbor, the success of the Marshall Plan—these are but a few of the incidents that served as the empirical basis for the traditional model in which nations were posited as serving (or failing to serve) their national interests through foreign policies that balance ends with means and commitments with capabilities. That the lessons of history might be variously experienced by different policy-making systems was not accounted for in the abstract models, and thus, to repeat, they were no more oriented toward comparative analysis than were the case histories that constituted the mainstream of foreign policy research.

Nor did the textbook editors take advantage of the opportunity afforded by the accumulation of materials about the external behavior of different countries and present concluding chapters that attempted to identify the similarities and differences uncovered by the separate, but juxtaposed, analyses of several policymaking systems. Ironically, in fact, the one text that used the word *comparative* in connection with the study of a foreign policy also explicitly raised doubts about the applicability of this form of analysis: in the first edition of this work the introductory chapter, "Comparative Study of Foreign Policy," written by Almond (1958), noted the "lack of the most elementary knowledge" about foreign policy phenomena and concluded that therefore "it will be some time before rigorous and systematic comparison becomes possible." Even more ironically, the comparable chapter of the second edition of the same text, written four years later by Thompson and Macridis, went even further and rejected the premises of comparative analysis on the grounds that foreign policy variables involve a "complexity [that] makes a mockery of the few 'scientific' tools we have," thereby rendering any attempt to generalize on the basis of comparative assessments "a hopeless task" (Macridis 1962, pp. 26–27).

The existence of this attitude of hopelessness and of the traditional inclination toward case histories raises the question of why pronounced signs of a major reorientation had appeared with increasing frequency in the mid-1960's. The answer would seem to be that two unrelated but major trends, one historical and the other intellectual, converged at this point; and while neither alone would have stimulated the impulse to compare foreign policy phenomena, their coincidence in time served to generate strong pressures in that direction.

Let us look first at the intellectual factors. It seems clear, in retrospect, that the rapid emergence of a heavy emphasis upon comparison in the analysis of domestic politics served as a potent impetus to reorientation in the study of foreign policy. The turning point for the field of comparative politics can be traced to the mid-1950's, when structural-functional analysis was first applied to political phenomena (Almond 1956), an event that in turn led to the formation of the Committee on Comparative Politics of the Social Science Research Council and the publication of its many pioneering volumes. These works highlighted the idea, explicitly set forth in the first chapter of the first volume, that certain key functions must be performed if a political system is to persist, and that these functions can be performed by a wide variety of structures (Almond 1960). Whatever the limitations of structural-functional analysis—and there are many (Nagel 1961, pp. 520–35; Dowse 1966)—this central premise provided a way for students of domestic processes to compare seemingly dissimilar phenomena. Until structural-functional analysis was made part of the conceptual equipment of the field, the most salient dimensions of political systems were their unique characteristics, and there seemed to be little reason to engage in comparison, except perhaps to show how different governmental forms give rise to dissimilar consequences. Indeed, until the mid-1950's it was quite commonplace to show that even similar governmental forms can give rise to dissimilar consequences. "Look at this Western parliament and contrast it with that non-Western legislature," a student at that time would observe with a sense of satisfaction. "They both go through the same procedures, but how diverse are the results!"

Then the breakthrough occurred. Structural-functional analysis lifted sights to a higher level of generalization and put all political systems on an analytic par. Thereafter, tracing differences was much less exhilarating than probing for functional equivalents, and students of domestic politics were quick to respond to the challenge and reorient their efforts. Since the mid-1950's political scientists have turned out a seemingly endless series of articles and books committed to comparative analysis—to a delineation of similarities and differences upon which empirically based models of the political process could be founded. A spate of comparative materials on governance in underdeveloped polities was the vanguard of this analytic upheaval, but its repercussions were by no means confined to Africa, Asia, and Latin America. No type of system or area of the world was viewed as an inappropriate subject for comparative analysis. Even the two systems which an earlier generation of political scientists viewed as polar extremes, the United States and the Soviet Union, were considered as fit for comparison and as apt subjects to a test of a "theory of convergence" (Brzezinski and Huntington 1964). Similarly, while the

West/non-West distinction had been regarded as representing mutually exclusive categories, it was now treated as descriptive of two segments of the same continuum of whatever class of political phenomena was being examined (Huntington 1965). Nor was there any reluctance to break systems down and look at only one of their components: political parties were compared (LaPalombara and Weiner 1966), and so were political cultures (Almond and Verba 1963), oppositions (Dahl 1966), revolutionary movements (Johnson 1966), Communist regimes (Tucker 1967), bureaucracies (LaPalombara 1963; Heady 1966), constitutional subsystems (Jacob and Vines 1965; Munger 1966; Froman 1967), military elites (Janowitz 1964; Johnson 1962; Fisher 1963), and so on, through all the major institutions, processes, and personnel of polities. As the comparative movement gained momentum, moreover, it generated efforts to clarify the methodological problems posed by the new orientation (Merritt and Rokkan 1966; Kalleberg 1966; Neumann 1957, 1959; Haas 1962; Eckstein 1964), and more importantly, to provide comparable data for most or all of the polities extant (Banks and Textor 1963; Russett et al. 1964). Like all major movements, the trend toward comparative analysis also evoked protests and denials of its legitimacy (Wolf-Phillips 1964).

If the ultimate purpose of political inquiry is the generation of tested and/or testable theory, then this upheaval in comparative politics had already begun to yield solid results by the mid-1960's. One could look only with wonderment upon the progress that had occurred in a decade's time: not only were data being gathered and processed in entirely new ways, but a variety of stimulating, broad-gauged, systematic, and empirically based models of domestic political processes in generalized types of polities had also made their way into literature (Almond and Powell 1966; Apter 1965; Hartz 1964; Holt and Turner 1966; Organski 1965). Curiously, however, foreign policy phenomena were not caught up in these tides of change. None of the new empirical findings, much less any of the new conceptual formulations, dealt with the responses of polities and their institutions, processes, and personnel to international events and trends. For reasons suggested elsewhere (Rosenau 1969a, pp. 1–17), everything was compared but foreign policy phenomena, and only belatedly have students of comparative politics even acknowledged the need to make conceptual allowance for the impact of international variables upon domestic processes.[5]

[5] The conference that occasioned this paper and the one that led to the volume edited by Farrell (1966) are among the few efforts to examine national-international

The recent signs of interest in comparative foreign policy, in other words, arise out of the work of students of international politics and foreign policy and not from an extension of the models and inquiries of those who focus on national or subnational phenomena. As indicated, however, it seems doubtful whether the former would have become interested in comparative analysis if the latter had not successfully weathered a decade of upheaval. This spillover thus constitutes the prime intellectual source of the reorientation toward comparative foreign policy: in large measure the reorientation stemmed from the desire of students of international processes to enjoy success similar to that of their colleagues in an adjoining field.[6]

The other major source of the reorientation is to be found in certain postwar historical circumstances that coincided with the upheaval in the field of comparative politics. At least two trends in world politics would appear to have attracted the attention of students of foreign policy to the virtues of comparative analysis. Perhaps the more important of these was the proliferation of nations that occurred during the decade from 1955 to 1965 as a result of the withdrawal of colonial powers in Africa and Asia. Not only did foreign policy phenomena also proliferate at a comparable rate during this period (there being more nations engaging in foreign policy actions), but more importantly, the recurrence of similar patterns was far more discernible and impressive in a world of some 120 nations than it had been when half this number comprised

---

relationships organized by students of domestic political systems. For another belated acknowledgment of the relevance of international variables, see Almond and Powell (1966, pp. 9, 203–4). Actually, in all fairness it should be noted that some years ago Almond did acknowledge that studies of "the functioning of the domestic political system . . . have commonly neglected the importance of the international situation in affecting the form of the political process and the content of domestic public policy. . . . We do not know until this day whether the differences in the functioning of the multiparty systems of the Scandinavian countries and those of France and Italy are to be attributed to internal differences in culture, economics, and political and governmental structure, or whether they are attributable to the differences in the 'loading' of these systems with difficult and costly foreign policy problems, or whether both and in what proportions" (1958, pp. 4–5). In his ensuing pioneering works on domestic systems, however, Almond did not follow the line of his own reasoning. Not even his highly general structural-functional model of the political process, presented two years later in *The Politics of the Developing Areas* (1960), made conceptual room for the impact of international variables or the functions served by political activities oriented toward a system's external environment.

[6] For evidence that the foreign policy field was not the only one to experience the spillover from the comparative movement initiated by students of national and subnational politics, see Useem and Grimshaw (1966, pp. 46–51), who outline developments that have recently culminated in the appointment of a new committee on comparative sociology by the Social Science Research Council.

the international system. Conversely, the larger the international system grew, the less did concentration upon unique patterns seem likely to unravel the mysteries of international life. Stated differently, as more and more nations acquired independence and sought to come to terms with neighbors and great powers, the more did contrasts between two or more of them loom large as the route to comprehension of world politics. The decolonization of sub-Sahara Africa was especially crucial in this respect. The resulting nations were so similar in size, cultural heritage, social composition, political structure, and stage of economic development, and the problems they faced in the international system were thus so parallel, that the analysis of their foreign policies virtually compelled comparison. At least this would seem to be the most logical explanation for the fact that many of the early efforts to derive theoretical propositions about foreign policy from the comparative analysis of empirical materials focused on Africa in particular (McKay 1966; Thiam 1965) and underdeveloped polities in general (Kissinger 1966).

The advent of the thermonuclear era and the emergence of Red China as a budding and recalcitrant superpower are illustrative of another historical trend that has fostered a reorientation in foreign policy analysis, namely, the emergence of problems that are worldwide in scope. As more and more situations have arisen toward which all national actors must necessarily take a position, analysts with a policy-oriented concern have become increasingly inclined to juxtapose and contrast the reactions and policies of nations that they previously treated as single cases. Analyses of the 1963 nuclear test ban treaty, the continuing problem of nuclear proliferation, and the Chinese acquisition of a nuclear capability are obvious examples. Indeed, the worldwide implications of China's emergence recently resulted in what is probably the first work to focus on an immediate policy problem by analyzing how a number of different nations are inclined to respond to it (Halpern 1965).

The Study of Comparative Foreign Policy and the Comparative Study of Foreign Policy

Reorientation of analytic modes never occurs without a period of transition and adjustment that is often slow and difficult. Apparently the study of foreign policy is not to be an exception. Some of the early changes suggest that the reorientation is based partly upon a headlong and ill-considered rush to get aboard the comparative bandwagon. Perhaps because the intellectual and historic factors that have fostered change converged and reinforced each other in such a short span of time, little thought has been given to what comparison of foreign policy phenomena entails. "After all," some students of foreign policy seem to say, "the comparative people are doing it, why shouldn't we?" What "it" is in this context, however, is rarely examined and is often assumed to involve no more than the juxtaposition of the foreign policy phenomena of two or more systems. What aspects of foreign policy should be compared, how they should be compared, why they should be compared, whether they can be compared—questions such as these are not raised. Rather, having presumed that simply by juxtaposing such phenomena an endeavor called "comparative foreign policy" is established, many analysts proceed in the accustomed manner and examine each unit of the juxtaposed materials separately as a case history.

A good illustration of the continuing predisposition to settle for juxtaposition without comparison is provided by the aforementioned work on how more than sixteen different nations are inclined to respond to Communist China (Halpern 1965). Despite the abundance of comparable material made available by the common focus of the various chapters, neither the editor nor the authors saw fit to contrast systematically the relative potencies of the variables underlying responses to China. Instead, each of the sixteen substantive chapters deals with the policies of a different country or region toward China, and the editor's introductory and concluding chapters are concerned, respectively, with presenting an overview of China itself and summarizing all the differences that were revealed to underlie policies toward it. In effect, the work consists of sixteen separate studies conveniently brought together in one place (Rosenau 1967e).

In short, comparative foreign policy has to some extent become a new label for an old practice. It is in this sense—in the sense that reference is made to comparative analysis without adherence to the procedures it requires—that some of the recent signs of reorientation are essentially no more than a passing fad, an emulation of form rather than of substance. Even worse, to the extent that the label is more than an empty symbol of modernity, it has been invested with misleading connotations. An unfortunate tendency, perhaps also stemming from ill-considered emulation, has developed whereby comparative foreign policy is viewed as a body of knowledge, as a subject to be explored, as a field of inquiry. Scholars and textbook publishers alike tend to refer to the study of comparative foreign policy as if there existed in the real world a set of phenomena that could be so labeled. Scholars speak of engaging in research on comparative foreign policy, and publishers talk of issuing eight or ten paperbacks as their comparative foreign policy series. Such nomenclature is unfortunate because the benefits of comparative analysis cannot be enjoyed if it is conceived in terms of subject matter rather than in methodological terms. Comparison is a method, not a body of knowledge. Foreign policy phenomena—and not comparative foreign policy phenomena—comprise the subject matter to be probed, and these can be studied in a variety of ways, all of them useful for certain purposes and irrelevant to other purposes. The comparative method is only one of these ways, and it is not necessarily the best method for all purposes. It is most useful with respect to the generation and testing of propositions about foreign policy behavior that apply to two or more political systems. Only by identifying similarities and differences in the external behavior of more than one nation can analysis move beyond the particular case to higher levels of generalization.[7] On the other hand, if the researcher is concerned with the processes of only a single system, then the comparative method may not be as valuable as the case history.[8]

Strictly speaking, therefore, it makes a difference whether one defines oneself as engaged in the comparative study of foreign policy or in the study of comparative foreign policy. The former, it is argued here, is a legitimate and worthwhile enterprise that may well lead to the formation of a disciplined field of inquiry, whereas the latter is an ambiguous label that serves to perpetuate a fad rather than to establish a field.

Still another kind of confusion has arisen out of the initial burst of enthusiasm for a more systematic approach to the analysis of foreign policy phenomena, namely, a tendency to posit such phenomena as encompassing the entire range of actions and interactions through which the interdependence of nations is sustained. Just as this ever-increasing interdependence has stimulated analysts to look more carefully at foreign policy, so it has spurred a greater concern with linkages between national and international political systems. Also referred to as "transnational politics" or "national-international interdependencies," these linkages are seen as comprising all the ways in which the functioning of

---

[7] For a discussion of the different levels of generalization at which the comparative analysis of political systems can be undertaken, see Tucker (1967), pp. 246–54.

[8] Under special circumstances, however, it is possible to apply the comparative method to a single system. If certain conditions remain constant from one point in time to another, then variables pertinent to the one system can be contrasted and assessed in terms of their operation at different historical junctures. For an extended discussion and application of this procedure, which has been designated as quantitative historical comparison, see Rosenau (1968c).

each type of political system is a consequence of the other (Rosenau 1969b). While the foreign policy and linkage approaches overlap in important ways, they are identical. The latter is broader than the former and can be viewed as subsuming it. Foreign policy phenomena comprise certain kinds of linkages, those in which governments relate themselves to all or part of the international system through the adoption of purposeful stance toward it, but there are other major kinds in which the links may be fashioned by nongovernmental actors or by the unintentional consequences of governmental action. These other kinds of linkages can, of course, be highly relevant to the formulation, conduct, and consequences of foreign policy, but they emanate from and are sustained by a set of processes that are analytically separable from the processes of foreign policy. Yet, impressed by the extent to which national systems have become pervaded by external stimuli, some analysts tend to emphasize the fact that in responding to these stimuli the national system is responding to elements "foreign" to it, an emphasis which leads to the erroneous equation of national-international linkages with foreign policy phenomena.[9]

Tracing the Outlines of a Field

To note that foreign policy phenomena involve governmental undertakings directed toward the external environment neither justifies treating them as a separate field of inquiry nor indicates where the boundaries of such a field lie. While it is possible to argue that the comparative study of foreign policy is a subfield of political science because many political scientists research such matters and see themselves as engaged in a common enterprise when they do so, plainly a field must have an intellectual identity apart from the activities of its practitioners. For a field to exist, presumably it must have its own discipline—its own subject matter, its own point of view, and its own theory. In the absence of a subject matter with an internal coherence of its own, of a viewpoint that structures the subject matter in unique ways, and of a body of theoretical propositions that have not been or cannot be derived from any other way of structuring the subject, researchers can never be sure whether in fact they are engaging in a common enterprise. Under such circumstances, they may actually be working on highly diverse problems that share only the labels attached to them. What is regarded as the "field" may be no more than a composite of several different enterprises that overlap in some

[9] See Hanrieder (1967a), and my critique of this article (1967b).

respects but that have distinctive subject matters, viewpoints, and propositions of their own.

Thus it is conceivable that the comparative study of foreign policy is not a field at all. Perhaps the search for its subject matter, viewpoint, and propositions will yield the conclusion that it is best viewed as a composite of national and international politics—as the appropriate concern of two fields, one treating foreign policy phenomena as dependent variables in the operation of national political systems, and the other, as independent variables in the operation of international political systems. Needless to say, it would make matters much easier if a separate field could not be delineated and comparative studies of foreign policy could be assessed in terms of the concepts and standards of either the national or international politics fields. Much preliminary conceptualization and argumentation could thereby be avoided, and analysts could push on to the main task of gathering data and advancing comprehension.

Tempting as such a conclusion may be, however, it must be rejected. The fact is that the national and international fields do not encompass all the phenomena to which the label "foreign policy" might be attached. No matter how much the viewpoints of these fields may be stretched, some phenomena remain unexplained. Reflection about the nature of these phenomena, moreover, reveals a subject matter that is internally coherent, that is distinctive in its point of view, and that is at least capable of generating its own unique body of theory.

Stated most succinctly, the phenomena that are not otherwise accounted for, and that we shall henceforth regard as the subject matter of the field of foreign policy, are those that reflect an association between variations in the behavior of nations and variations in their external environments. The distinctive point of view of this field is that inquiry must focus on the association between the two sets of variations and that this association can only be comprehended if it is examined and assessed under a variety of conditions. The theoretical propositions unique to the field are those that predict the association between the two sets of variations rather than only the behavior of the national actor or only the events in its environment.

Let us first look more closely at the subject matter of the field and indicate those aspects which render it internally coherent. Thus far we have loosely referred to foreign policy phenomena as if their nature was self-evident. Obviously, an enumeration of the major phenomena encompassed by this terminology is necessary if an assessment is to be made of whether they constitute a coherent body of data. Such an enumeration seems best begun with the premise that at the heart of foreign policy analysis is a concern with sequences of interaction, perceptual or behavioral, which span national boundaries and which unfold in three basic stages. The first, or initiatory, stage involves the activities, conditions, and influences—human and nonhuman—that stimulate nations to undertake efforts to modify circumstances in their external environments. The second, or implementive, stage consists of the activities, conditions, and influences through which the stimuli of the initiatory stage are translated into purposeful actions directed at modifying objects in the external environment. The third, or responsive, stage denotes the activities, conditions, and influences that comprise the reactions of the objects of the modification attempts.[10] The three stages so defined encompass, respectively, the independent, intervening, and dependent variables of foreign policy analysis.

The independent variables can be usefully divided into two major types, those internal to the actor that initiates a foreign policy undertaking[11] and those external to it. The former include any human or nonhuman activities, conditions, and influences operative on the domestic scene that stimulate governmental officials to seek, on behalf of the national actor, to preserve or alter some aspect of the international system. Examples of internal independent variables are elections, group conflicts, depleted oil reserves, geographic insularity, demands for higher tariffs, historic value orientations, a lack of societal unity, executive-legislative frictions, and so on, through all the diverse factors

[10] This three-stage formulation of foreign policy sequences derives from a conception, elaborated elsewhere, which posits certain kinds of efforts to modify behavior, together with the modifications that do or do not subsequently ensue, as the essence of political behavior (Rosenau 1963).

[11] The use of the word "undertaking" throughout is intended to emphasize that by "foreign policy" is meant considerably more than mere pronouncements indicating present or future lines of action. Such a designation helps to remind us that foreign policy can arise out of complex sources and require the mobilization of complex resources as well as lengthy and continuous efforts to bring about modifications of situations and conditions in the external environment. Stated differently, it seems insufficient to describe foreign policy solely in decisional terms. The central unit of action is too multi-dimensional to be seen as merely a choice that officials make among conflicting alternatives. By the time officials have mobilized resources in support of their decisions and coped with the responses of those toward whom the decisions are directed, decision-making is no longer enough to describe the action in which the analyst is interested. For officials to translate the stimuli to external behavior into behavior intended to be effective externally requires a vast undertaking that encompasses many decisions by many people. Hence it seems desirable to use nomenclature that is descriptive of the complexity and scope of the behavior being examined.

that contribute to national life and that can thereby serve as sources of foreign policy. External independent variables also include human and nonhuman activities, conditions, and influences, but these occur abroad and operate as foreign policy stimuli by serving as the objects that officials seek to preserve or alter through their undertakings. Diplomatic incidents, deteriorating economies, crop failures, military buildups, elections, and historic enmities are but a few of the many diverse circumstances abroad that might stimulate official action. Obviously, foreign policy undertakings cannot be completely divorced either from the society out of which they emanate or from the circumstances abroad toward which they are directed, so that some external and internal independent variables will be present in every undertaking, albeit the mix of the two types may vary considerably from one undertaking to the next.

The intervening variables in foreign policy analysis are hardly less extensive. They include not only any attitudes, procedures, capabilities, and conflicts that shape the way in which governmental decision-makers and agencies assess the initiatory stimuli and decide how to cope with them, but they also embrace any and all of the resources, techniques, and actions that may affect the way in which the decisions designed to preserve or modify circumstances in the international system are carried out. The priority of values held by officials; their tolerance for ambiguous information; their capacity for admitting past errors; their training and analytic skills; the hierarchical structure of their decision-making practices; the rivalry of agencies for money, power, and prestige; the administrative procedures employed in the field; the readiness to threaten the use of military force and the availability of men and matériel to back up the threats; the appropriateness of propaganda techniques; and the flexibility of foreign aid programs are examples of the many intervening variables that can operate in foreign policy undertakings.

The dependent variables comprising the responsive stage are equally complex and extensive. They include the activities, attitudes, relationships, institutions, capacities, and conditions in the international system that are altered (or not altered) or preserved (or not preserved) as a result of the foreign policy undertakings directed toward them. As in the case of the independent variables, the dependent variables can be divided into two major types, those that involve an alteration or preservation of behavior internal to the object of the foreign policy undertaking and those that pertain to the object's changed or unchanged external behavior. Again a number of obvious examples can be cited. The readiness of another actor to enter into and/or conclude negotiations, the inclination to comply with or resist demands for support on issues in the United Nations, and the strengthening or weakening of an alliance exemplify external dependent variables. The ability or inability to put armies into the field as a consequence of military assistance, the continuance or downfall of a hostile government, and the emergence of a new social structure or the persistence of an old one as a result of a multifaceted foreign aid program are illustrative of circumstances that would be treated as internal dependent variables whenever they become the focus of foreign policy undertakings.

The field of foreign policy is thus seen to cover a vast range of phenomena. Circumstances can arise whereby virtually every aspect of local, national, and international politics may be part of the initiatory or responsive stage of the foreign policy process. Indeed, the foregoing examples indicate that students of foreign policy may often be led by their subject matter to move beyond political science to investigate phenomena in the other social sciences. They may even find themselves investigating phenomena in the physical sciences. This might occur, for example, if the foreign policy undertakings of interest aim to modify the external environment by compensating for depleted oil reserves. To comprehend the behavior of the national actor and the resistance or compliance of the actors abroad whose oil deposits make them the objects of modification attempts, investigators must acquire some familiarity with the geology, technology, and economy of discovering, mining, and transporting oil.[12]

Yet, despite its breadth of coverage, the subject matter of the foreign policy field is internally coherent. All the phenomena of interest to foreign policy analysts acquire structure and coherence through their concern with the three stages of the interaction process through which national actors purposefully relate themselves to the international system. If individual, group, organizational, or societal phenomena are not relevant to one of the stages of a particular foreign policy undertaking, then the analyst does not investigate them. A vast range of phenomena may fall within the scope of his concerns, but they always do so in a

---

[12] Of course, this is not to say that the individual student of foreign policy should or can be so broad-gauged as to be able to handle all the phenomena that fall within his purview. We have been tracing the outlines of a field to be probed by many persons and not of a research design to be implemented by one. Plainly the diversity and range of materials encompassed by the field are too great for one analyst to master fully. On the other hand, the individual researcher must be capable of communicating with the many types of specialists to whom he may have to turn for guidance on those aspects of undertakings that lie outside his competence.

specific context—that of whether variations in the initiatory and implementive stages can be related to variations in the responsive stage. Often,
to be sure, the analyst may find that the two sets of variations are unrelated to each other. Some, perhaps many, foreign policy undertakings
are totally ineffective and thus do not reflect an association in the two
sets of variations. The internal coherence of the subject matter of a
field, however, derives from logical possibilties and not from empirical
realities. It is the legitimacy of the search for, not the fact of, association
between the two sets of variations that renders foreign policy phenomena
internally coherent.

This is not to deny that the subject matter of the foreign policy field
overlaps many other fields at many points. As already indicated, the
phenomena encompassed by the initiatory and implementive stages can
be of considerable concern to students of national politics, just as those
comprising the responsive stage can be highly relevant to the analysis of
international politics. Furthermore, variations in any one of the stages
may also be related to variations in sequences of behavior that span national boundaries but are not part of either of the other two stages.
Foreign policy undertakings do have unintended consequences for social,
economic, and political life, and to the extent that they do, the phenomena of the field become central to these other disciplines. Yet notwith-
standing such overlap, the foreign policy analyst structures his subject
matter in such a way as to distinguish it from that of any other field.
He is interested in the entire relationship that national actors establish
with their external environments and not in only one segment of it.
None of the three stages has any meaning for him by itself. The characteristics of each stage hold his attention only insofar as they may be
associated with the characteristics of the other two. For him, foreign
policy becomes intelligible only to the extent that its sources, contents,
and consequences are considered jointly. This is the distinctive viewpoint
of the field. No other field concerns itself with the association between
variables on both sides of national boundaries. The phenomena em-
braced by this association are the ones that always remain unexplained
even after the fields of national and international politics are stretched
to their limits. Students of national (or comparative) politics have no
theoretical justification for sustaining an interest in foreign policy once
the behavioral sequences it initiates are extended into the external environment. Although slow to make theoretical allowance for the point,
they do have a vital concern with the internal consequences of the
processes of foreign policy formulation and with the feedback effects

that may result from the alterations which foreign policy undertakings bring about in the external environment. The responsive stage itself, however, lies outside the scope of their field. Similarly, nothing in the theoretical foundations of international politics provides students of that field with justification for probing the sources of foreign policy that are located within national actors or the response to foreign policy undertakings that are confined to the target society and do not become foreign policy initiatives on the part of that society. Theories of international politics focus on the interactions of national actors and not on the sources or consequences of interaction which are not part of previous or subsequent interactions.

Although the problems posed by the third requirement for the existence of a field, a unique body of theoretical propositions, are discussed at greater length in a later section, it can be seen from the foregoing that the study of foreign policy also meets this condition. Propositions about the association between variations in the behavior of nations and variations in their external environments cannot be derived from any other field of inquiry. Foreign policy theory necessarily borrows from theories of local and national politics in order to manipulate properly the internal independent variables of the initiatory stage, the intervening variables of the implementive stage, and the internal dependent variables of the responsive stage. It must also rely on theories of international politics for guidance in manipulating the external independent and dependent variables of the initiatory and responsive stages. Yet, by virtue of combining theory about domestic and international processes, foreign policy theory is neither domestic nor international theory. It bears the same relationship to these allied fields as social psychological theory does to psychology on the one hand and sociology on the other.[13] Like social psychology, it alone consists of propositions that relate the behavior of an actor both to its own functioning and to its environment. The list of foreign policy theorists is not long and contains no names comparable to Lewin, Hovland, Newcomb, Asch, or Festinger in social psychology, but presumably this is due to the fact that the reorientation toward the comparative analysis of foreign policy has just begun, rather than to an inherent inability of the field to support its own unique body of theory.

---

[13] For a discussion of how the distinctiveness of social psychology is not diminished despite the large extent to which it borrows from psychology and sociology, see Newcomb (1950) and Deutsch and Krauss (1965).

Some Underlying Assumptions

Having traced in bold strokes the outline of the field, some finer touches are in order. A number of problems require further discussion. Perhaps the most important of these is the question of why the responsive stage must be part of foreign policy analysis. Why not treat governmental decisions as the dependent variables and bypass the responsive stage? After all, it might be argued, aspects of the international system are being taken into account as external independent variables; why must they also be regarded as dependent variables? If the focus is on the national actor in relation to its environment, why is it necessary to investigate the consequences of foreign policy undertakings for other actors? Furthermore, how is one to know whether the presumed or modified behavior that constitutes the responsive stage is in fact a response to the foreign policy undertaking being examined? Are there not insurmountable methodological problems inherent in the task of separating responses to external influences from behavior generated by other factors?

A similar line of questioning can be pursued with respect to the initiatory and implementive stages. Since foreign policy undertakings are being treated as purposeful, why not regard the governmental decisions that launch them as the independent variables and bypass the initiatory stage? Why not focus on the purposeful behavior directly, rather than positing it as an intervening process? If the interaction of national actors and their environments constitutes the subject matter of the field, why does not its scope include unplanned actions as well as purposeful ones? How does one assess the relative potencies of all the independent variables that may be operative as a source of a foreign policy undertaking? Indeed, how does one determine whether the undertaking is a consequence of the external and internal independent variables being examined rather than of the decision-making process that launched it.

Another set of problems posed by the suggested outline concerns the nature of foreign policy theory. What are the main questions that such theory is designed to answer? Are not all the interesting questions answered by other fields? Do not national and international political theories, respectively, cope with the ways in which foreign policy phenomena are functional or dysfunctional for national and international systems? Posed differently, theories of national and international politics deal with the fascinating questions of why systems endure or collapse and how they do or do not achieve equilibria—but what kinds of systemic questions can be asked about foreign policy phenomena? If foreign policy analysis does not pose functional and systemic questions, what theoretical challenges does it have to offer? To repeat, is it a fantasy to aspire to the construction of generalized theories of foreign policy that are viable and relevant? If so, why compare? Why not simply examine the particular relationships that particular national actors established with their particular environments?

Obviously this is not the place to develop full answers to all these questions. But, an explication of some of the basic assumptions underlying our delineation of the foreign policy field should clarify some of these problems and point the way to a more formal and extended attempt to resolve all of them.[14]

The centrality of the responsive stage is unquestionably the most radical conclusion of our effort to trace the outlines of the foreign policy field. Probably because of the enormous methodological difficulties they pose, responses to foreign policy are usually examined with much less care than are the variables comprising the initiatory and implementive stages. Ordinarily analysts tend to settle for a brief account of the international environment in which the nation is located, noting any limitations and opportunities that the environment may impose and offer, and then moving on to examine what the actor seeks to accomplish in this environment and why.[15] The problem of sorting out the consequences of foreign policy undertakings from the events that would have occurred anyway is so awesome that, in effect, the responsive stage is ordinarily viewed as consisting of constants rather than variables. Yet, here we are insisting that it cannot be bypassed, that it is a central aspect of the field, and that the methodological obstacles must be confronted and surmounted.

Several reasons and one assumption underlie this insistence. The assumption—perhaps better called an article of faith—is that the methodological problem is at least theoretically solvable. Differentiating between responses intended by political actors and those that would have occurred anyway is the central problem of political analysis and haunts

---

[14] For a more detailed discussion of the problems posed by the independent and dependent variables of the field, see Rosenau (1968b).

[15] Interestingly, and perhaps significantly, works concerned with nations passing through periods of dynamic readjustment to the international system stand out as exceptions to this general tendency. Recent works on postwar Germany, for example, are notable for the equal attention that they pay to the interaction of all three of the stages comprising the foreign policy field (Deutsch and Edinger 1959; Richardson 1966; Hanrieder 1967b).

research in all areas of the discipline. Yet it has not deterred inquiry into the responses of voters to candidates, of legislatures to interest groups, of bureaucracies to leaders. Why, then, should it block the analysis of attempts to modify behavior that span national boundaries? To be sure, the crossing of national boundaries renders foreign policy situations more complex than others, but this is a difference in degree and not in kind. More variables may have to be examined in foreign policy analysis, but the problem remains that of identifying behavior that would not have occurred in the absence of a specific stimulus. The fact that the methodological equipment presently available rarely permits a satisfactory solution of the problem does not mean that it can never be solved. For political scientists to abandon inquiry on these grounds would be the equivalent of astronomers having long ago ceased theorizing about the far side of the moon because it could not be observed through telescopes. Old methodological techniques do get perfected and new types of equipment do get developed in political science as well as in astronomy. Political science is still a long way from having the equivalent of the space capsule, but recent progress with simulation and with other procedures for tracing the flow of influence indicates that methodological innovation is far from over. Hence what is important is whether it is at least theoretically possible to translate responses to foreign policy undertakings into observable behavior. The answer seems to be clearly in the affirmative and is the basis for the assumption that the methodological obstacles to treating the responsive stage as a set of dependent variables can be surmounted.

As for the substantive reasons for insisting that the responsive stage cannot be bypassed, one is the simple fact that a concern for foreign policy cannot be sustained without the question of its effectiveness and consequences arising. Some conception of the receptivity of the international system to the behavior of the nation being examined is necessary even if the degree of receptivity is treated as a constant rather than a variable. Whether their research is oriented toward the solution of practical policy problems or the building of theoretical models, foreign policy analysts cannot avoid assessing the likelihood that one or another type of undertaking may bring about the desired modifications in the structure of the external environment. All their conceptual tools lead to such assessments. If one examines any of the standard concepts of the field, it soon becomes clear that what we have called the responsive stage is a central element. To refer, say, to foreign policy attitudes is to denote judgments about general or specific conditions abroad that ought to be preserved or altered; to describe foreign policy issues is to depict either conflicts at home about what constitutes effective action abroad or conflicts abroad that may have adverse consequences at home if attempts to modify them are not undertaken; to study foreign policy decision-making is to analyze what officials hope to preserve or alter through their external behavior. Since the responsive stage thus cannot be bypassed, it seems only prudent to treat its variability as a central aspect of the field.

But there is an even more important reason for placing the responsive stage on an analytic par with the initiatory and implementive stages. Not only do the responses that unfold in the environment provide a means of assessing the effectiveness of foreign policy undertakings, but they also lead the analyst to treat the foreign policy process as dynamic rather than static, since many of the dependent variables that comprise the responsive stage of one undertaking operate as independent variables in the initiatory state of a subsequent undertaking. For example, having fostered viable social and political institutions abroad through an effective foreign aid program, the aid-giving nation may then be faced with a changing alliance system as the newly strengthened recipient societies are able to follow more independent foreign policy lines of their own. Neither the national actor nor its environment, in other words, ever remains constant. Both are in a state of flux, altering in response to each other in a dynamic fashion that serves to maintain the distinction between the actor and its environment. The foreign policy process is thus marked by continuity, and it is only for analytic convenience that undertakings are examined separately. The ultimate goal is comparison across many undertakings, since only then can higher levels of generalization about national actors in their environments be attained. Treating each undertaking as an analytic unit facilities movement toward this goal, while the inclusion of the responsive stage serves as a means of bridging the artificial discontinuity to which such a procedure gives rise.

There is another important advantage in the notion that the dependent variables of the responsive stage may operate as independent variables in the initiatory stage of subsequent undertakings. It provides a basis for drawing a boundary beyond which the student of foreign policy no longer need analyze the consequences of attempts to modify behavior abroad. If the foreign policy analyst were to examine all the repercussions of an undertaking, eventually he would become, in effect, a student of the society toward which the undertaking was directed. Such a transformation from foreign policy analyst to national politics specialist, however, is prevented by utilizing the distinction between those dependent variables that are and those that are not likely to serve as independent variables in subsequent undertakings. That is, having examined the responsive stage with a view to establishing whether it is associated with variations in the initiatory and implementive stages, the foreign policy analyst loses interest in the responses if they do not emerge as stimuli to further action on the part of the nation whose undertakings are the focus of his attention.

Much the same line of reasoning underlies the inclusion of the initiating stage as a major aspect of the field. While the analysis of foreign policy would be greatly simplified if predecisional determinants were treated as constants and governmental policymaking processes as independent variables, such a procedure would omit from consideration an important body of phenomena of interest to students of the field. As in the case of the responsive stage, both the analyst oriented to policy and the analyst interested in building theory have substantive concerns that lead them to inquire into the factors that give rise to foreign policy undertakings and to assess the relative potencies of the factors they identify. In his effort to improve the quality and direction of undertakings, the policy analyst must examine their sources or he cannot account for the variation in their degrees of success and failure. Likewise, his theoretically oriented colleague must differentiate among the many domestic and foreign influences acting upon decision-makers in order to construct models that are both susceptible to empirical proof and capable of explaining an even wider body of phenomena. To be sure, both the policy analyst and the theorist could follow the precepts of the decision-making approach and analyze the predecisional determinants in terms of the stimuli to which government officials see themselves as reacting (Snyder et al. 1954, p. 37). In doing so, however, they would nevertheless be treating the antecedents of decision as independent variables. They would still be asking whether variations that occurred before decision were associated with those that occurred subsequently. Hence, it seems preferable to examine the initiatory stage directly rather than indirectly through the perceptions of officialdom. That is, since assessing the strength of causal factors is at best extremely difficult, it seems unnecessarily complicating to make the task that of first determining how others (officials) assess the relevant factors and then assessing these assessments (Rosenau 1967d). Besides, officials may not reconstruct the world in such a way as to highlight the variations in the initiatory stage that the analyst is interested in correlating with variations in the responsive stage, in which case he would have to forego the decision-making approach anyway. The procedure of focusing on the initiatory stage directly does not, however, neglect the fact that the way officials perceive and experience the world is crucial to the action they take. It will be recalled that the dimensions of purpose, timing, and style given to undertakings by the way in which decision-makers experience the initiating stimuli are treated as intervening variables in the implementive stage. Furthermore, those aspects of the decision-making process itself that operate as initiatory stimuli (e.g., competition for prestige, power, or appropriations among agencies and their personnel) are regarded as independent variables and analyzed accordingly.

Turning to the question of why purposeful behavior serves as an organizing focus of the foreign field, it must first be emphasized that by *purpose* is meant nothing more than the fact that officials do not act at random. They always have some goal in mind, some notion of how the action they take will help to preserve or modify one or more aspects of the international environment. The goals need not be highly concrete or rational. Nor need they be integral parts of an overall plan. On the contrary, our conception of goals allows for them to be ambiguous, tentative, and not fully formed. They might amount to no more than a stalling for time or be no clearer than an effort to "muddle through."[16] They might well be unrealistic goals and give rise to a host of unintended and undesirable consequences. Imprecise, ineffective, and counterproductive as they may be, however, foreign policy undertakings are launched for some reason. They do envision some future state of affairs as being served, and it is in this sense that they are regarded as purposeful.

The emphasis on the purposefulness of foreign policy undertakings serves two needs. One is obvious. Without the presumption of goal-oriented behavior, there would be no basis for knowing which variations in the external environment should be examined in order to determine whether they are associated with variations in the behavior of foreign policy actors. The variable circumstances in the environment are so

16 Although policymaking designed to "muddle through" situations is here conceived to be goal-oriented behavior, some analysts tend to posit it as lacking this characteristic (Lindblom 1959). The latter position arises out of the unnecessarily narrow view that only behavior directed toward long-range, well planned, and duly considered ends can be goal-oriented. Ends may be short-range, poorly planned, and impetuously considered, but action designed to serve them is nonetheless goal-oriented. Even the "muddler" hopes to get "through," and thus it is difficult to conceive of his behavior as purposeless.

numerous that many are bound to be associated merely by chance with the foreign policy undertakings being considered. The student of foreign policy, however, is interested in systematic associations and not in those founded on happenstance. The goal-oriented nature of foreign policy provides the analysts with a reference point for selecting associations around which to organize his inquiry. To be sure, he may be interested in associations involving variations in the initiatory stage that officials do not formally include among their purposes; and he may also wish to probe associations involving variations in the responsive stage that are unintended consequences of the purposeful undertakings. But, even in cases where his focus extends beyond the goal-oriented nature of foreign policy, such orientations still serve as a baseline for his assessments.

A second reason for emphasizing the purposefulness of undertakings is that it helps to distinguish foreign policy from the total set of inter-actions that occur between a society and its environment. As previously indicated, foreign policy phenomena constitute only one kind of linkage that a society establishes with its environment. Others are established by businessmen, scientists, artists, and tourists, to name but a few of the many types of private individuals and groups whose interactions span national boundaries. These cultural, social, economic, and scientific linkages can be so relevant to the processes of foreign policy that the analyst may often find it appropriate to treat them as independent and/or dependent variables operative in undertakings. In themselves, how-ever, such linkages are not of interest to the foreign policy analyst. He is interested in the national actor, not in the subnational one—in public individuals or groups, not in private ones. Stated in another way, the foreign policy analyst is concerned with the linkages that the entire so-ciety, rather than a segment of it, establishes with the external environ-ment. Only governments can link the personnel and resources of the entire society to situations abroad, and this, to repeat, governments always do for some purpose. On the other hand, whether nongovern-mental linkages are or are not intended by those who sustain them, there is a limit beyond which they cannot be controlled by governmental purposes. Up to a point travel can be forbidden, and so can trade and scientific and other types of exchange. But, if only because some of the interaction is perceptual, government cannot arrogate to itself total con-trol over external ties. Hence, from the perspective of the national actor, the linkages established by subnational groups or by individuals are not purposeful. From this perspective, the actions of governments are the only goal-oriented external undertakings of the entire society. This characteristic distinguishes foreign policy from all other national-international linkages.

There remains the problem of what questions foreign policy theory is designed to answer. As implied earlier, the foreign policy analyst is not faced with the kinds of systemic and functional challenges that impress his counterparts in the national and international fields. Foreign policy theory can never in itself explain why and how a national system manages to persist or why and how it collapses. Such theory can shed light on one of the functional requirements of all national systems—the necessity of adapting to the environment—but it does not pretend to deal with the full range of integrative mechanisms through which national systems maintain their internal coherence. Thus it can never provide more than partial answers to the intriguing questions of systemic persistence. Similarly, the endurance or deterioration of international systems lies outside the competence of the foreign policy theorist. By explaining why and how one or more nations interact with their environments, foreign policy theory provides some of the material needed for a functional analysis of international systems, but it does not address itself to the sum of the separate patterns of interaction maintained by different actors and thus the student of foreign policy must again stand aside when the fascinating questions of systemic stability and change are posed by his colleagues in the international field.

It is exactly at this point that foreign policy theorists run the risk of engaging in unrealistic fantasy. Those who wish foreign policy theory to explain and predict systemic coherence and collapse are bound to be thwarted. The fantasy is enticing and the aspiration is worthy, but neither can ever be realized. Foreign policy is the only field that relates the behavior of a national actor both to its environment and to its own functioning, but the price of such a focus is that the boundaries of the field do not correspond to those of any empirical political system. While a foreign policy undertaking can be judged as functional or dysfunctional for the national system that undertakes it and functional or dysfunctional for the international system with respect to which it has consequences, there is no concrete foreign policy system for which its functionality can be assessed.

What, then, are the theoretical challenges posed by the foreign policy field? The answer is that the challenges are endless if aspirations are scaled down to the level of middle-range theory and not cast in systemic terms at the highest level of generalization.[17] The question is paralyzing only if the foreign policy analyst wants to construct broad-gauged models that account for the dynamics of concrete systems of action whose boundaries are rooted in historical experience and political authority. Once he accepts the fact that his subject matter does not permit emulation of colleagues in allied fields who employ functional analysis and systems theory, a host of theoretical tasks that enliven thought and compel inquiry come into view.

Before identifying these tasks, it is useful to note that the act of identification is itself important. Too many first-rate theorists have forsaken foreign policy because of its failure to excite their imaginations. For example, two of the most distinguished empirical theorists in the modern era of political science, Almond and Dahl, started their careers with important works dealing with foreign policy (Almond 1950; Dahl 1950) and subsequently turned their talents to phenomena that originate and unfold within national boundaries. Neither ever returned to the study of foreign policy, apparently finding the construction of theory about units bounded by a common system of authority more challenging. Hence the drama of foreign policy undertakings, of nations coping with their environments, needs to be emphasized if the field is to recruit and keep theorists capable of exploiting the reorientation toward comparative analysis.

The many challenges inherent in foreign policy phenomena are most succinctly identified by calling attention to two main types, those that derive from the truly political quality of the field's unit of analysis, the undertaking, and those that are posed by the adaptive function of national systems. The former set of challenges is rarely appreciated. Many political scientists do not seem to recognize that while comprehension of foreign policy undertakings may not explain or anticipate systemic stability and change, it will provide fundamental insights into the dynamics of politics. For the attempt to modify behavior across national boundaries is perhaps the purest of all political acts. Unlike their domestic counterparts, foreign policy officials cannot appeal to the common ties of culture and history to secure the compliance of those whose behavior they are attempting to modify. Unlike domestic officials, they can-

---

[17] The distinction between middle-range and general theories is best described by Robert K. Merton (1957, pp. 5–6), who notes that the former are "intermediate to the minor working hypotheses evolved in abundance during the day-by-day routines of research, and the all-inclusive speculations comprising a master conceptual scheme from which it is hoped to derive a very large number of empirically observed uniformities of social behavior."

not merely rely on the structures from which their own authority is derived to induce compliance. The foreign policy official is the only politician whose actions are directed toward persons and situations that are normally responsive to cultural standards, historical aspirations, and sources of authority different from his own. Hence the foreign policy undertaking is the most delicate of political actions and the most fragile of political relationships. It involves a degree of manipulation of symbols that is unmatched in any other political situation. It requires a balance between the use of persuasion on the one hand and the use or threat of force on the other that is more precarious than it is in any other kind of politics. It reveals the limits of legitimacy, the sources of loyalty, and the dynamics of bargaining. It demonstrates the inertia of habit as well as the continuities to which habitual behavior gives rise. It exposes the universality of resistance to change, and correspondingly, the large extent to which change can be introduced only in small increments at the margins of organized life.

In short, the field of foreign policy contains the promise that virtually every dimension of politics will be examined in its purest form. In a profound sense the challenge of foreign policy theory is, at the middle-range level, hardly less than that of empirical political theory itself. The empirical political theorist confronts no problem—whether it be that of authority, law, influence, responsibility, federalism, rationality, order, sovereignty, community, leadership, communications, or revolution—that cannot be fruitfully investigated in the foreign policy field.[18]

The other clearly identifiable set of theoretical challenges arises out of the notion that foreign policy undertakings perform an adaptive function for national systems. General systems analysis may lie beyond the scope of the foreign policy theorist, but the functional problems posed within the area of his concern are nonetheless compelling. Even though national systems may collapse for strictly internal reasons, they cannot persist without coping with their environments, and this never-ending effort to maintain boundaries and achieve an accommodation with the environment commands attention and provokes inquiry. It is just as dramatic as an adolescent's search for identity in a world that seems to engulf independence and demand acquiescence, a marriage's endeavor to survive in a world of possessive relatives and tempting lovers, a business firm's struggle to keep up with technological change and a world of aggressive competitors, a minority group's fight to bring about

[18] For an elaboration of the notion that the quintessence of politics can be found in the foreign policy field, see Rosenau (1963, 1967c).

a world of fair and equal treatment, a political party's striving to extend its popularity and create a world that it can govern. For none of these—or for any of the many other actors that could be listed—is accommodation with the environment easy or predetermined. At any moment the boundaries separating a system from its environment can give way and suffer drastic revision, if not elimination. At no point can a nation assume that a permanent accommodation has been attained. Performance of the adaptive function is never completed. It must be continuously serviced. Thus foreign policy undertakings are inherently intriguing, both in the basic emotional sense that they are rooted in human efforts to survive and prosper and in the theoretical sense that it is no simple matter to fathom why and how national systems manage to remain differentiated from their environments.

But why compare? Granting the challenges inherent in the study of foreign policy undertakings, why is it also necessary to reorient the field toward comparative analysis? Although a full discussion of the reasons would constitute an essay in itself, they can be asserted simply and concisely here. Comparison is necessary because the two major theoretical challenges we have identified cannot otherwise be met. Comprehension of the external activities undertaken by one national system is not sufficient to answer the questions of systemic adaptation and political process that are inherent in foreign policy phenomena. The repeated experiences of two or more systems must be carefully contrasted for an answer to such questions to begin to emerge. Only in this way can the theorist begin to satisfy his curiosity and the policy analyst begin to accumulate reliable knowledge on which sound recommendations and choices are made. Only in this way will it be possible to move beyond historical circumstance and comprehend the continuities of national life in a world of other nations.

Postscript

The prediction made eight years ago that the comparative study of foreign policy would become a major preoccupation in the 1970's has already been confirmed. A trend that was described in 1967 as an "occasional" paper, book, dissertation, or text on the subject can now be fairly characterized as an incessant outpouring of research and teaching materials. This outpouring has been so great, in fact, that it can only be highlighted here; the important task of compiling a full bibliographic essay must be postponed to another time or left to others.

That the prediction has been upheld in the realm of teaching is perhaps most clearly indicated by the publication of a separate volume of twenty syllabi (out of "approximately" forty submitted) for courses in which some kind of comparative approach to foreign policy phenomena was undertaken (Hermann and Waltz 1970). Moreover, the prescience of textbook publishers has resulted in such a proliferation of texts and books of readings that the number of courses presently being given on the subject is probably much greater than it was when the anthology of syllabi was compiled. Or at least it is now possible to organize such a course around a few basic works rather than relying on fugitive papers or noncomparable treatments. To be sure, the latter treatments are still available, both in the form of innumerable texts on American foreign policy and in compendia of single-country analyses. Macridis's compendium, for example, is now in its fourth edition (1972) and it still characterizes (p. 25) efforts to compare foreign policy phenomena rigorously as a "hopeless task." But a pronounced trend in this proliferation of teaching materials has been the use of a comparative context. This has been done both in single-author texts (e.g., Jones 1970; Lovell 1970; and Wilkinson 1969) and in books of readings (Chittick 1974; Jacobson and Zimmerman 1969; Hanrieder 1971a; Rosenau 1974), of which this volume is still another instance. Indeed, even selected dimensions of foreign policy phenomena, such as conflict behavior and reactions to crises, have become the focus of comparative treatment in texts (George, Hall, and Simons 1971; Halper 1971; Wilkenfeld 1973a). No less indicative, teaching packages that allow students to work out problems in the comparative analysis of foreign policy (see Chap. 9, for example) or to engage in foreign policy simulations (Schleicher 1973) have also become readily available. Equally indicative are signs that highly analytic examples may be replacing historical narratives as the means used by teachers to expose their students to real-world events. At least the popularity of monographs such as Allison's 1971 analysis of how three different models might be used to explain U.S. behavior in the Cuban missile crisis suggests that even single-country case studies are being treated comparatively in the classroom. Finally, for teachers who prefer to open or close courses on an abstract note, short essays elaborating and extolling the virtues of a comparative approach to foreign policy can now be assigned (Hanrieder 1971b; Singer 1972).

On the research side, too, the prediction has been confirmed. The proliferation of comparative studies has been nothing short of astonishing over the past seven years. Now dissertations in this vein are not only in progress (Hitlin 1972), but a number of important ones have also been completed that compare, both theoretically and empirically, selected aspects of the external behavior of either all the nations in the world or some analytic subsample of them (e.g., Blong 1973a; Kegley 1971; McGowan 1970c; Moore 1970; Salmore 1972). Collaborative research efforts spanning several universities have been launched, and in one case, at least temporarily completed (Rosenau, Burgess, and Hermann 1973). Attempts to generate quantitative materials that will facilitate comparative analysis of the sources of foreign policy behavior have mushroomed, and many data sets have been created with substantial financial support from federal sources (e.g., Azar 1970a; Burgess 1970a; Corson 1969; C. F. Hermann 1973; McClelland et al. 1971). The resulting flow of articles and monographs devoted to the comparative analysis of foreign policy is too great even to begin to enumerate, but the appearance of a yearbook designed to provide an outlet for the increase (McGowan 1973c) is a good indication of their number.

But the original questions remain: Does all this activity add up to more than a fad? Does it still express an unrealized fantasy? Does it reflect the characteristics of a field? My own answers are resoundingly negative to the second question and even more emphatically postive to the first and last.

It might be argued that fads are by definition momentary and that any mode of inquiry that has persisted for nearly a decade has passed the test of being more than mere craze. There are, however, more persuasive reasons for judging these eight years of effort as more than a passing phase. The vast research output it has spawned does more than pay lip service to the comparative method. It reveals an intense, restless, and creative use of models, variables, and methodologies in which comparisons are hypothesized or made. The complexities of foreign policy phenomena have yielded to the scientific mode, and increasingly parsimonious conceptions that are not bound by time and place have been built, extended, and revised. Descriptions have been supplemented by analyses, implicit assumptions have given way to explicit propositions, unrelated examples have been replaced by recurring patterns, and noncomparable case studies have been complemented by careful replications. Where past investigations focused on either concrete single countries (such as England or China) or concrete clusters of countries based on geographic location (such as those in Europe or the Far East), now the nations to be examined are chosen on the basis of analytic categories as well, with small ones being perhaps most intensely probed (Rothstein 1968; Sveics 1970; Vital 1967, 1971) but with comparisons between large and small nations, between open and closed ones, and between developed and underdeveloped ones by no means being neglected (Butwell 1969; Hermann and East 1974; Moore 1970; Rosenau and Hoggard 1974; Salmore 1972; Singer 1972; see also Chap. 6 of this volume). Indeed, a rich literature is beginning to emerge in which comparisons are organized around even more precise and narrower, but no less analytic, foci. The degree to which a society has been penetrated by another (Blong 1973b), the role played by personality variables in foreign policy making (M. G. Hermann 1972), the interaction of racial stratification and foreign policy behavior (Eldridge n.d.), the impact of regime structure and change on foreign policy behavior (Salmore and Salmore 1972), the role of common markets and other situational variables as sources of foreign policy (Axline n.d.; Brady 1973); the tendency to found present policies on previous ones (Phillips and Crain 1972)—these are but a few of the more creative analytic categories that have been employed to compare the external behavior of nations.[19] Furthermore, the comparative mode has even begun to affect single-nation studies, in which the behavior of a nation has been compared at different points in time and with respect to different dimensions of behavior in different parts of the world (Brecher 1972; Eley 1973; Rummel 1972b; Weinstein 1972; Winham 1970). That these efforts amount to more than old wine in new bottles, that instead they reflect a basic reorganization of foreign policy analysis, can be demonstrated by noting that it has already proven possible to derive 118 propositions from 203 comparative studies in which foreign policy phenomena are compared across a number of nations (McGowan and Shapiro 1973).

The comparative study of foreign policy, in short, is a serious enterprise, one that seems likely to be around for a long time and to entice an ever larger number of students to its ranks. And as the early faddishness has yielded to sustained inquiry, it has become clear that the idea of analyzing foreign policy phenomena in terms of independent, intervening, and dependent variables that are operational and manipulable is no mere fantasy. A field has emerged around a welter of variables that describe one or another aspect of the initiatory, implementative, and responsive stages identified seven years ago as necessary to delineate foreign policy phenomena as separate and distinctive subject matter.

[19] For abstracts of fifty-one empirical studies employing still other categories, see Jones and Singer (1972).

The responsive stage has been relatively neglected, and much remains to be done in tracing the links among the variables encompassed by the three stages, but as this volume again so clearly illustrates, there can be no gainsaying that the collective efforts of many researchers have brought the study of foreign policy into existence as a rigorous, self-sustaining field of inquiry.

This conclusion is reinforced even further by another conception of what constitutes a field, namely, Kuhn's notion of a "normal science" (1970b). In my original article I asserted that for a field to exist it must have substantive discipline, that is, a specified subject matter and a theoretical perspective that structures the subject matter in a distinctive way. Kuhn, however, suggests that a field can be defined by looking at what researchers do in relation to one another, regardless of the content of the phenomena they investigate or the theory they follow. He sees the practitioners of a normal science as a community of like-minded investigators who share certain premises about how and when "truths" about the subject are established and who thus build on each other's work. They are commonly concerned, to use his phraseology, with solving certain "puzzles," and "no puzzle-solving enterprise can exist unless its practitioners share criteria which, for that group and for that time, determine when a puzzle has been solved" (1970a, p. 7). Furthermore, in order to solve the puzzles and thereby extend understanding, the practitioners have a common interest in, and commitment to, building on each other's work and tying the loose ends of earlier solutions or unresolved puzzles:

Mopping-up operations are what engage most scientists throughout their careers. They constitute what I am here calling normal science. Closely examined, whether historically or in the contemporary laboratory, that enterprise seems an attempt to force nature into the preformed and relatively inflexible box that the paradigm (i.e., shared puzzle-solving orientations) supplies. No part of the aim of normal science is to call forth new sorts of phenomena; indeed those that will not fit the box are often not seen at all. Nor do scientists normally aim to invent new theories, and they are often intolerant of those invented by others. Instead, normal-scientific research is directed to the articulation of those phenomena and theories that the paradigm already supplies. (1970b, p. 24)

In short, Kuhn's formulation of a normal science allows for a field to be said to emerge when the degree of methodological and philosophical consensus among researchers is such that their contributions are merely elaborations and refinements of each other's work.[20] Viewed in this way, developments in the comparative study of foreign policy over the last seven years amply justify the conclusion that those engaged in the enterprise have nurtured a field into existence.

The vitality and pervasiveness of the events data movement is one indication of the emergent field. It has, in effect, provided a basis for consensus-building. Before large and wide-ranging data sets depicting the actions that foreign policy actors direct toward each other became available, researchers worked in isolation, confining themselves to case studies or imprecise observations of ambiguous phenomena that came under the general heading of "foreign policy." But the events data movement changed all this by making available a measure of repeated, concrete, and specifiable forms of behavior on the part of foreign policy actors which, in turn, made it possible for investigators to compare and cumulate their findings. As the ensuing essays in this volume plainly reveal, the construction, perfection, application, and analysis of data sets that reflect what international actors are doing—act by act, day by day, and nation by nation—in contiguous, regional, and global situations has become a central preoccupation of researchers, involving them in a continual process of criticizing, revising, and extending each other's work. One need only pursue this and other compendia (Azar, Brody, and McClelland 1972; Azar and Ben-Dak 1974; Burgess and Lawton 1972; Sigler, Field, and Adelman 1972), or scan the agendas of panels at the annual meetings of the International Studies Association or the American Political Science Association, to appreciate that mopping-up operations have begun and that what was once lip service to the virtues of behavioral research has now become a set of concrete premises and practices shared by a wide and ever-widening number of investigators.

Nor are these mopping-up operations confined to the realm of methodology. Events data present a host of methodological problems that continue to command the energy and attention of many researchers. But these do not constitute the only concern. Much energy and attention is also given to genuine substantive and theoretical problems, such as tests of hypotheses about the role of environmental factors (Zinnes 1972); formulations in which the sources of conflictual foreign policies in Africa (Collins 1973; McGowan 1973b), Latin America (Eley and Petersen n.d.), and the Middle East (Burrowes and Spector 1973) are sub-

---

[20] Kuhn gives the label *revolutionary science* to those rare instances when a researcher breaks with the prevailing puzzle-solving orientations and arrives at genuinely new theories that identify new puzzles.

jected to intensive empirical scrutiny; evaluations of whether a cognitive balance model of the behavior of foreign policy officials better explains their actions than a role model (Stassen 1972); assessments of the relative strength of internal and external factors as sources of foreign policy in one data set (Rosenau and Hoggard 1974) and across data sets (Rosenau and Ramsey 1973); and—perhaps most indicative of all— replications of concrete substantive findings (Powell et al. 1974; Wilkenfeld 1973b), as well as findings pertaining to source coverage and category reliability.

All of this is not to say that comprehension of foreign policy phenomena lies immediately ahead. Normal science, as Kuhn notes, has limitations, an important one being that it tends to discourage theoretical venturesomeness. As a result, obstacles to understanding are sometimes swept under the rug instead of being mopped up. Two aspects of the field come to mind as obstacles that have not been adequately confronted. One is the possibility that the capacity of national governments to solve international problems is declining. The growing interdependence of societies and the resulting emergence of important international actors other than nation-states thus creates the possibility that foreign policy behavior may become increasingly less important as a factor in world affairs. If this is so, and if the field continues, as a normal science, to blind itself to theory and data that are not nation-state centered, then the progress of the last seven years may be short-lived. An exclusive focus on foreign policy behavior that fails to allow conceptually for other types of transnational interdependencies would surely negate not only the long-range aspiration for a deeper understanding of world politics, but in the short range it might also preclude adequate solutions to the puzzle of why nations act as they do in international affairs. To solve this puzzle, theoretical and empirical account must be taken of the differences between the kinds of issues to which foreign policy officials address themselves and those that they willingly or otherwise permit other international actors to process.

While there is reason to be concerned about the tendency of many, even most, investigators to be too nation-state centered in the hypotheses they frame and the data they gather to test them, happily the field is not without its gadflies who remind us that mopping-up operations can get out of hand (Handelman et al. 1973; Keohane and Nye 1972). In their enthusiasm for revolutionary science, some of these critics assert that nation-state–centered data and models of foreign policy behavior are becoming so obsolete that they should be replaced with a "world policy process" framework (Handelman et al. 1973). Such enthusiasm serves the field well, and one may hope that the response to it will be empirical investigation rather than outright rejection. My own view, elaborated elsewhere, is that the immediate problem is empirical rather than theoretical, that the world may be entering an asymmetrical era in which nation-states are the predominant actors in certain key issue-areas while subnational and supranational actors predominate in other areas, and that therefore we must develop data which will allow for the identification of the several types of issue-areas and the boundaries that divide them (Rosenau 1972).

A second obstacle to continued progress in the field stems from the neglect of the responsive stage relative to the initiatory and implementive stages of foreign policy. As even this brief evaluation of the progress of the last eight years suggests, most of the effort has involved testing theories and cumulating findings about the sources of foreign policy behavior and the processes whereby policies come into being. The event rather than the undertaking has emerged as the basic unit of analysis, thus tending to preclude empirical inquiries into the responses to foreign policy behaviors evoked abroad and the feedback of these responses into subsequent behaviors. It is easy to see why the event is a more manageable unit of analysis than the undertaking. As noted in the original article, undertakings pose the enormous methodological problem of differentiating between responses to foreign policy acts and those that would have occurred anyway, and given all the work that was needed, researchers found valid reasons for not confronting it. The reasons for focusing on the responsive stage are no less compelling today, however, than they were seven years ago, especially in view of the insights yielded by the small amount of theoretical work that has included this stage (McGowan 1970a; Rosenau 1970; Thorson 1974). Furthermore, perhaps the methodological obstacles to empirical inquiry into the responsive stage have been lessened by the advent of events data sets. Although events data are not necessarily constructed for the purpose of tracing feedback processes, it does seem possible to manipulate them in such a way as to allow for the creation of undertakings as analytic units by juxtaposing acts of different nations toward each other. Such a procedure is a poor substitute for the direct creation of undertakings data, but it may suffice to maintain forward movement until such time as more appropriate data sets become available.

In sum, there is still much to be done, but if progress in the next few years is anything like that which has marked the past eight, there is reason to believe that the dynamics of foreign policy will begin to yield rapidly to greater understanding. And in greater understanding there lies the greatest contribution that the field could offer: an enlarged capacity to apply human intelligence to the alleviation and solution of real problems.

Part II

Methodological Issues

Introduction:
Comparative Analysis and Nomological
Explanation

GREGORY A. RAYMOND

Professor Rosenau's introductory article suggests that we use techniques of comparison when examining theoretical propositions about foreign policy output behavior. By comparing either several nations at one point in time (synchronic analysis), or one nation with itself at specific intervals over time (diachronic analysis), he contends that it is possible to test empirically the maxims and rules of thumb frequently voiced by observers of international affairs. In this section we will focus upon various research design issues which confront the individual preparing to engage in these empirical tests.

Before considering specific methodological questions, however, it is important to understand the central aim of inquiry. Though scientific investigation involves a search for regularities, we seek more than just correlational knowledge. One is reminded of "the fabled gentlemen who got experimentally drunk on bourbon and soda on Monday night, Scotch and soda on Tuesday night, and brandy and soda on Wednesday night— and stayed sober on Thursday night by drinking nothing. With a vast inductive leap of scientific imagination, they treated their experience as an empirical demonstration that soda, the common element each evening, was the cause of the inebriated state they had experienced" (Simon 1969, p. 70). Rather than merely establishing associations, our

41

ultimate goal is explanation. Consequently any methodological discussion should not only refer to data collection, processing, and analysis, but also indicate the "criteria for admissible explanation that exist independent of these instrumentations and routines" (Holt and Turner 1970, p. 4).

Scientific explanations are fashioned from theoretical statements which relate specific events to generalized patterns. As shown in Figure II–1, the procedure utilized for their construction is both dynamic and circular—dynamic because theories may spiral upward or downward with respect to their generality; and circular insofar as once theory is applied

FIGURE II–1

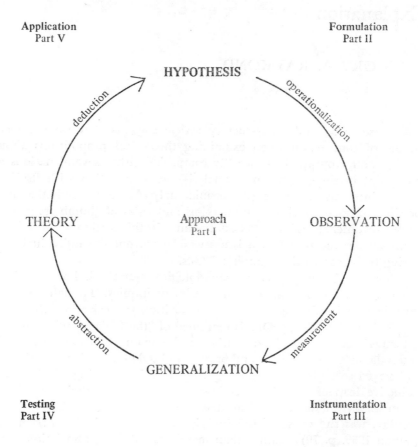

Application
Part V

Formulation
Part II

HYPOTHESIS

deduction

operationalization

THEORY

Approach
Part I

OBSERVATION

abstraction

measurement

GENERALIZATION

Testing
Part IV

Instrumentation
Part III

for predictive purposes, new observations prompt another research cycle.[1] To quote Wallace:

Individual *observations* are highly specific and essentially unique items of information whose synthesis into the more general form denoted by empirical generalizations is accomplished by measurement, sample summarization, and parameter estimation. Empirical *generalizations,* in turn, are items of information that can be synthesized into a theory via concept formation, proposition formation, and proposition arrangement. A *theory,* the most general type of information, is transformable into new hypotheses through the method of logical deduction. An empirical *hypothesis* is an information item that becomes transformed into *new observations* via interpretation of the hypothesis into observables, instrumentation, scaling, and sampling. (Wallace 1971, p. 17; emphasis added)

Schematically each of the ensuing sections in this volume can be conceptualized as representing an arc in the circular *modus operandi* described above: Part II centers upon design problems encountered between hypothesis and observation; Part III deals with the use of events data in moving from observation to generalization; Part IV contains works which employ events data comparatively in an effort to establish generalizations that can be used to build theory; and finally, Part V covers the transition from theory to new hypotheses and observations in forecasting foreign policy output behavior.

Contending Explanatory Systemizations

Although the verb *explain* pervades contemporary foreign policy studies, there is no consensus among researchers or philosophers of social science regarding the logical structure of the explanatory process. Table II-1 illustrates eight common uses of the word. Other than its use simply as (1) a political justification, perhaps the most frequent use is that of portraying the meaning of some foreign policy undertaking. On the one hand, this may imply (2) defining the policy in a precise manner. On the other, it may connote (3) delineating all the policy's implications. Besides these customary uses, "explanation" is also employed in

---

[1] We do not contend that all scientific research follows this reconstruction. Rather, to quote Kaplan's baseball metaphor, "There are ways of pitching, hitting, and running bases; ways of fielding; managerial strategies for pinch hitters and relief pitchers; ways of signaling, coaching, and maintaining team spirit. All of these, and more besides, enter into playing the game well, and each of them has an indefinite number of variants" (Kaplan 1964, p. 27).

TABLE II-1

Types of Explanations

Explanatory mode	Conceptual discussion[a]	Substantive example: explanations of U.S. foreign policy toward Vietnam
1. Justification	Meehan 1969, p. 111	"We are there because we have a promise to keep" (L. B. Johnson, as cited in Effros 1970, p. 36).
2. Meaning: specification by precise definition	Brecht 1959, p. 63 Bridgman 1927, p. 37 Kaplan 1964, pp. 327–28	"Vietnam is essentially an American intervention against a nationalist revolutionary agrarian movement which embodies social elements in incipient and similar forms of development in numerous other Third World nations" (Kolko 1969, p. 89).
3. Meaning: presentation of ramifications	Palmer 1969, pp. 20–22 Schrag 1967, pp. 279–80 Kaplan 1964, pp. 358–59	"The Vietnamese war will eventually have to be . . . understood . . . as one of the less agreeable manifestations of the American world role. This role implies the necessity to define . . . the terms on which regional balance of power are evolved. . . . In this perspective, the war no longer appears a unique event" (Liska 1967, p. iv).
4. Understanding actor intentions	Anscombe 1957 Brown 1963, pp. 58–74 Collingwood 1946, p. 24 Isaak 1969, pp. 117–20 Winch 1958	"We have fought a costly war in South Vietnam to carry out our threat. . . . The next time an adventurous Kremlin leader thinks about pressuring us in Berlin he will remember Vietnam" (Payne 1970, p. 139).

[a] This column suggests references where these explanatory patterns are discussed more fully.

Table II–1 (continued)

Explanatory mode	Conceptual discussion[a]	Substantive example
5. Reference to actor reflexes, habits, or impulses	Brown 1963, pp. 75–98 Hempel 1965, pp. 457–63 Isaak 1969, pp. 115–17	"What seemed in retrospect to have made large-scale military intervention all but inevitable in 1965 was a fateful combination of the President's uncertainty and sense of insecurity in handling foreign policy, and a prevailing set of assumptions among his close advisers that reinforced his own tendency to think about the external world in the simplistic terms of appeasement versus military resolve" (Hoopes 1969, p. 7).
6. Tracing temporal sequence of acts	Brown 1963, pp. 47–57 Gallie 1959 Hempel 1965, pp. 447–53 Isaak 1969, pp. 126–29 Oakeshott 1933	"Through a series of small steps, none extremely important or irrevocable in itself, the United States gradually took over the French commitment in South Vietnam" (Fulbright 1966, p. 117).
7. Identifying simultaneous occurrences	Burns 1968, pp. 55–56	"In 1954 two things were very clear: that in the absence of external help communism was virtually certain to take over the successor states of Indochina . . . and that with France no longer ready to act . . . no power other than the United States could move in to help fill the vacuum" (W. P. Bundy, as cited in Effros 1970, p. 33).
8. Subsumption under generic concept	Dray 1959 Hempel 1965, pp. 453–57 Walsh 1942, pp. 133–35	"There was what you might call the 'falling domino' principle" (Eisenhower, as cited in Effros 1970, p. 48).

[a] This column suggests references where these explanatory patterns are discussed more fully.

several other ways. For example, the term may pertain to (4) under-standing the intentions of those agents responsible for an event. It like-wise has been applied to (5) describing actor reflexes, habits, and im-pulses; (6) tracing the temporal sequence of acts antecedent to an event; (7) identifying simultaneous incidents which together aggregate into the occurrence of an action; and (8) subsuming discrete events under a generic concept such as "national interest." Hence not only are there contending explanations of foreign policy behavior, but the logical structure of these explanations may also vary.[2]

In contrast to the explanatory modes outlined above, a deductive-nomological explanation accounts for an event by showing it to be an instance of a general regularity. As Figure II–2 indicates, this approach has two notable features. First, the *explanans,* or statements which ac-count for an event, must contain a set of initial conditions (C_1, C_2, C_3, . . . , C_n), and a series of covering laws (L_1, L_2, L_3, . . . , L_n) govern-ing the universality of an event occurring in precise circumstances. Secondly, the *explanandum,* or event (E_1) to be explained, must be deduced from the explanans. To clarify this formulation, let us examine the following simple model based upon Rosenau's (1966, 1970) pre-theory of foreign policy:

C_1: State Q is a small, developed, open society.
L_1: For any state x: if x is a small, developed, open society, then systemic level variables are the most potent sources of foreign policy output.
L_2: For any state x: if systemic level variables are the most potent sources of foreign policy output, then the foreign policy of x is acquiescent.

E_1: The foreign policy of Q is acquiescent.

Clearly the above explanandum is logically deductible from information found in the explanans. If, however, the covering laws in the explanans were to be replaced by contingency generalizations which merely per-tained to the probability of an event happening under certain condi-tions, then we could confer only inductive support upon the ex-planandum. While our goal is to establish those covering laws necessary

[2] This list is not intended to be exhaustive. Other explanatory modes include demonstrating the logical steps which resulted in a particular conclusion (Sprout and Sprout 1965, p. 44); referring to rational action (Hempel 1965, pp. 463–83); dis-playing the functional requiredness of an entity to some dynamic system (Parsons 1951; Radcliffe-Brown 1957); and revealing isomorphism between the entailments of a formal calculus and a cluster of empirical referents (Meehan 1968). Moreover, as Isaak (1969, pp. 129–30) reminds us, "Practically speaking, one notices a great number of explanations in political science that are really combinations of patterns."

FIGURE II-2

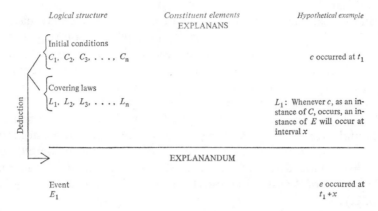

Logical structure   *Constituent elements*   *Hypothetical example*
EXPLANANS

Initial conditions
$C_1, C_2, C_3, \ldots, C_n$ c occurred at t_1

Covering laws
$L_1, L_2, L_3, \ldots, L_n$ L_1: Whenever c, as an instance of C, occurs, an instance of E will occur at interval x

Deduction

EXPLANANDUM

Event e occurred at
E_1 $t_1 + x$

for deductive-nomological explanation,[3] current research findings rest upon contingency generalizations; therefore, our explanations are inductive-statistical.[4] Nonetheless, these "probabilistic accounts play a fundamentally important role in such fields as statistical mechanics, quantum theory, and genetic theory" (Hempel, cited in Donagan 1966, p. 132). Moreover, they are nomological in the sense that events are explained by disclosing their conformity with a general constancy.

Aspects of Nomological Explanations

Explanations of foreign policy behavior generally are envisioned as being tantamount to a disclosure of causation. Yet causality "apparently is one of those scaffoldings inside which you can build a sermon of any type" (Samuelson 1965, p. 99). Despite its great intuitive appeal and

---

[3] Meehan (1968) has argued to the contrary: "This line of reasoning elevates the deductive paradigm into a privileged position in the conduct of inquiry—where it becomes an albatross around the neck of the social scientist. For social science simply cannot meet the requirements for deductive explanations. We do not have, and we are unlikely to get, the nomic empirical generalizations or empirical laws that deductive explanations demand. It follows, if the deductive paradigm is accepted, that the social scientist's capacity to explain is severely restricted and is likely to remain so for the indefinite future" (p. 3).

[4] Greeno (1970), Jeffrey (1969), and Salmon (1970; 1971) contend that statistical explanations need not be interpreted as inductive inferences. Their explanatory model is based upon the view that to call "a certain factor . . . *statistically relevant* to the occurrence of an event means, roughly, that *it makes a difference to the probability of that occurrence*—that is, the probability of the event is different in the presence of that factor than in its absence" (Salmon 1971, p. 11).

frequent use in common parlance, there is little intersubjective agreement on the nature of the concept. Not surprisingly, then, long-standing philosophical debates have continued to rage over its empirical status. Some individuals have rejected the term *à la* Russell, others have followed Hume in questioning the capacity of *a priori* reasoning to establish causation, and still others have agreed with Dewey that the differentiation between cause and effect is solely a device for regulating inquiry. In short, despite attempts to employ surrogates in lieu of cause (for example, a change in the value of independent variable X "produces" a change in the value of dependent variable Y), disagreement still abounds over the nature of causality. Consequently the question of whether nomological explanations are causal can be answered "only if it is first made determinate, by indicating in which of the many specific senses of 'causal' the question is to be understood" (Nagel 1965, p. 21).

When causal explanations of foreign policy events involve universal laws that connect initial condition C and event E, Popper (1959, p. 59) claims that they are deductive-nomological—albeit Hempel (1965, p. 350) adds the caveat that because both the explanans and explanandum contain spatio-temporally bound statements, it is possible only to say that the discrete occurrence c, as an instance of C, caused individual event e, as an instance of E. Aside from this qualification, since we seldom have detailed information regarding initial conditions, and since the contingency generalizations in the explanans of our inductive-statistical explanations disclose only covariation, we cannot infer the necessary and sufficient conditions for a given occurrence. For instance, empirical tests may provide evidence that intense and conflicting demands from allies abroad and pressure groups at home are sufficient to account for the transformation from a promotive to a preservative foreign policy strategy. But they may not be a necessary cause of the alteration if, as Rosenau (1970, p. 19) posits, "all that is required is that any of a variety of systemic, societal, and governmental variables become highly potent relative to the individual preferences of the officials who occupy the top policy-making posts."

Whether or not the above perspective on causation resolves any of the philosophical questions bearing upon free will and determinism, it does raise the issue of the relationship between nomological explanation and the description and prediction of foreign policy events. Scientific explanation often is contrasted with description and prediction. In Part IV of this book, for example, Wittkopf maintains that explaining Soviet and American political successes from one General Assembly session to the next is a different task from describing them. But although description and explanation may be differentiated for analytic purposes, this does not imply that they function independently. In the first place, they are intertwined in a researcher's "logic-in-use." In the second place, an explanans is composed of descriptive statements; as Kaplan (1964, p. 329) comments, an explanation "does its work, not by invoking something beyond what might be described, but by putting one fact or law into relation with others. . . . each element of what is being described shines, as it were, with the light reflected from all the others; it is because they come to a common focus that they throw light on what is being explained." Aside from these bonds with description, nomological explanations also are linked to prediction through their structural congruence with respect to deductive systemization (Hempel and Oppenheim 1948, p. 164; Tanter 1972, p. 46).[5] As Azar indicates in Part V of this volume, one's predictive capability is enhanced by having a nomological explanation of an event. Thus, while the combination of operational classification and statistical analysis may provide a basis for short-run foreign policy predictions, in the final analysis, explanatory knowledge remains our ultimate goal.

Existential Limitations on Explanation

At the outset of this essay empirical research was cast in terms of a dynamic, circular process undertaken for the purpose of acquiring explanatory knowledge. Presently our explanations of foreign policy output behavior are incomplete in several ways. First, as Braithwaite (1968, p. 347) insists, explanations are indeterminate:

[5] Many, following Scheffler's (1963) lead, have contested this perspective. Much of the present dispute is a product of disregarding those nuances which distinguish the retro-dictive and pro-dictive character of nomological models and their predictive and explanatory uses. According to Rudner (1966, pp. 63–64):

A retro-dictive explanatory argument is one whose *explanandum* describes an event that is temporally antecedent to any events described by the particular-circumstance statements of its *explanans*. A pro-dictive explanatory argument is one whose *explanandum* describes an event temporally posterior to at least one of the particular-circumstance statements of the *explanans*. It should be clear that the pro-dictivity or retro-dictivity of an explanatory argument . . . does not determine whether a given use is a predictive or an explanational use of that explanatory argument; for this latter fact depends *only* on a temporal relation between the *explanandum* and the date on which the use occurs.

To explain a law . . . is to incorporate it in an established deductive system in which it is deducible from higher-level laws. To explain these higher-level laws is similarly to incorporate them, and the deductive system in which they serve as premises, in an established deductive system which is more comprehensive and in which these laws appear as conclusions. To explain the still-higher-level laws serving as premises in this more comprehensive deductive system will require their deduction from laws at a still higher level in a still more comprehensive system. At each stage of explanation a "why?" question can significantly be asked of the explanatory hypotheses; there is no ultimate end to the hierarchy of scientific explanation, and thus no completely final explanation.

Secondly, explanations are indecisive; that is, rather than being absolute truth, they merely eliminate alternative theories. Third, explanations are conditional insofar as they cover only a specific range of phenomena. Fourth, explanations are limited because they are relevant exclusively within particular contexts of inquiry (Kaplan 1964, pp. 352–55). Finally, explanations may remain unconsummated because of their not being testable, their containing laws which do not completely account

FIGURE II–3

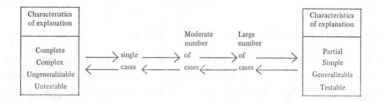

for their explanandum, or their foregoing a presentation of the entire explanans (Hempel 1965, pp. 415–25).

Given these limitations, the researcher is continuously subjected to countervailing pressures "to search for data or to formulate hypotheses, to construct theories or to perform experiments, to focus on general laws or on individual cases, to construct molar studies or molecular ones, to engage in synthesis or in analysis" (Kaplan 1964, p. 30). More specifically, the analyst faces the issue of "trade-offs," where, as Figure II–3 shows, methodological choices affect the characteristics of one's explanatory mode. Take, for instance, Eddington's illustration of the ichthyologist trawling with a net of two-inch mesh (cited in Toulmin 1960, p. 125). Obviously fish less than two inches long will escape him, and he will find only fish two inches or longer upon retrieving the net. Generalizing from this experience he might proclaim that all fish are two or more inches long. But until he examines his methods of catching fish, he will never realize that his methods, not the biological facts, are what led him to his conclusion. The following chapter also encourages us to examine our methodology. By highlighting some of the key problems in making meaningful comparisons in foreign policy studies, Professor McGowan suggests the need to be attentive to the implications our methods and explanatory models have for the kind of knowledge we obtain.

2

Meaningful Comparisons in the Study of Foreign Policy: A Methodological Discussion of Objectives, Techniques, and Research Designs

PATRICK J. McGOWAN

What is new and important in comparative foreign policy analysis is the application of new methods of research to the study of an old subject—foreign policy behavior. This chapter will discuss aspects of social science methodology as they apply to foreign policy research. Students sometimes do not like to study methods; rather, they prefer to go straight to the study of "relevant" topics, such as why and how the United States got involved in Southeast Asia or what the impact of monetary crises on the foreign policies of the industrialized nations of Europe, North America, and Japan will be. These are certainly important questions, and there are hundreds of other equally relevant and interesting questions one could pose. But let us look at these two questions a moment. They ask, respectively, for descriptions and explanations of U.S. intervention and for predictions concerning the future course of relations among the modern industrial nations. Any relevant or important question about foreign policy that one can ask will *always* ask for a description, an explanation, a prediction, or an evaluation (such as whether it was "wrong" for the U.S. to intervene in Vietnam). Social science methodology helps one to describe, explain, predict, and evaluate. Methodology can be applied to answer any questions we now want to ask or may want to ask in the future. Methods show one how to go about asking answerable questions and how to arrive at answers. An understanding of the comparative method is therefore essential, because once the student has this understanding, he will have a tool of analysis that he can apply to any foreign policy question of interest to him. Being general, social scientific methods are perhaps the most relevant subject of all (for excellent recent surveys of general methodology in political studies, see Graham 1971; Mayer 1972; and Holt and Turner 1970).

As a method of inquiry, comparison can be applied in a variety of ways to achieve a diversity of goals. There is no agreement on definition of the comparative method. Each writer whose ideas we shall examine in this chapter gives a different emphasis to the term. Some scholars view comparison as a form of measurement (Hempel 1952; Kalleberg 1966); others view it as a technique for clarifying the meaning and empirical referents of concepts (Sartori 1970; Goodenough 1970); still other social scientists regard comparison as being synonymous with the logic of scientific analysis in general (Mill 1843; Nadel 1951; Zelditch 1971); some see comparison as a particular type of research design (Naroll 1968; Lijphart 1971); finally, some scholars view the comparative method as a solution to the problems of valid cross-cultural measurement and explanation (Przeworski and Teune 1970). And there are yet more subtle distinctions that can be drawn among the views of writers on this subject. What I shall do in this paper is to review the various meanings that comparison and the comparative method have for social scientists and to illustrate the application of each meaning to the comparative study of foreign policy behavior. In so doing, I hope to convey some basic principles of reasoning that students can apply in asking and answering relevant foreign policy questions of interest to them in our interdependent world of the 1970's.

Before we move on to a discussion of the comparative method as applied to foreign policy, we must first outline a conceptual definition of foreign policy behavior and a series of assumptions related to it. Foreign policy behavior can be thought of as the official behavior of the authorities of states that aims to control the behavior of other authorities beyond the jurisdiction of the acting state for the purpose of adapting the national state in an optimal fashion to its external environment (Rosenau 1970; 1971). Let us assume that we have agreed upon some sort of paradigm (Kuhn 1962) or pretheory (Rosenau 1966) for the comparative study of foreign policy that indicates the possible causes of foreign policy behavior, how these predictor variables relate to foreign policy, and how foreign policy feedback affects the acting national state and its environment (McGowan and Shapiro [1973] present one such framework). Furthermore, we shall have to assume that we have developed a valid and reliable way to observe and measure the foreign policy behavior of national states, perhaps by use of events data, as discussed elsewhere in this volume. Finally, we shall simply have to assume that we agree to study foreign policy in a scientific fashion, for we cannot justify this decision within the space of this chapter. In fact, this entire book seeks to make a case for such an approach, as does Rosenau (1971). We have now assumed that we have a definition of foreign policy behavior adequate for comparative research; that we have a conceptual framework that tells us where to begin research; that we can and have measured the behavior in question; and that we want to ask and answer scientific questions about foreign policy. If we can accept, for a time, this set of assumptions, then we can discuss how meaningful comparison is the basic method for the scientific study and measurement of foreign policy behavior.

The Objectives of Comparison

In its widest sense, comparison involves looking at two or more instances of the phenomenon under investigation. Although this mode of thought is inescapable whenever we try to explain or to generalize, the long dominant mode of research in foreign policy studies has been to look at a single case. Diplomatic history, political narrative, and international law all tend to be idiographic—they tend to result in case studies—and these disciplines have long been the backbone of foreign policy studies (e.g., Macridis 1968, 1972). Case studies are very good if one aspires merely to describe what is going on in some area of inquiry. Except in special circumstances, however, they cannot meet the requirements of scientific research. Such research aims to establish relations between variables and to account for these relationships in terms of some general theory. Case studies cannot explain. It is for this reason that researchers who want to study foreign policy scientifically have become comparativists.

Methodological Objectives of Comparison

The first object of comparative research is that of validating facts. It is generally accepted among social scientists that the most reliable means for validating facts is through replication (Glazer and Strauss 1967, pp.

21–31; Suchman 1964). Thus, one way to compare is to ask similar questions about foreign policy in regard to different national states. Another is to repeat someone else's questions in a new situation or in the same state at a later point in time. The most striking use of this approach in comparative foreign policy studies is Tanter's (1966) replication of Rummel's (1963) research. Comparative replication, as in this instance, can lend greater credence to the original findings, but it can also question them, as has evidently occurred frequently in social psychology. In either case, the student can better evaluate research if it is replicated. Not only does he gain a greater appreciation of the meaning of the results, but he also gains a better idea of the reliability of the data and the adequacy of the descriptions involved. Thus, comparative analysis can help refine our tools for the description of foreign policy.

A second methodological object of comparative research is to specify the meaning of a concept (see Hempel 1952; Kalleberg 1966; Sartori 1970). One can spin out endless definitions in an effort to clarify the meaning of a theoretical concept, which as a variable enters into our theories of foreign policy. If, however, the concept is to enter into testable if-then hypotheses, it must be open to operationalization. One may begin with an abstract definition of a concept such as aggressive foreign policy, but it is only by engaging in comparative research, with its many operational and procedural decisions, that the empirical meaning of aggression will emerge. Of particular importance in this respect is the fact that most concepts are culture-bound and refer to what may be the very limited range of behavior particular to the culture in which it originated. By engaging in comparative research, and in this sense we mean both historical and cross-cultural comparison, we broaden the range of empirical variation which our conceptual variables must encompass. This has the important consequence of determining whether our concepts are specific to some culture or historical period, or whether they are the cross-culturally valid general categories we want (Przeworski and Teune 1970). Also, by enlarging the scope of variation we seek to explain, comparison requires theory to explain more than it has before (Marsh 1964). Comparative researchers can, therefore, document the range of variation in behavior, specify the empirical content of concepts, and demand more inclusive theories.

A final methodological use of comparison is in the development of simple descriptive generalizations. How generally valid are the facts in our field? For example, Rummel (1972a) has asserted that the level of participation of national states in foreign affairs is associated with their size and level of development. The bigger and more modern the national state, the more it participates in foreign policy activities. But if we look at thirty-two states of tropical Africa, we find that while size is associated with participation, level of development makes no difference to the state's rate of participation (McGowan 1973a). It would seem that Rummel's "fact," or descriptive generalization, is not as universally valid as he presumes. In any case, foreign policy specialists must heed the warning of one anthropologist: there is no imaginable social arrangement so *outré* that it "cannot be found as a normal part of life in one place or another. One can give many plausible reasons why polyandry cannot work, but work it does in Tibet; one can give many plausible reasons why 'the principle of legitimacy' has to be universal, but it seems not to apply among the lower classes in the British West Indies" (J. Manfredi quoted in Marsh 1967, p. 8). Only through comparative research can we establish the generality of what exists and the relationships among what exists, such as the roles of size and development in foreign policy behavior.

In sum, the central aim of scientific inquiry in foreign policy studies is to explain observed relationships between variables. Comparative analysis makes it possible to accomplish this task. The only social science that has long used comparison is anthropology (see Eggan 1954; Evans-Pritchard 1963; Nadel 1951), which has used the method for two rather distinct purposes. One has been the *idiographic* study of specific cultural histories or traits. The other has been the search to find or test basic laws of society or culture applicable in any society, anywhere, any time (Naroll 1968, p. 236)—a *nomothetic* analysis. Both of these applications of comparison are appropriate for students of foreign policy. When the comparative technique is applied idiographically, it is used as a research tool. Nomothetic uses of comparison focus on theoretical problems. The latter is the main interest of the present chapter.

Theoretical Objectives of Comparison

The idiographic objectives of comparison are largely technical and involve improved description, concept clarification, and descriptive generalization about the truth range of facts. There are five nomothetic, or theoretical, uses of comparison: (1) theory verification through hypothesis testing, (2) theory generalization, (3) theory generation, (4) explanation, and (5) prediction. Most of these aims are straightforward and need little discussion.

The logic of science is general and is the same in its three major forms of application: experimentation, statistical analysis, and comparison (Mill 1843; Lasswell 1968; Zelditch 1971). We may, for example, deduce from a theory an hypothesis which purports to say something meaningful about the real world. Depending on the nature of the phenomena to which the hypothesis relates, we may test the truth of the statement by experiment, by statistical analysis of many natural cases, or by comparative analysis of a few natural cases. The validity of our test—that is, our confidence in the results achieved—depends on our control over the empirical phenomena. Wherever possible, then, we will experiment. If we cannot experiment, we will statistically compare many cases, and where this is impractical, we will qualitatively compare a few (Lijphart 1971). There is no question that comparative data permits the strongest nonexperimental test of deductive hypotheses (Glazer and Strauss 1967, pp. 21–31).

Hypotheses may also be generated inductively on the basis of field work. Since most foreign policy theory has been developed on the basis of research in one rather small corner of the world— (our own) —it may be extremely limited in terms of a general explanatory scheme. Comparative studies need to test in other societies propositions which have been developed about foreign policymaking in the United States, where there has been considerable research on this topic. In one sense this is but another example of hypothesis testing. On the other hand, as Marsh (1967, pp. vii, 5–6) so strongly argues, such tests will lead to the generalization of theory to new contexts, which is the second nomothetic use of comparative analysis.

Explanation and prediction are the fundamental objects of science and of comparative foreign policy analysis. But to explain and predict, the researcher must first of all have an adequate theory of the phenomena involved. It becomes quite clear, then, that the central reason for the application of comparative methods to foreign policy is the generation and validation of theories of foreign policy behavior (Zetterberg 1964). If such fundamental human behavior as visual perception varies across cultures, then there can be little doubt that complex behavior like foreign policy does as well (Segall, Campbell, and Herskovits 1966). If our theories are to account for this variation, then they must be based on the widest possible comparative data. The application of comparative methods allows us to isolate relationships among variables that form the beginnings of causal models of behavior.

One possible type of predictor variable which may have a causal impact on foreign policy behavior is the establishment type. A number of phenomena belong to this class of variables, one of which would be the degree of differentiation among structures in the foreign policy bureaucracy of a national state. The degree of differentiation of a foreign policy bureaucracy can be defined as the number of structurally distinct and functionally specialized organizations in a foreign policy establishment. For the United States, such organizations are the Central Intelligence Agency, Department of Defense, United States Information Agency, United States Agency for International Development, Peace Corps, State Department, Congress, White House Staff, and so on, including all units of government that deal with the foreign relations of the United States on a continuing basis. The comparative analysis of government organization manuals and secondary studies of the foreign policies of the states under analysis would permit the construction of a scale of foreign policy establishment differentiation. It should be noted that the concept of differentiation is abstract and formal, and hence, it can be used to classify and characterize the most diverse societies and foreign policy establishments (Marsh 1967, pp. 31–32).

It seems quite reasonable to hypothesize that the more differentiated the foreign policy establishment, the greater will be the need for interdepartmental coordination by committees and other *ad hoc* bodies. The greater the involvement of committees in foreign policy formulation, the less likely changes in foreign policy will be, since committees are notorious for their inertia. This chain of reasoning suggests the following hypothesis which could be tested comparatively: if a national state has a highly differentiated foreign policy establishment, then its foreign policies will manifest continuity (see Kissinger 1969, pp. 17–26). I have just outlined how differentiation might be measured. Continuity in foreign policy is also open to measurement. Assume for the sake of illustration, however, that both concepts have been operationalized and measured for a sample of fifty contemporary national states. Comparative analysis then proceeds by correlating the two scales of differentiation and continuity.

Correlation is nothing more complex than a comparison of the scores of each national state on the two scales to determine whether a knowledge of that state's differentiation score will improve the ability to predict its foreign policy continuity score. There are four possible relationships between the scores for the sample and for any subset of the sample, as summarized in Table II–2. As the table makes clear, the type of relationship found is determined by the pattern of variation in the scores on the two variables.

TABLE II-2

Relationships between Two Variables Found by Comparative Analysis

Type of relationship	Does the independent variable vary among the units compared? (differentiation)	Does the dependent variable vary among the units compared? (continuity)	Does the dependent variable vary with or independently of the independent variable?	Statistical relationship (such as r)
Replication	No	No		0.0
Universal generalization	Yes	No		0.0
Contingency generalization	Yes	Yes	With	+1.0 to −1.0
Specification	Yes or no[a]	Yes	Independently	0.0

Source: Modified from Marsh 1967, p. 41.

[a] Whether the independent variable varies or not is unimportant for specification. What is important is that the dependent variable varies independently of the independent variable. Because of this, knowing the degree of differentiation would not materially improve our ability to estimate the degree of continuity in foreign policy.

Let us first examine what Marsh (1967, p. 41) has called a contingency generalization. In a contingency generalization the units compared manifest variation in the phenomena measured, and the pattern of variation is shared. Such a relationship is usually expressed as a correlation coefficient, the particular coefficient depending on how we have measured the variables (Blalock 1972). The size of the coefficient expresses the improvement in estimating continuity in foreign policy, given our knowledge of the degree of differentiation in the foreign policy establishments. We have hypothesized that this would be a positive relationship, that is, that national states with high differentiation scores would also have high continuity scores and vice versa. If the correlation which summarizes a contingency generalization is both large and positive in sign, we would regard our hypothesis as being confirmed. Moreover, since the hypothesis derives from some theoretical expectations, if we could show that other factors were equal, we might be willing to infer that this is a causal relation, that differentiation causes continuity. The correlation coefficient, however, might be large and negative in sign. This would mean that highly differentiated establishments are associated with low continuity and vice versa. This is not what we expected, and we would have to reject our hypothesis and seek a reason for this observed relationship. Contingency generalizations can become confirmed general explanatory sentences that are the basis of theory and comprise the most common form of generalization used in explanation and prediction in social science. This role will be discussed subsequently, but first, what about the other three types of relationships?

The correlation associated with each of the other three possible findings would be near zero. All too often, such a result is treated as providing evidence of no relationship, and hence, of being of no importance. Nothing could be farther from the truth. Let us begin with the relationship called specification. As Table II–2 makes clear, our dependent variable varies independently of the independent variable, differentiation. If we found this to be the case, Kissinger's hypothesis would be shown to be false. It has been argued by Karl Popper (1959) that tests which result in the rejection of theories are often the best we can do in science. There are so many plausible theories in the study of foreign policy that the quicker we eliminate the unsatisfactory ones, the better off we will be. In brief, if we have a theoretically derived hypothesis, the finding of no statistical relationship is theoretically as important as finding an expected relationship.

Even if we have a correlation of zero, however, and therefore believe we have an instance of specification, or of no relation between the variables, we may well have a relation hidden in the data. First of all, the relation may be curvilinear rather than the predicted positive linear relationship tested for. That is, a low degree of continuity may be associated with both high and low differentiation, and great continuity, with intermediate levels of differentiation. Thus, both over- and under-administered foreign policy establishments may produce rapid and frequent changes in foreign policy, while establishments with a moderate institutional mix may create continuous policies. Such possibilities should always be looked for in comparative analysis, and the simplest method by which to do so is to plot a scattergram of the national states in terms of the two variables (Tufte 1969).

A second reason why we might have a zero correlation and hence think that there is no relationship among the variables might be because we have come across an instance of a replication or a universal generalization. In each instance at least one variable does not vary significantly, and hence the covariations will be very small or zero. Nevertheless, relationships exist in both instances, and they may be important. Let us suppose that we can introduce a new variable and divide our original fifty states into two categories, old states and new states, based upon whether or not they were independent before 1945. Let us say that we get twenty old states and thirty new states by this method.

Suppose that after division into old and new states, we found no or very little variation in differentiation and continuity among the thirty new states. Thus, all the new states have just a few structures engaged in foreign policy formation, and all manifest great discontinuities in foreign policy. Neither variable varies, and hence the statistical relationship would be zero. But the theoretical relationship found in this instance of a replication could well be very significant. This is only a particular instance of the truism that there is a profound difference between statistical relationships and theoretical relationships. Table II–3 depicts a finding of a replication where all new states are in one cell.

Table II–3 also gives an instance of a Universal Generalization. For the twenty old states the independent variable, differentiation of foreign policy establishment, varies, but continuity in foreign policy as measured is invariant and high. This too is an important finding, for we have located a constant, or parameter—that is, a conceptual variable that in fact does not vary when it should. This universal generalization is universal only for old states, but within that context it can be expressed as follows: for old states, whatever the complexity of administrative ar-

TABLE II–3

Illustration of Replication and Universal Generalization

Continuity in foreign policy	Level of differentiation		Row totals
	Low	High	
High	10 old states	10 old states	20 old states
Low	30 new states	0 new states	30 new states

rangements for making foreign policy, the foreign policies produced will manifest continuity. The reader is left to judge whether or not an actual finding such as this would be of importance to political scientists and policymakers.

The main purpose of comparative research on foreign policy is to build theory. We have seen in this discussion of the four types of relations among variables that each type is important *if* we begin our comparative research with a well formulated hypothesis about the relationship we expect to find. Of these four types, contingency generalizations have the widest possible explanatory ability.

The contingency generalizations developed in comparative research are statistical laws which express associations among the observed variables. When we make a contingency generalization, "we argue from a regularity observed in a number of instances to one taken to hold in all similar instances; we predict that the regularity will be verifiable in the stipulated instances, and we also invite further clarification" (Nadel 1951, p. 246). Such arguments are clearly statistical, and as such, state the probability of the relationship's holding in circumstances stipulated in the law-like generalization. As Nadel (1951, pp. 246–55) points out, two things follow from the nature of the general explanatory statements we can make in the comparative study of foreign policy. First, the truth-probability associated with the law may vary with the number of instances we have examined. The more cases examined, the greater will be the likelihood that the general statement is true for as yet un-examined cases. This is another reason why one cannot make general explanations from a case study, for the probability of any explanation made from one case study being true for other cases is near zero. Thus, because of the nature of the laws we are likely to discover, it is wise to examine comparatively as many cases as restraints of time, money, skill, and access permit.

The second characteristic of the laws that can be developed about foreign policy relates to their universality. Contingency generalizations do not imply determinancy: "A single or infrequent event going counter to any formulated 'law' cannot contradict it since [the law's] validity is only statistical and does not hold for individual cases" (Nadel 1951, p. 254). Since contingency generalizations have this characteristic, the theories of foreign policy that we are likely to develop will describe classes of events and states of affairs as tending to be of a certain kind. The realm of foreign policy is one where more or less likely, or even alternative possibilities hold, where some play must be given to accident, chance, uniqueness, and hence, indeterminancy. But these are questions only of degree, not differences in kind. The law of falling bodies does not absolutely hold near the surface of the earth; it holds only in the assumed vacuum of space or in laboratory vacuum chambers. Quantum physics has even elevated indeterminancy to a principle of science, since at that level of physical events "we cannot . . . in the essence of things, even by any conceivable experiment find out at the same time where an electron is and how fast it is moving" (Andrade 1957, p. 146). Students of foreign policy must learn to live with greater degrees of indeterminancy than physicists, but that does not imply that their theories cannot, *in principle*, offer satisfying explanations of foreign policy or useful predictions about future conditions in foreign affairs.

Several times in this chapter, I have noted that the object of the comparative study of foreign policy is to build theories to explain and predict foreign policy phenomena. But students of foreign affairs are frequently confused about this basic role of theory in social research. Since explanation, prediction, and evaluation are the ultimate objectives of comparative foreign policy analysis, a demonstration of why theory is essential to their achievement will make an appropriate conclusion to this section.

What does it mean to say that we have "explained" something? Explanation may be contrasted with description. It tells us not just what happens, but why. As Raymond has pointed out in the Introduction to Part II, we explain a fact by showing that it is a particular instance of a general tendency. In Kaplan's words: "Explanation is often said to mean the discovery of like in unlike, of identity in difference. We *see* the explanation when we discern the identity, recognizing that what is going on is nothing other than something already known" (Kaplan 1964, p. 338). When we make meaningful comparisons of foreign policy phenomena, we seek contingency generalizations that obtain between an event to be explained, such as foreign policy behavior (effects), and one or more initial conditions, like governmental and societal attributes (causes). As we have seen, if we do find a contingency generalization between the phenomena we are investigating, such as bureaucratic differentiation and continuity in foreign policy, it will express the statistical probability of continuity, given a certain level of differentiation. Any contingency generalization will state that if A occurs, then B will occur with a probability of $1 - e$, where e is error. Now, if e is small, high inductive probability is conferred on the statement that where A_i, there B_i.

An example of a general explanatory sentence, confirmed to some degree as a contingency generalization, might be that, of the national states that have a differentiated foreign affairs establishment, 90 percent also manifest continuity in their foreign policy behavior. This is a statistical law in the form, if A, the probability of B is 0.9. If someone asks why changes in administration from the Democratic to Republican parties and back again in the United States have not greatly affected the nature of American foreign policy, we could refer them to our "law" for an explanation. Our generalization states that 90 percent of the states that belong to the class of states that have differentiated foreign policy bureaucracies also are members of the class of states that show continuity in foreign policy. Thus, because the United States has a differentiated policy establishment, it is a member of the first class and very likely, but not certainly, a member of the second class; it is for this reason that changes in political leadership seem to have no effect. In order to explain foreign policy, we must be able to do two things. First, we must show that some initial condition holds, such as the fact that the U.S. government is bureaucratically differentiated. Second, we must demonstrate that this condition is linked in a *validated general explanatory sentence* to the phenomenon we want to explain—continuity in foreign policy. Such explanations are not nomological; they are based upon contingency generalizations, and therefore they admit of exceptions. But there is no other recognized way to explain observable phenomena.

This example demonstrates how any foreign policy phenomena can be explained and formulates a research program for the field. At the level of description there is the need to establish the most accurate possible factual records of what has happened in foreign affairs. These descriptions will specify both the possible causes and their effects. At the level of inductive theory building we need to create as many useful contingency generalizations and other relationships as possible (see

Table II–2). These statistical laws should be at a number of levels of abstraction, ranging from the rather concrete case just discussed to broad correlational patterns among abstract variables like development and aggression. Finally, comparativists must engage in deductive theorizing in an effort to relate empirical statistical laws to general causal forces, such as the need for national security and for adaptation to the international environment.

Our capacity to predict and evaluate foreign policy is dependent upon the adequacy of our theories. A theory is, after all (as the foregoing example has shown), "an explicit formulation of determinate relations between a set of variables in terms of which a fairly extensive class of empirically ascertainable regularities (or laws) can be explained" (Van Dyke 1960, p. 101). Now, if we know the factors that caused X at time t and hence were able to explain the occurrence of X, it is quite simple to see that if we had known all these causes beforehand, we could have predicted the occurrence of X. Since this is true, if we have generated a theory of the causes of X, like war, we can predict its future occurrence; X would take place when the necessary and sufficient conditions reoccur. This is prediction based on explanatory theory. We can, however, predict on the basis of a mere correlation or contingency generalization. Thus, the United States has had the highest per capita income in the world for a number of years. Knowledge of this simple correlation is sufficient to allow us to predict that next year, Americans will be individually the wealthiest people in the world. Predictions based on reliable contingency correlations are at times useful; however, they are much inferior to predictions based on explanatory theory. This will be made clear when we come to the issue of the evaluation of foreign policy behavior.

Many people study foreign policy because they want such things as a more peaceful world or one in which wealth is more equitably distributed among societies (Dahl 1968). Since neither of these conditions apply in today's world, this means changing it. But how do we change today's foreign policies? The answer is quite clear: by changing the conditions that lead to war and to the poverty of the Third World. But what causes war and the present inequalities of wealth between national states? We really do not know for sure. It is quite clear that if we wish to change the world we must first understand it, and that means building theories of foreign policy. If we have a good explanatory theory, for example, of why wars occur, it will tell us what variables to manipulate to reduce the likelihood of war. The most socially relevant research on foreign policy, then, is theoretical research that is focused on particular problem areas such as war, imperialism, and dependence.

Techniques and Logic of Comparison

Comparison is a method of inquiry, not a field of study. Our subject matter is foreign policy. We propose to study foreign policy via the methods of science; as we have seen, comparative analysis is the heart of the logic of scientific inquiry. As comparison is a method, it can be formalized into a set of five rules that comprise the logical foundations of meaningful comparisons (Zelditch 1971, p. 167). These are as follows:

1. Comparability: two or more instances of a phenomenon may be compared if and only if there exists some variable, say V, common to each instance.
2. Mill's First Canon: no second variable, say U, is the cause or effect of V, if it is not found when V is found.
3. Mill's Second Canon: no second variable U is the cause or effect of V if it is found when V is not.
4. One Variable: no second variable U is *definitely* the cause or effect of V if there exists a third variable, say W, that is present or absent in the same circumstances as U.
5. Causality: no variable is the cause of V if not antecedent to V.

In this section we shall examine the application of these logical rules to the techniques of comparative analysis.

First, let us make sure that we understand these rules and the limits of their sufficiency. The rule of comparability (1) indicates that comparison of objects or events is possible if the researcher can conceptually isolate at least one attribute or condition common to the objects or events and can then proceed to validly and reliably measure the score of each case on this variable. The issue of whether or not apples and oranges or the foreign policies of Ghana and the U.S.S.R. can be compared may be resolved via the identification of concepts like "taste" and "conflict" and the adequate measurement of "sweetness" and "hostility-friendship" (Przeworski and Teune 1966, 1970).

The rule of causality (5) is really general to all scientific inference. Our conception of cause and effect relations almost always includes the idea that the cause, or initial condition, must precede in time the effect, or consequence (Blalock 1964). We will not therefore discuss this rule further, except to note that it implies that hypothetical causes should be observed and measured at points in time prior to their hypothetical effects. This is not always done.

The remaining rules relate to the analysis of relationships among variables, which, as we have already indicated, is the heart of the process of comparison. If we have measured variables U, V, and W, what logical rules must be followed in order to be able to infer correctly from contingency generalizations that U causes V? Mill's first canon states that if we find V, then we must also observe U; and his second canon says that if we find U, then we must also find V (Mill 1843). But there may be other variables involved. Thus, the rule of one variable (4) states that besides Mill's canons' holding, we must be able to rule out the effects of third variables. Psychologists try to rule out such effects by randomization and by carefully controlling the conditions of their experiments. Researchers in comparative foreign policy studies try to rule out the effects of third variables by careful case selection and by statistical procedures such as partial correlation and multiple regression (Naroll 1968; Lijphart 1971; Verba 1967; Blalock 1964, 1971). But even if all five of these logical rules are met in a research study, they are not alone sufficient to support the inference of a causal relation between U and V. To be sure, if one or more of these rules is broken, an inference of causality would be illogical; but alone they are not sufficient to make a causal inference both logical and true and comparison meaningful.

As Zelditch (1971, p. 269) warns, "There is no mechanical procedure that assures any fool of making correct inferences if only the rules are obeyed." In a meaningful comparative foreign policy study, say, of the causes of nuclear armament and national policies toward the nuclear nonproliferation treaty, substantive knowledge and theoretical knowledge would have to be combined with an application of these rules in order to make warranted inferences about the causes of these behaviors. Subject-matter knowledge about how nuclear weapons are made and about the scientific and industrial resources necessary for their production would be necessary for the selection of the cases to be compared. One would be foolish to include in such a study the independent nations of Jamaica, Togo, and Western Samoa, for their leaders have never had to seriously consider the option of going nuclear and thus have never been influenced by certain presumed causes. Knowledge of previous research on this subject would be necessary in order to select an appropriate set of variables to investigate; or would one want to look at the language of the nation or the sex of its head-of-state as reasonable explanatory factors? In any case, the number of factors to be taken into account is literally infinite, and it is only knowledge of subject matter and theory that permits one to select a workable set. Finally, without empirical knowledge and theoretical assumptions, tests of hypotheses concerning proliferation are inconclusive. Is a negative result evidence against the hypotheses in question, or is it evidence of measurement error or faulty reasoning from basic premises? How can one puzzle out the causal relations between variables U, V, and W without making *a priori* assumptions about their relations (Blalock 1964, 1971)? Thus, the five rules of comparison cannot, in themselves, produce meaningful comparisons. When related to the techniques of comparison, they can, however, prove highly useful in the hands of knowledgeable investigators.

Because comparison is a method, it is also a form of measurement. It forms a midpoint between the first step of science, observation, and the end product of our work, generalization. As a program of activity, the scientific study of foreign policy involves five steps: (1) observation, (2) classification, (3) comparison, (4) analysis, and (5) generalization. Since our generalizations are seldom perfect, yet always empirical, two other activities are necessary. First, their imperfection requires us to begin again with improved techniques of observation in search of stronger contingency generalizations. Second, we must depart from science to evaluate the empirical patterns we have found. These activities frequently overlap or are accomplished in a different order than listed. But they are all part of the systematic study of foreign policy and worthy of discussion.

The problems of observation in the scientific study of foreign policy are not peculiar to this field but are common to all the social sciences and are properly discussed in that context (Kerlinger 1964). Only two points seem worth making in the context of the present study. Reliable observation is the foundation upon which the house of science stands. Science, first of all, "seeks to know what exists" (Kalleberg 1966, p. 72). This is as true of foreign policy studies as of any other area of research. Students of foreign policy have been slow to adopt techniques of data gathering that have proven to be reliable methods in other branches of the social sciences. There is a legitimate basis for controversy over whether or not concepts drawn from psychology, anthropology, and sociology should be used by foreign policy specialists, but there seems little basis for debate on whether or not we should increase our use of their techniques of observation (see Kerlinger 1964; and Webb et al. 1966).

The second point about observation in foreign policy studies has to do with basic research strategies. One way of distinguishing among research designs is between field studies and library research. If we engage in field research on comparative foreign policy phenomena, the methods of data gathering used by the behavioral sciences—participant observation, survey research, elite interviews—are particularly appropriate. But if we do field research, we will very likely have only a few societies to compare. Our gain in richness of observational detail will be counterbalanced by the limited generalizations we can make from our few cases. We need such field studies. But if our object is the development of nomothetic generalizations of wide applicability, then most comparative research on foreign policy will be library research, as this permits the examination of many cases.

Library research, a means of indirect observation, involves the collection of documentary data of essentially two types: (1) reports of current and historical events, and (2) aggregated data on national states. Current trends in comparative foreign analysis indicate that aggregate and events type data are being increasingly used by investigators in this field. The nature of these data, how they are made, and their particular strengths and weaknesses are beyond the scope of this methodological essay. Both types are discussed in Merritt (1970); studies of events data are represented in Part III of this book; aggregate data are surveyed in Merritt and Rokkan (1966) and Taylor (1968). Suffice it to say that data-gathering techniques are well developed; what is needed is their intelligent application to the study of foreign policy.

Once data have been gathered, or even while they are being gathered, the student of foreign policy confronts the basic problem in the use of comparison in the social sciences, the variability of human culture. In this context Kluckholm (1953) has observed that "genuine comparison is possible only if non-culture-bound units have been isolated." He speaks of "invariant points of reference" or "universal categories" which the comparativist must use so that his explanations are not merely reflections of the cultural values of his own social system. Abstract, typological categories are necessary so that the raw data of comparative studies can be "classified in some reasonable preliminary way, so that they can be communicated, cross-tabulated, and thought about" (Lazarsfeld and Barton 1951, p. 156). Classification must precede comparison, because "comparison is valid only between two facts of the same type

and between facts with analogous structures" (Duverger 1964, p. 262).
This is merely another way to state the rule of comparability.

The categories of classification that are established by the comparativist should meet three criteria. First, they should be "natural" classes which are theoretically relevant because they "can enter into many and important true propositions about the subject-matter other than those which state the classification itself" (Kaplan 1964, p. 50). Second, classifications for comparative research should be abstract and formal rather than concrete in order to establish the necessary invariant points of reference (Sjoberg 1955, p. 109). Finally, definitions of categories for classification must be operational so that coding decisions as to which category a particular fact belongs can be generally agreed upon, "lest," as Nadel (1951, p. 224) warns, "the study of co-variations be reduced to private computations of individual observers."

The coding rules which, in fact, form the actual definitions of categories must therefore be as clear-cut and logically consistent as possible. Clarity can be achieved by making the rules as detailed as proves necessary so that every case is coded. Criteria for logical consistency can be easily specified. Nominal categories must be mutually exclusive and jointly exhaustive. No observation should be codable in more than one category, and every observation must be coded. To classify, one establishes a set of two or more coding rules such that every entity in a domain D (for instance, foreign policy acts) satisfies only one of the rules. Each rule then defines a class or category, namely the class of all objects in D that satisfies the rule (Kalleberg 1966, p .73).

Once having engaged in the elaboration of coding categories and the classification of objects or events into the categories, the comparativist has left the first stage of scientific research, observation, and moved on to the crucial process of measurement. Nominal classification is a form of measurement, although the most primitive. As Kalleberg (1966, p. 73) has observed: "Science must first of all discriminate. This is the ultimate ground of all scientific measurement, from the simplest procedures of empirical classification based on observation, to comparison, and finally to the complex constructions of quantitative theory." Primitive though it may be, nominal measurement is fully sufficient for comparison (Przeworski and Teune 1970: Zelditch 1971) and for establishing contingency generalizations. In many cases it is as complex a measurement as the nature of observation permits.

Logically, comparison follows classification. We compare by means of rank ordering all of the units in one class according to the order of magnitude they manifest with respect to their common characteristic. Conceived this way, comparison is based upon the rule of comparability. Since classification has preceded comparison, we know that all objects or events in our category have at least one variable on the basis of which they can be compared. Thus, for any two objects in the same class, there are only two logical possibilities in terms of their rank with respect to the variable: (1) they have an equal degree or amount and are therefore in a state of coincidence with respect to it, or (2) one has more than the other object and is in a state of precedence vis-à-vis the second object. Kalleberg (1966, pp. 75–76) has formulated six logical rules which every comparative operation must meet:

1. Coincidence (C) is transitive; that is, whenever unit 1 stands in C to unit 2, and unit 2 stands in C to unit 3, then unit 1 stands in C to unit 3.
2. Coincidence (C) is systematic; that is, whenever unit 1 stands in C to unit 2, then unit 2 stands in C to unit 1.
3. Coincidence (C) is reflexive; that is, any unit stands in C to itself.
4. Precedence (P) is transitive; that is, whenever unit 1 stands in P to unit 2 and unit 2 stands in P to unit 3, then unit 1 stands in P to unit 3.
5. Precedence is coincidence-irreflexive; that is, if unit 1 stands in coincidence to unit 2, then unit 1 does not stand in precedence to unit 2.
6. Precedence is coincidence-connected; that is, if unit 1 does not stand in coincidence to unit 2, then unit 1 stands in precedence to unit 2 or unit 2 stands in precedence to unit 1.

The primary methodological point of these rules is that "*two objects being compared must be of the same class*—they must either *have* an attribute or *not. If* they have it, and *only* if they have it, may they be compared as to which has it more and which has it less" (Kalleberg 1966, p. 76). This rule of comparability is frequently ignored in comparative research. It would be foolish, for example, to compare France and Ghana in terms of the wars they have fought overseas since 1945 and to conclude that Ghana is a less warlike society than France. Because it lacks the capacity to undertake military operations outside its territorial boundaries, Ghana belongs to a different class of states from that to which France belongs. The only logically meaningful comparison is to compare France to other societies with the variable attribute, the capacity to conduct an overseas war. We must remember that "classification is a matter of 'either/or'; comparison is a matter of 'more or less.' Two 'objects' being compared must already have been shown to be of the same class" (Kalleberg 1966, p. 81). To conclude, it must be stressed that to make meaningful comparisons, foreign policy research must be seen as being at heart a conceptual exercise. Adequate classificatory concepts which permit the comparativist to sort foreign policy observations must be developed. Adequate comparative concepts which allow one to rank order foreign policy actors must also be developed. In addition, these concepts must be defined in terms of explicit and concrete procedures. Because a diamond will scratch all other gemstones, but none of them will scratch a diamond, we can say it is the hardest gem (Kalleberg 1966, pp. 75, 81). Such a straightforward, commonsense test of comparative "hardness" is a model to which we should aspire in the study of foreign policy.

Comparison, then, can be defined as a form of nonmetrical or ordinal measurement. Once data have been observed and measured on the appropriate scale, they are then analyzed. In most instances, analytical techniques will be statistical. Statistical techniques give fairly precise estimates of the strength of contingency generalizations, in such form as correlation coefficients, and of their plausibility, in the form of significance tests. In some situations, particularly in the analysis of field research materials on a limited number of cases, the method of concomitant variations will be more appropriate (Lijphart 1971). Nadel (1951, pp. 229–36) has ably described how this technique may be used by field workers in social anthropology, and the method is equally applicable for comparative foreign policy studies.

The method of concomitant variation is based upon Mill's canons and the rule of one variable. One begins with social situations which are comparable, which share common features while differing in others, or which have the common features in somewhat different degrees. Thus, when Waltz (1967) compared foreign policy formation in the United Kingdom and the United States, he held constant many cultural factors and political variables, since both are liberal democracies with far-flung involvement in world affairs. Two important features varied, however: the contrast between parliamentary and presidential democracy and the more pronounced elitism of the British establishment. Waltz was able to conclude "that in matters of foreign policy . . . the American Presidential system is superior to British Parliamentary government," because "American institutions facilitate rather than discourage the quick identification of problems, the pragmatic quest for solutions, the ready confrontation of dangers, the willing expenditure of energies, and the open criticism of policies" (pp. 307–8).

This somewhat literary proposition can be formalized into a contingency generalization in the following form: presidential systems of government (U) in industrially developed, democratic societies, with deep involvement in international politics facilitate open criticism of foreign policy (V). This generalization seems to hold for Britain and America. But what about Fifth Republic France, which was presidential, industrial, democratic, involved, and yet, apparently, lacking in effective criticism of de Gaulle's policies? Does the generalization hold in preindustrial societies? Many such questions could be asked. The method of concomitant variations clearly invites further testing because the rule of one variable is so difficult to meet. Sewell (1967, pp. 208–9) has summarized what a comparativist working with concomitant variation techniques can do with Waltz's tentative findings:

He can check this hypothesis by trying to find other societies where U occurs without V or vice versa. If he finds no cases which contradict the hypothesis, his confidence in its validity will increase, the level of his confidence depending upon the number and variety of comparisons made. If he finds contradictory cases, he will either reject the hypothesis outright or reformulate and refine it so as to take into account the contradictory evidence and then subject it again to comparative testing. By such a process of testing, reformulating, and retesting, he will construct explanations which satisfy him as convincing and accurate.

In sum, this is the method of concomitant variation studies. That the method ends in explanatory generalizations demonstrates its unity with comparative statistical studies (Lijphart 1971). The logic of control is the same, the only real difference being in the number of cases examined. But this discussion of concomitant variation as a method of data analysis was necessary because so many students of foreign policy use it on an implicit basis without trying to introduce into their studies the rigor and clarity which it can share with other scientific approaches to the study of foreign policy.

The end product of the scientific study of foreign policy is generalization and theory development. It does not appear that theories of foreign policy behavior will present any particular problems that are not shared with other behavioral sciences. This includes what may be the ultimate impossibility of devising direct empirical tests of the basic, most general theoretical propositions of foreign policy theory. Thus, direct tests of adaptation hypotheses put forward by Rosenau (1970) are unlikely. This problem may be overcome by devising "linkage systems," which involve theoretical assumptions that bridge the gap between operational —that is, measurable—variables and the unmeasured concepts of our macrotheory. These and other problems involved in empirical theory construction are discussed by Blalock (1968, 1969) and Stinchcombe (1968).

While the scientific-comparative study of foreign policy ends with validated theories, the systematic study of foreign policy should not. In the comparative study of foreign policy, as in all political studies, "after discovering what are the facts and explaining why they are what they are, there is the final task of ethical evaluation" (Lipson 1957, p. 381). Values, private and public, are involved in any study of foreign policy. The private values of the researcher or the public values of his employer invariably influence his choice of problems to research. To the extent that his empirical findings relate to policy issues, they can have an impact on public values. If the student of foreign policy has a scientific orientation to his subject, he is aware of this role of values in research. Just because of this he adopts scientific procedures in order to reduce as far as possible the chance that his or anyone else's values will influence his findings. That this can or should be done is open to some dispute (see Brecht 1959), but responsible scholarship which aims at establishing reliable knowledge must eschew the clamor for relevancy if this means allowing personal or public values to predetermine research results. Students of the problems involved also conclude that a scientific approach to human behavior can reduce to negligible levels the role of preferences and values in determining findings. Since there are so few reliable and valid generalizations in the field of foreign policy, many scholars are loath to claim a special voice in public debate about foreign policy issues. This is presently a defensible position, but as our field develops, this position will become less responsible.

Research Designs in Comparative Foreign Policy Studies

One way of distinguishing among comparative studies is on the basis of how the data were collected. If one adopts this approach, three possible collection methods emerge: (1) library studies, (2) field work, or (3) studies that blend field work with library research (Lewis 1961). Very often considerations of time, money, and access determine the researcher's choice among these possibilities. The field of comparative foreign policy needs all three approaches, and it is always preferable to choose the approach best suited to providing answers to the questions one is asking.

Another way of looking at the issue of research design focuses on the questions being asked. The comparative method is a way to experiment artificially by selecting cases so as to maximize desired variation in the research variables and to control unwanted variation among other possibly confounding variables. We can distinguish among four research designs on the basis of the number and type of cases selected: (1) the case study, (2) concomitant variation designs, (3) regional comparisons, and (4) the intersocietal survey. Since each of these designs can be either cross-sectional or longitudinal, there are really eight basic research designs of theoretical importance (on general research design considerations in social science, see Campbell and Stanley 1966).

Case Studies

The basic rule in comparative research design is, of course, that *"we should use for comparison whatever social systems will be useful in determining the validity of our hypotheses"* (Sewell 1967, p. 215). Thus, as in almost every other area we have treated in this chapter, the ideal basis of choice is always theoretical, although practical considerations like money or personality may intervene (Glazer and Strauss 1967, p. 49). All comparative research designs, including the case study, should give prime emphasis to building nomothetic theory. It is the fact that the case study of a single society's foreign policy can contribute to such theory that gives it scientific status. It takes the observation of only one black swan to falsify the universal hypothesis that all swans are white. Likewise, the recording of an instance in which an international arms race did not end in an international war would falsify an hypothesis which said arms races always lead to wars among the competitors. Case studies, consequently, are a form of scientific study of foreign policy *if* the case is selected in order to determine whether or not a theory of foreign policy is false. Falsification is stressed, because showing that the theory held in only one more instance would add little to its credibility.

This theoretically oriented use of case studies is limited for two reasons, however. It implies, first, that there already exist explicit, testable propositions in the discipline. Moreover, for the case study to achieve its greatest impact, these testable propositions should be rather central ones with some degree of universality. Now, in the field of foreign policy, propositions which are at the same time testable, nontrivial, and universal are few and far between. This severely limits the scientific use of case studies. Second, since most of the generalizations that do exist in this field are in the form of statistical laws, finding one case that goes against the "law" does not invalidate it, as previously noted. For these reasons I am persuaded that at the present stage in the development of the scientific study of foreign policy, case studies are of limited use (an opposite view is found in Paige 1968, pp. 9–12).

This harsh conclusion can be moderated somewhat, since case studies can serve what we might call accessory purposes in scientific study. A case study can generate data and description, which are then grist for the comparativist's mill. Such basic research is indispensable and can achieve the highest standards of scholarship. It is not, however, social science if one agrees that science is concerned with building nomothetic theory. While science must first of all observe, it must do much more to be worthy of the name. Case studies can also generate interesting concepts and provocative insights. Both can be extremely useful for others, although they are unfortunately seldom followed up on a systematic basis. A third way a case study can be useful is when it is an explicit comparison to another case study. The case study may also be used to generate hypotheses that can be validated subsequently in actual comparative research. A very useful type of case study is what can be called a deviant case study. This fifth type involves the study of a case that does not fit an already well-established contingency generalization. The analysis of such cases can refine and improve theory considerably (Lijphart 1971).

A final application of the case study approach is the examination of one nation's foreign policy over time, with similar instances of its action compared to each other. As with all case studies, the student is still unable to determine how typical the national state selected is, but this approach at least permits the elaboration of some valid generalizations about how this particular state manages its external relations. Much of the literature on American foreign policy is of this type, although the comparisons are seldom as explicit and rigorous as a true comparativist would like. Such studies can be genuinely comparative, but to the extent that they are, they become a type of most-similar design wherein one compares policies rather than different actors (e.g., Ness 1969).

Concomitant Variation Designs

The method of analysis involved in concomitant variation studies has already been discussed. In terms of research design problems there are two basic types of concomitant variation designs: Most-similar and most-different comparisons (Przeworski and Teune 1970, pp. 31–46). Most-similar comparisons have long been favored by social and cultural anthropologists (Eggan 1954; Evans-Pritchard 1963). It is their view "that *differences arising from similarities* are the most fruitful field from which to derive generalization" (Southall 1965, p. 136). When one engages in most-similar comparison, two or more cases are selected which are as similar as possible. The object is to hold constant, and thus control, as many factors as possible—such as culture, level of development, or geographical zone—so that variations in independent and dependent variables will stand out and permit the clear demonstration that they covary. The factors that differ should be the concepts representing the causes and effects of the theoretical hypotheses one is investigating. Nadel's (1952) comparison of witchcraft in four African societies is a classic instance of a most-similar comparison, as is Redfield's (1941) famous study of Yucatan social organization. In foreign policy studies, examples of the most-similar design are Wolfers (1941), Waltz (1967), and Ness (1969). Most-similar comparison is "essentially a substitute for the experimental method" (Duverger 1964, pp. 265–67) and is especially appropriate for field studies where one wishes to test explicitly formulated hypotheses.

A second type of concomitant variation design manipulates differences rather than similarities and is what Przeworski and Teune call the most-different systems design (1970, pp. 34–39). In such designs one chooses cases that are clearly dissimilar in most respects, but which present at least two common features. If one can identify similar relationships within widely diverse contexts, one is able to isolate invariant features of foreign policy behavior. Thus, it does make sense to compare foreign policy formulation in Ghana between 1960 and 1966 to the same process in the United States. Such a study would investigate the hypothesis that whatever the gross differences in socioeconomic development and international posture between these two states, presidential leadership in foreign affairs with a crisis-type decision situation will lead to a common pattern of decision-making in the two greatly different foreign policy establishments. Most-different comparison can be particularly useful in the search for uniformities, applications, and universal generalizations that may enter into the elaboration of typologies and theories of foreign policy behavior (see Table II–1).

Most-similar and most-different comparisons are a marked improvement over the case study in their capacity to yield nomothetic generalizations. The findings produced by such studies, however, can hardly be regarded as conclusive for three reasons. First, although concomitant variation studies claim to control for all unwanted variation in confounding variables (hence their frequently used alternative name, *controlled comparison*), they in fact hold constant only certain macrophenomena such as economy or language. This is clearly more scientifically rigorous than ignoring control problems altogether, as so often happens in foreign policy case studies; but concomitant variation studies seldom actually list all possible relevant factors and demonstrate that they are being held constant by the judicious selection of cases. They therefore violate the rule of one variable. The incomprehensive, informal, and unsystematic efforts at control one finds in most concomitant variation studies greatly weaken the conclusiveness of their findings (Naroll 1968, pp. 240–41).

A second limitation of this type of design derives from the small number of cases examined. While the method can establish correlations, they are not open to causal analysis. Either there are too few cases or there is too low a level of measurement for statistical inferences about causal influence to be drawn. Most available methods of causal inference require an interval level of measurement and a sufficient number of cases to establish meaningful product-moment correlations (Blalock 1964, 1971). Concomitant variation studies seldom examine more than three or four cases at a time. Variables are measured on nominal scales—the presence or absence of features—or on ordinal scales—the few cases being rank-ordered by the degree to which they manifest certain characteristics. Designs which are longitudinal and thus permit the specification of the temporal sequence of events can overcome this handicap, however.

Another difficulty of concomitant variation studies is Galton's problem —the possibility that observed correlations do not represent functional relationships among variables measured by independent trials but are rather "artifacts of culture-trait borrowing from a common source" (Naroll 1968, pp. 241, 258). This is a clear problem for anthropologists seeking valid contingency generalizations, and it also applies in comparative foreign policy. For example, one might investigate legislative control of foreign policy in Africa and find that in Kenya, Tanzania, and Zambia, legislatures do not have specialized committees dealing with foreign relations. Is this correlation a valid finding about the African approach to the conduct of foreign policy, or is it rather an instance of borrowing the British organizational procedure in these matters? Most-similar designs cannot overcome this problem. Galton's problem can be avoided by engaging in most-different comparison, which should always be used as a check on the possibility that findings based upon most-similar comparisons are spurious. In the above example, if former British colonies in Asia and the West Indies also lacked parliamentary foreign relations committees, we would have a clear-cut example of the diffusion of an aspect of foreign policy making, rather than an example of a fundamental tendency regarding the involvement of Third World legislative bodies in the conduct of foreign policy.

Regional Comparisons

A third possible research design is the regional comparison. Regions may be defined in terms of geography or in terms of behavior (Russett 1967). Students with area interests will frequently wish to compare the foreign policies of the societies which comprise their area of interest, such as Africa (e.g., McGowan 1968, 1969, 1973a). Methodologically, such regional comparisons hold many factors constant and are concomitant variation studies on a larger scale (Naroll 1968, p. 242). But because of the increased number of cases—about forty for Africa and twenty for Latin America—the problems involved are reduced. Galton's problem of diffusion remains, as does the problem of not really controlling for all possible confounding factors. Galton may be circumvented by accepting diffusionally caused similarities and searching for differences or variations within the context of similarity. The increase in number of cases examined permits one to control statistically for a number of, but not all, confounding variables. It also necessitates quantitative measurement, and hence, causal inference becomes a possibility.

A very exciting possibility is opened up by Russett's (1967, 1968) research. He has identified a number of varying regional groupings on the basis of national state characteristics and policy similarities such as United Nations voting and international trade patterns. The student of comparative foreign policy could select for more intensive analysis one of these regional groups, such as the twenty-three nation Afro-Asian group identified by the analysis of General Assembly voting patterns; and beginning with this empirical similarity, he could see if other foreign policy patterns were associated with it. Such research designs would create a more cumulative science of foreign policy studies. Finally, regional studies can provide a useful check on the validity of generalizations generated from intersocietal surveys. Collins (1973), for example, has found that for African states there is a relationship between internal disorder and externally aggressive behavior. This specifies more clearly the scope of the work of Rummel (1963) and Tanter (1966), which found no such relation in a world-wide survey of states.

Intersocietal Surveys

The research design most capable of yielding valid and reliable contingency generalizations is the intersocietal survey. At its most comprehensive, the intersocietal survey would examine the foreign policies of all independent societies, present and past. There has, however, never been agreement on a list of all the states that have ever existed that were free to make foreign policy; much less do we have data on their foreign policies. Therefore, the universe of societies to be examined would have to be limited in some way, such as all societies which exchanged ambassadors with at least one other society since A.D. 1500, or all societies at present exchanging ambassadors with at least one other society. The latter definition of the universe to which our generalizations would apply would include the present membership of the United Nations and a few nonmembers, such as Formosa and the two Koreas—somewhat over 140 states.

The advantage of the intersocietal survey is that since it looks at all possible cases, it encompasses the totality of possible variations in behavior. The limitation of the case study—its external validity—is removed because generalizations emerging from an intersocietal survey are descriptive of all cases and not inferential to yet unexamined cases. In brief, if we seek to find nomothetic generalizations that hold for any society, at any time, anywhere, then intersocietal surveys provide the most direct route to this goal. This design, however, shares certain problems with both concomitant variation and regional comparisons. They are (1) making causal inferences from correlations, (2) unit of analysis definitions, (3) sampling bias, (4) Galton's problem—interdependent cases, (5) data quality control, and (6) concept formation (Naroll 1968, pp. 244–73). I shall briefly discuss each in turn.

Our fundamental objective is to make causal inferences from observed relations. This is the most general problem of all. We wish to establish correlations which, when properly tested, can be inferred to represent causal regularities between an effect and one or more initial conditions. Having established empirical correlations through our methods of analysis, the other five issues become problems of causal inference if there is reason to think that the variables correlated are being similarly biased or distorted by one or more of these factors. If they are in fact being biased, then correlations will be mere statistical artifacts rather than indicators of causal relations.

A number of techniques are available for causal inference. If we have a model which represents the causal patterns between, say, four independent variables and one dependent variable, the Simon-Blalock technique may be used to test the goodness of fit of the model (Blalock 1964). Estimates of the causal potency of the paths linking the independent variables to the effect may be made with path analysis (Land 1969; Blalock 1971). Since these approaches to causal inference make a number of restrictive assumptions, Naroll has developed another technique, influence analysis. This technique uses statistical and logical criteria in combination to test the model. If the four statistical tests Naroll uses consistently show that the independent variables are uncorrelated but that each is highly correlated with the supposed effect, and if logical analysis demonstrates that there is no other explanation which so parsimoniously accounts for the observed data, then the explanation embodied in the model is accepted. The causes of the effect have been established (Naroll 1968, pp. 244–48).

When the intersocietal survey is used in the comparative study of foreign policy, the researcher is confronted by two definitional problems: (1) When one counts national states that have foreign policies, what is one in fact counting? (2) What is the sampling universe from which one draws a probability sample for data collection and analysis? (Naroll 1968, p. 251.) Another way of putting these two questions is to ask what are the acting units, and how many are there, or have there been? To say glibly that the societies whose foreign policies we should study are the members of the United Nations plus a few outsiders is unsatisfactory. Such a definition would obviously be inapplicable to the comparative study of nineteenth-century foreign policy. Even worse is to define our units as those that report to the United Nations Statistical Office so that their gross national products can be recorded in the *Statistical Yearbook*. Many social collectivities conduct meaningful external relations; churches, labor unions, international businesses, and international organizations are only a few examples.

What, then, are the actors and the actor attributes that comparative foreign policy analysis investigates? Decisive answers to this question are not, at present, available, but they are needed if we are to make meaningful comparisons. It has been argued elsewhere (McGowan 1973a) that the primary actors are national states; that what we seek to explain is the official collective behavior of national states toward other actors in their external environments; and that what accounts for this foreign policy behavior is a set of actor attributes ranging from the individual personalities of key decision-makers to changes over time in the actor's international environment. The comparative analysis of foreign policy therefore works at levels of analysis ranging from individuals to international systems (Singer 1969b). The units observed are individuals, subnational groups, nations and their attributes, and international organizations and structures. Meaningful comparison in foreign policy requires the consideration of explanatory factors within national systems, among national systems, and beyond national systems (Przeworski and Teune 1970, pp. 47–87).

We must also develop a standard definition of the behavior we study. This is a particularly troublesome problem because such units may not be independent behaviors, but those associated with each other over time. In fact, this is what we mean when we talk of foreign *policies*. Such serial correlation can be tested for. Behavioral units of analysis can be defined as foreign policy acts, as reported in public records of current and historical events. This defines the foreign policy acts that are correlated with attributes of foreign policy actors and their environments. What the sampling universe of such acts is we do not know and probably can never determine, given the inherent limitations of observation in our field (McGowan 1973b). What we must accept, then, is the need for careful and extensive reliability checks on our data sources in an effort to specify the biases inherent in the number and types of events they record (see the discussion in Part III of this volume).

Sampling bias may arise in two ways, first, in the selection of societies whose foreign policy behavior is to be studied, and second, in the selection of acts representing foreign policy behavior. The most direct way to get around the problem of sampling societies is not to sample, but instead, to survey all the units in the universe. But in view of the fact that there have been an estimated five thousand independent societies on earth and that some documentation exists for about two thousand of these societies, a survey presents immediate problems. If we chose to concern ourselves only with contemporary national states, we would still have over 140. Examining even this markedly reduced number of foreign policy actors would be a difficult task and would greatly reduce the richness of the data we could collect on them. Some research on foreign policy will use an intersocietal approach that includes all contemporary societies. I suspect, however, that the really interesting questions can be answered only when we study a smaller number of actors for which we have good data. This, therefore, implies some sampling procedure.

Before we can sample societies, we need a list of the population from which we can draw our sample. Russett, Singer, and Small (1968) have established a very useful list of national and quasi-national entities that have existed since 1900. It contains 156 societies which, by their criteria, have been at some time independent since 1900. A comparativist interested in doing an intersocietal survey of the societies on the list could randomly sample them, but this would be an inappropriate procedure for two reasons. First, data on the foreign policies of these units are very unevenly distributed. While we have plenty for France and the United States, what about Eire, Upper Volta, Asir, Yemen, and Western Samoa, which are also part of this universe of 156 states? Thus, prior to sampling, the list must be stratified on the basis of bibliographically acceptable limits. If we are using a source of publicly available data like *Deadline Data,* we would have to exclude from the list societies like Newfoundland, Austria-Hungary, Estonia, and the Hejaz Sultanate, which ceased to be independent before the commencement of this source. If we are using narrative histories of foreign policy as our data source, societies whose foreign policies have been described only in scant detail would have to be eliminated. How many national states on the Russett list have at least a hundred pages of descriptive history devoted to their foreign policies? This would have to be determined before a sample was drawn, or it would be unduly biased by very scant data on many of the states sampled. This sort of problem shows why descriptive case studies remain important. The second reason why random sampling procedures would be inappropriate is Galton's problem. Of the societies on Russett's list, forty-four, or nearly 30 percent, are in Africa. Yet, the closer any two societies are to each other geographically, the more likely they are to share characteristics of common historical origin. The correlation among variables in our sample might represent an African syndrome, rather than functional relationships true for all societies.

The answer to these problems is straightforward. First, Russett's list should be reduced to include only societies for which adequate documentation is available. Note must be made of the biases introduced in doing this. Second, the reduced list should be stratified by geographical or political regions as established by Russett (1967) or by genotypes as defined by Rosenau (1966). Then a probability sample can be selected by drawing cases from each of the strata according to assigned probabilities. Thus, since 30 percent of the list might be African and about

15 percent Latin American, the comparativist would make it twice as likely for a Latin American society to be selected as an African society. Such a procedure would ensure equal representation in the sample to societies from the major sociocultural regions of the world, and thereby reduce the likelihood of spurious correlations emerging from historical diffusion.

Once a probability sample of, say, fifty societies has been drawn, the comparativist is still confronted with the problem of sampling the behavior of his actors. Again, one could try to record all identifiable acts during a given period of time. But if this time period is long enough and the data sources rich enough, the number of events available for coding will increase to unmanageable proportions. Since there is no reason to believe that there are seasonal variations in foreign policy, one can randomly select a limited number of days or months from each year for which acts will be coded for the societies under analysis. We do know, however, that international crises provoke flurries of foreign policy activity, and therefore, before sampling selected days, we would want to stratify the sample in such a fashion that crisis behavior would not be overrepresented in the sample. Thus, a study that randomly selected foreign policies of Middle Eastern states since 1965 could well produce correlations describing the events of June 1967 rather than being true of the entire period under analysis. How samples of actors and acts are drawn will vary depending on our research questions. All we need to do is to be aware of the consequences of the sampling decisions we make (Sartori 1970).

A related issue, Galton's problem, is associated with the fact that through geographic propinquity and/or historical associations the national states that we observe are not statistically independent but rather are interdependent, and thus knowledge of one society will help us predict characteristics of the other society. Since industrialization diffused from a common source, Great Britain, the closer any society is to Britain, the more likely it is to be industrialized, as is generally the case when we move eastward from the English Channel. Since the Ivory Coast and Malagasy were both colonies of France and achieved independence under the Fifth Republic, we should not be surprised to find them sharing similar governmental structures modeled after de Gaulle's constitution, although geographically and culturally they are far apart. As Naroll (1968, p. 259) has commented, "Galton's problem . . . is to test apparently functional correlations between traits to see if they are

mere artifacts of historical relationship—i.e. to control for diffusion."
When engaging in intersocietal surveys, the student of comparative
foreign policy should make sure he gathers data both on geographical
distances between his units and on their historical relations. Simple
partial correlation analysis will then permit him to determine whether
such diffusions have biased his findings.

Data quality control is a problem inherent in any research design. We
must never forget that we are not directly observing foreign policy behavior or attributes of international actors and their environments.
Rather, we study statistical tables, current events series, and historical
monographs about foreign policy. Very briefly, our task is to make reliable inferences and generalizations from more or less unreliable sources.
It is insufficient to test for intercoder reliability, which, when successful,
shows only that coders agree on what the source says. Such tests, although they should always be done, say nothing about observational
errors in the source itself. Intercoder reliability tests check for error
produced by measurement, not that produced by observation. It is common knowledge, for example, that many less developed countries inflate
their literacy and per capita income figures in order to enhance their
international prestige. The problems of the quality of quantitative data
have been ably discussed elsewhere (Taylor 1968; Merritt and Rokkan
1966) and will not be examined here. But what about the trustworthiness of qualitative, documentary materials?

First, as with data already quantified, we need to watch out for
systematic bias rather than random error. The artificial inflation of
literacy rates is an example of such bias. Systematic bias will give spuri-
ously large correlations; random error will, if anything, reduce the size
of the correlations, making any significant ones even more worthwhile
because of their capacity to emerge from the confusion of inaccurate observation. The key to controlling for systematic bias is to observe the
observer as well as what he says. For example, in an English-language
source of current events like *Deadline Data,* one might suspect systematic
bias caused by the overrecording of the foreign policy behavior of
English-speaking states. To check this, one could compare the frequency
of reported acts for Britain and France, Ghana and the Ivory Coast, and
a number of other pairs. If the English-speaking nation invariably has
more acts reported for it, then we have identified a bias in *Deadline
Data* for which we must control.

Data quality control of narrative materials proceeds in similar fashion.

Essentially one asks what sort of reputation for reliable, objective, thorough reporting the political historian has. One way of doing this is to ask a panel of historians to tell you. Their expert judgement will provide the comparativist with a quality control scale which can be correlated with other variables to test for bias. When such a direct approach is precluded, one can infer the trustworthiness of the observations from the mode of publication and characteristics of the author. Who, for example, published the book? If all one's descriptions of Soviet foreign policy appeared under the imprint of the Hoover Institution and all reports of American foreign policy came from the Monthly Review Press, one might have a serious bias problem. Was the author a central participant in the events he describes? If not, give him points for reliability. How did he collect his data? Did he use only one source of information, such as documents, or did he combine library research with interviews? The more methods used, the greater his chances of accurate observation. How well does he know the society whose foreign policy he describes? How long did he live there, does he speak the language, has he returned since he did his research? A long period of residence and language fluency should increase trustworthiness. If he has returned to the society since he published his study, one may suspect that he did not tell the whole truth, at least if his research focused on one of the Afro-Asian states. Of course, historians have been asking such questions for centuries. The comparativist engaged in an intersocietal survey systematically asks these questions, records the answers, and intercorrelates his data quality control measures with the indicators of his conceptual variables to test in a rigorous fashion for systematic bias (Naroll 1962). For example, foreign-policy making in the United States is notorious for the amount of conflict, bargaining, and generally political behavior involved in reaching decisions. When American scholars describe foreign-policy making in other societies, do their reports evidence greater emphasis on the political aspects than do descriptions by scholars from other societies? If they do, the comparativist has identified a likely candidate for systematic bias in observation among his political historians.

A final possible source of problems in all comparative research designs is that of conceptual definitions. More than anything else in the comparative study of foreign policy, we need a set of basic, theoretically relevant concepts which are logically coherent and operationalizable in order to process data collected from many national states (Goodenough 1970, pp. 98–130).

Conclusion

As a process, science is a circular activity. We may begin with what we think are perfectly adequate definitions of concepts and plausible hypotheses. But it is only by engaging in comparative research that we can determine if the concepts are open to operationalization, if they encompass the range of variation exhibited by our data, and if the hypotheses serve any purpose in explaining the patterns we find. More likely than not, our conceptual definitions and hypotheses will fail to serve us well in one of these respects, and we will have to reformulate them and begin again. Clearly then, it is only by doing comparative research on foreign policy that we can improve both our methods and our theoretical knowledge. In the study of foreign policy, as in the study of all things political, Grosser's (1972, p. 123) dictum applies: "Connaître pour comparer, comparer pour connaître!"

Part III

Indicators of Foreign Policy Behavior

Introduction:
The Generation and Use of Events Data

CHARLES W. KEGLEY, JR.

The authors of the preceding chapters have argued that it is possible to build reliable and verifiable knowledge about the behavior of nations through the application of the comparative method to the study of that phenomena (Rosenau) and have outlined some of the analytic procedures by which meaningful comparisons of foreign policy might be made (McGowan). A necessary step in the process of empirical inquiry is the collection of data regarding the behavior of states in the international arena, for only then can one move from hypothesis to empirical generalization. In order to study foreign policy comparatively, one must observe and classify the kinds and volume of actions that states direct toward one another. Evidence is required to build scientific knowledge, because without observational data we are unable to estimate the plausibility of theories. As Jones and Singer (1972, pp. 3–4) have cogently expressed it, "Whether we seek to understand the past or anticipate the future, we need something more than vague recollections or a vivid imagination. We need evidence. Without evidence, there is little basis for selecting among the contending (and often, equally plausible) models and explanations of the international politics we have experienced, and until we can adequately account for the past and present, our predictions of the future will remain mere conjecture."

Until recently, the student of foreign policy had few systematically collected bodies of data to analyze in order to arrive at empirical generalizations. This paucity of data was due in part to the fact that there are few publicly available records of foreign policy behavior, and partly because that behavior does not possess many empirical referents—ones which are visible, and therefore, open to independent inspection. The activities that represent state conduct are not directly observable, because much of foreign policy behavior is conducted in secret, behind closed doors. While it is indeed possible to study national foreign policy indirectly by inferring its character from such things as the state's voting record in international organizations, the speeches its representatives make about foreign policy, and the treaties it enters into, these sorts of information comprise at best a second-order reality and are exceedingly difficult to collect systematically for a large number of national actors in the international system. Hence, the attendant difficulty of monitoring the activity flowing across national borders on a cross-national basis has hitherto limited the quantity of data with which the comparativist could study what nations were doing to each other.

Data-Making for the Study of Foreign Policy Behavior

In order to rectify this problem, a number of quantitatively inclined researchers began to investigate alternate solutions to the observation of external conduct. The result of these efforts was the events data research movement, which consisted of a large number of scholars with disparate interests sharing the common desire to derive new measures of interstate behavior.[1] Two assumptions guided their endeavors.

First, it was recognized that systematic observation of foreign policy required a prior agreement on the meaning and defining attributes of foreign policy. One cannot reliably observe a phenomenon until one conceptualizes it in terms which allow him to specify what constitutes an instance of it. Unfortunately, one of the problems plaguing foreign policy analysis has been that "no agreement exists on the meaning of foreign policy" (Hermann 1972, p. 70). People use the term in different and often contradictory ways: some define foreign policy in terms of the goals states pursue ("country X is expansionist"); others, in terms of the process by which policies are made ("X's policy is democratic"); and still others in terms of national effect ("country X is conflictual") or

---

[1] The events approach has a long intellectual history, with roots going back to Grotius (1583–1645). For a statement of the origins, legacy, and theoretical underpinnings of the events approach, see Phillips (1973b).

alignment dispositions ("country X is a neutral"). Such imprecision invites semantic confusion and encourages polemics rather than disciplined inquiry. To circumvent this problem, events researchers reasoned that foreign policy should not be defined in terms of the motives or intentions of policymakers; such a definition would preclude observation of foreign policy, since it is impossible to "get inside their heads" in order to discover what their true goals are. Instead, the assumption was made that foreign policy could most meaningfully be defined as overt state behavior. While motives are not observable, actions are. Most events data collections thus share the concept of foreign policy defined by McGowan (1970d, p. 10): "A foreign policy act may be initially defined as any observable activity wherein the polity of a society or its official representatives interact with other polities or their representatives that are part of the society's environment."

Second, events researchers assumed that the foreign policy acts of states must be operationally defined; that is, a definition must be provided that states the operations to be performed, in order to classify and measure each act. Definitions of this type delineate concepts in terms of their observable properties. Science, it is frequently noted, deals exclusively with observations which may be related to concepts. As Kerlinger (1964, p. 35) notes: "There can be no scientific research without observation, and observations are impossible without clear and specific instructions on what and how to observe. Operational definitions are such instructions." Thus, events researchers sought to define a concept of foreign policy by specifying the types of observable behavior in empirical reality that could be used as an indicator of these policies and by delineating the procedures that must be performed in order to differentiate them from other observable empirical phenomena. It is assumed that such a definition, in itself, enables us consistently to recognize a foreign policy act when it occurs.

It should be emphasized that the product of this operational process of observation (data) differs from the layman's conception. Data consist of more than the mere accumulation of information and opinion regarding the activities of states abroad. "Data-making"[2] is a process whereby the supply of existing diplomatic records and documents are converted into scientifically useful data through systematic examination, classification, and tabulation: "Data . . . only emerge after large and

---

[2] This term was coined by J. David Singer to distinguish data from mere information, and to emphasize that while records may be used as a source of data, they do not constitute data themselves.

unassorted heaps of facts have been screened and codified by the systematic application of consistent, visible, and replicable procedures for observation and classification. When such operational and scientific procedures have been so utilized, we may speak of *data-making*, as distinguished from the more anecdotal and intuitive procedures of fact-accumulating and information-gathering" (Singer 1968, p. 2). Hence data-making involves collecting and organizing the amorphous mass of available information and facts about interstate phenomena into a form amenable to hypothesis-testing and empirical generalization. The reader is referred to Chapter 9 for illustrations of the derivation and formulation of such data, and to Part IV for illustrations of the analytic manipulation of data for hypothesis testing.

Sources for International Events Data

Once the problems of defining foreign policy had been addressed, events data researchers turned to the question of where data on foreign policy behavior could be obtained. Among the most potentially rewarding sources of information, they suggested, were the reports of elite newspapers, which could be classified systematically to yield a large body of data. The assumption underlying this approach to observation is that "fundamental review of major patterns of policy, foreign and domestic, is as a rule conducted *in camera,* attended by press and public. The changing of gears is usually noisy and the process open and frequently awkward, whether by design or otherwise" (Gregg and Kegley 1971, p. 4). Events data collections require that the events or behavior of international actors be recorded at least once in a publicly available source. As Burrowes, Muzzio, and Spector (1974) note, "Events data are perhaps best distinguished by their ready accessibility, by *where* rather than *what* they are. They are data which are systematically recorded and ordered in newspaper indexes, chronologies and other compilations of public affairs. These public sources make data readily accessible because they are formatted in such a way as to facilitate the identification, abstraction and coding of actions of nations and other international actors."

It is appropriate to ask whether newspapers monitor transnational governmental acts in a sufficiently comprehensive manner. A number of reasons can be offered as to why they may be relied upon. Perhaps most cogent is the argument that policymakers themselves rely on this type of source for information about the international system, and in fact, have their image of international affairs—their "reality worlds"—partially molded by the news they read. Since statesmen make extensive use of the daily newspaper for their information, it is reasonable for scholars to utilize the press as a source of data (McClelland and Hoggard 1969). Bernard C. Cohen (1961, p. 220) has commented on the propriety of this judgment by noting: "One frequently runs across the familiar story: 'It is often said that Foreign Service Officers get to their desks early in the morning to read the *New York Times,* so they can brief their bosses on what is going on.' This canard is easily buried: The 'bosses' are here early, too, reading the *New York Times* for themselves."

A second reason for using the press as a source of data is because of convenience and document availability. There are only three methods of obtaining data in social research: (1) asking people questions; (2) observing directly the behavior of the people, groups, and organizations being investigated; or (3) utilizing existing records or data already gathered for other purposes (Festinger and Katz 1953, p. 240). Since decision-makers are seldom willing to be interviewed and international conduct is seldom open to direct observation, the only apparent alternative for students of foreign policy is to rely on existing public documents.[3] But most such information is either classified, unavailable for public inspection, or unrecorded; so "unless we are prepared to wait for extended periods of time until state papers and compilations of documents of international relations are released by governments, we have no real alternative but to base our knowledge of contemporary world affairs mostly on day-to-day reporting of the wire services, newspapers, and other mass media agencies" (McClelland and Hoggard 1969, p. 711). Given the proclivity of most governments to selective perception and memory, it might be held that the press is as objective a source of information as that which could be provided by governments and decision-makers, even if they were amenable to revealing their actions.

Third, not only is the press one of the few existing sources of data, but it may be posited that it is the most competent source. McClelland (1968c, pp. 43–48) makes several points in support of the capability, reliability, and breadth of coverage of the press:

1. There is no doubt that the volume, detail, and accuracy of international news reporting have greatly increased over the past half century. . . .
2. The professionalization of journalism and the maturing of the newsgathering organizations are important forces in increasing the effort toward accuracy.

[3] For an innovative example of how direct observational techniques might be utilized to gather international relations data, see Alger (1968).

3. Multiple sources and channels of information provide some safeguard against the systematic falsification of reports. The sovereignty of states and the diversity of national interests contribute some beneficial effects, globally, against news management.
4. The real source of large numbers of international news stories is the government agency. The news media are, essentially, pipelines between the regime and the public. One of the oldest maxims of statecraft, stated by Machiavelli among others, is that it does not pay to lie too often.

These opinions have been echoed by both friend and foe of the press. The columnist William F. Buckley, Jr., himself no fond admirer of the news establishment of which he is a part, commented after hearing a radio report that Nasser had died: "I slipped off to telephone the *New York Times* to see if the report was correct (one always telephones the *New York Times* in emergencies. The State Department called the *New York Times,* back in 1956, to ask if it was true that Russian tanks were pouring into Budapest)" (Syndicated Column, 29 November 1969). And John Kenneth Galbraith, a former American policymaker, has testified to the effectiveness of elite newspapers to gather "all the news that's fit to print": "I've said many times that I never learned from a classified document anything I couldn't get earlier or later from the *New York Times*" (reported in a roundtable discussion, "The Power of the Pentagon," *The Progressive* 33 [June 1969]: 29).

Fourth, we would do well to recall that no monitoring instrument is able to record "all the diplomatic exchanges fit to observe." Any particular observational instrument is incapable of recording everything. Some conceptual reduction of any phenomena is not only necessary but scientifically useful; as Rosenau (1971, pp. 11–12) couched it: "Unable to perceive and depict the universe of international phenomena in its entirety, the observer is forced to select some of its dimensions as important and in need of close examination, while dismissing others as trivial and unworthy of further analysis. . . . Though there may be an objective truth about world politics, the observer can never know it. He must select in order to know reality, and in so doing he must distort it."

Since some distortion is inevitable in the observational process, to attack the press for its failure to record every foreign policy act is to judge it against an unfair standard. It is obvious that not all foreign policy acts will be recorded by the mass media, and that therefore this source of observations, like any source, will be far from complete in its coverage. Many of the minor, less dramatic, and less noticeable foreign policy acts will go unrecorded. The events reported by the press therefore should not be interpreted as a full and accurate summary of all the foreign policy actions that have occurred everywhere. Rather, these records are best seen as indicators of what happened, as a sample of the behavior that has been undertaken. Given the fact that we can never know everything that is occurring, it would seem pointless to try to observe all international events, so "students of international relations have little alternative but to use the materials at hand with an awareness of their defects" (McClelland and Ancoli 1970, p. 6).

Research Utility of Events Data

We must now examine several questions regarding the use of events data in research. Most generally, it is important to ask what information international events data provide us about interstate behavior that is of use in constructing indices of foreign conduct. More specifically, we must inquire about the conceptual boundaries of "events." Are there special attributes of events which limit their meaning and restrict them to descriptions of particular dimensions of foreign behavior? Can events data be employed to analyze all aspects of foreign policy, and can international events data be regarded as a multipurpose indicator of external behavior?

A perusal of the events data coding manuals suggests that a number of implicit theoretical assumptions influence the substantive meaning of "events." As we have seen, events are commonly construed, following McGowan (1970d), as "the *acts* initiated by national governments on behalf of their societies, and pursued beyond their national boundaries, to effect changes in the behavior of other nation-states and international actors in the international system." Some salient features of this definition can be delineated. First, the emphasis on *acts* means that events refer to behavior, to the things states do and say to others abroad. Adoption of the discrete foreign policy act as the unit of analysis places the study of comparative foreign policy within the philosophical and theoretical tradition of those such as Mead (1938), Parsons and Shils (1962), Rescher (1967), Schuetz (1951), and Riker (1957), who emphasize the act in the scientific analysis of social behavior. Tapping overt and manifest behavior, events do not measure national goals, national interests, or the content of national policy orientations. Second, events are empirical referents for foreign policy actions that are *official* and *governmental*, that is, external behavior which is a direct result of governmental action. For the purposes of most event collections, the actors, or initiators of events, are usually the official representatives of sovereign states. This definition hence excludes "informal access" activity (A. M. Scott 1965) —behavior such as anti-foreign demonstrations conducted by national citizens but not officially inspired by the government—and agrees with Blake's (1969) contention that "behavior of non-government actors . . . is not a measure of foreign policy behavior unless such action is implemented on behalf of or in the name of the government" (p. 17).

Third, because they are extracted from public sources, events are, by definition, newsworthy. Since news sources are exclusively interested in reporting out-of-the-ordinary activities, events are only empirical referents of nonroutine and extranormal foreign policy behaviors of states. Consequently, events researchers assume, with McClelland (1968b), that events are indicators of dramatic *interactions* between states, but are not measures of routine intersocietal behavior, or transactions, between states.

From this, a fourth assumption follows. By the nature of events data sources, we may infer an underlying motivation behind the initiation of all international events: to influence the behavior of other actors in the international system. That is, what the press monitors and deems newsworthy are the attempts of one state to affect the behavior of another state to the advantage of the former. International events, therefore, are expressly "influence attempts" (Coplin and O'Leary 1972), designed for the explicit purpose of getting others to do what they would not otherwise do. Conceptually, international events are essentially *political* actions. If events, then, are foreign activities motivated by the desire to influence, events data logically are used more meaningfully as indicators of interstate *politics* than of international *relations*.[4]

If foreign policy events are seen as politically motivated, then a concomitant fifth assumption is that the foreign policy activities indicated by events are goal-directed, purposeful forms of behavior. Foreign policy acts are therefore seen as deliberate activity, directed toward consciously entertained ends; they are undertaken with rational motives in mind.[5]

What these characteristics of international events suggest is that the

---

[4] For a discussion of the conceptual differences between these terms, see Holsti (1972, pp. 20–24) and Sondermann (1961, pp. 8–17).

[5] As Charles A. McClelland (1969, p. 1) has argued, "Even irrational foreign policy, as exemplified in some of Hitler's wartime moves, is based on some anticipated outcome although that may be nothing more than a leader's self-image or his personal convictions."

concept "event" has very precise conceptual boundaries.[6] This means that event-interactions may not be used as multipurpose indicators of abstract, general, and multifaceted conceptions of foreign policy, because by definition the term *events* refers explicitly to specific dimensions of interstate behavior: namely, the *official, nonroutine, deliberate, overt actions* of *governmental* representatives, directed at external actors, for the express *political* purpose of modifying the behavior of those targets. The conclusion which inescapably follows is that while events data provide the student of comparative foreign policy with a useful base for analysis, many theoretical and substantive aspects of foreign policy may not be investigated meaningfully with this type of data.

Abstraction Procedures in Events Data Generation

Of equal importance to the issues of data source and the conceptual meaning of events is the cluster of problems associated with the operational procedures for identifying those foreign policy activities reported in that source. Explicit coding rules must be devised, outlining the operations performed in converting journalistic accounts into quantified data. Excellent discussions of these operations are found in McGowan (1970*d*) and Azar (1970*a*).

A perhaps oversimplified statement of the major premise of the events-data technique is that the coding rules enable the data collector to decide which accounts in the press may be considered interstate events. These sets of directions define foreign policy acts and instruct the coder in how to convert accounts into data. Most coding manuals require the data collector to condense the account into "the most discrete, meaningful printed statement about foreign policy that we can identify" (McGowan 1970*d*, p. 13). By convention, the account is abstracted so that it can be recorded in a "who (nation) did what (action) to whom (nation)" format. Thus, the coding operation "makes" data about

---

[6] Some events data collection enterprises, such as the World Event/Interaction Survey (WEIS) project, have taken great care to describe, explicate, and defend the conceptual definition of "event" which they believe their coding rules provides. Others have been remiss in specifying the analytic boundaries of "event" connoted by their coding procedures, arguing that the coding manual itself adequately provides an at least implicit conceptual definition of events. This latter practice may be questioned on grounds of logic and on grounds that it violates the norms of scientific rigor. Regardless, it may be contended that every event data collection employs definitions and coding procedures which restrict the meaning of events to a particular interpretation and thereby limit the research purposes to which the data may be employed.

foreign policy activity, because the transitive verbs in these declarative sentences identify instances of foreign policy acts. When a news report is summarized by the sentence "The United States threatens South Africa," that sentence then becomes the unit of observation, and the verb *threatens* becomes an instance of a foreign policy act initiated by the national actor, the United States. The resultant frequency of verbs recorded in these sentences, categorized according to a mutually exclusive and exhaustive *ad hoc* typology of the types of acts states may initiate, become quantified indicators of foreign policy behavior.

An example will help to illustrate how these rules and assumptions operate in the derivation of events data. On 30 November 1973, the *New York Times* reported a foreign policy action in a story headlined "Brezhnev Signs 15-Year Pact with India to Solidify Relations." This is an identifiable international event because it was observed by a publicly available news source. In collecting data from this observation, the data collector applies a set of coding rules (explicitly defined in a coding manual to the *Times'* description of that event. This abstraction process would result in a datum which might look something like this:

Description of the event (in a declarative sentence):	The U.S.S.R. reached an agreement with India on 30 November 1973.
Abstraction:	U.S.S.R. Agree India 11/30/73 (Actor) (Action) (Target) (Date)

Thus, the event is abstracted in a who-did-what-to/with-whom format, wherein the subject refers to the initiator of the act, the verb refers to the type of foreign policy action, and the object refers to the target of the behavior. The date records the temporal aspect of the event. This, of course, is a simple example. Needless to say, other variables related to the event could be abstracted and coded as well; for instance, the purpose (to solidify relations), the affect component of the behavior (in this case, friendly rather than hostile), or the channel through which action was taken (diplomatic visit) could be classified as well to enhance the richness of the data set. Note also how the assumptions about foreign policy behavior are operative in this process. The event refers to overt action, or behavior; it records the activities of government officials acting on behalf of their states; the behavior recorded is unusual, dramatic, and extraordinary; the action is political because it is designed to influence the relationship of the two societies; and finally, the action is rational in the Weberian sense of being goal-directed.

Problems and Prospects in Events Data Research

While the problems inherent in the events data generation effort are too important to be dismissed lightly, they are much too complex to be treated adequately here. Indeed, it may be said that the vast proportion of effort in the events data movement has been directed toward the resolution of data quality problems instead of toward substantive foreign policy research. Table III–1 outlines some of the salient issues confronting events data collection. While the number and complexity of the problems outlined in this table should caution the reader to possible limitations of events as indicators of external conduct in comparative research, it would be incorrect to infer that these problems vitiate their applicability. These problems are endemic to all research and all data, whether qualitative or quantitative. To acknowledge their presence is to follow the scientific credo against accepting evidence at face value. It is only by making explicit the assumptions and limitations of the observational procedure that the researcher can estimate the credibility of his evidence and of the conclusions he derives from his analysis of it. While we should not treat events data as a panacea in comparative foreign policy research and exaggerate what it can do for us, we should not be overly hesitant about its use, because it is the best data currently available for the comparison of national external behavior.

Table III–2 (from Burgess and Lawton 1972, pp. 56–57), which summarizes the characteristics of the major current events data collections, gives some indication of the breadth, extent of development, and scale of effort of the events data generation movement. As this table indicates, the events data movement is vigorous, in terms of sheer quantity, and the movement has succeeded in realizing its primary objective: providing the scientifically oriented student of foreign policy with a rich data base with which to conduct empirical analysis. The amount of energy expended and rigor exercised to generate this large data base, derived from many sources and covering the external behavior of many nations over long time periods, attests to the magnitude of the movement and its growing sophistication. It also suggests the significant contribution events research has made, and will continue to make, to the growth of scientific theories of foreign policy. Without data a science of interstate behavior is impossible. As Burgess and Lawton (1972, p. 76) conclude:

TABLE III–1

A Typology of Major Issues Confronting Events Data Generation and Analysis

Problem	Related issues
I. Definitional characteristics of an event: how are events to be conceptualized and identified? (Hermann 1971; McGowan 1970*d*)	A. Conceptual boundaries of an event: abstraction procedures of formal definition B. Temporal boundaries of an event: discrete vs. continuous actions C. Observation problems
II. Codification procedures: what are the scientific requirements of a systematic coding scheme, and what are the consequences of alternate coding procedures? (Phillips 1972)	A. The problem of the ideal number of event categories; aggregation considerations B. Multitheoretical vs. unipurpose typologies (Leng and Singer 1970) C. Interpreting the meaning of events intersubjectively D. The problem of whether to account for contextual and situational components of an event E. Dyadic vs. monadic coding
III. The question of measurement: should events be measured simply by categorizing types, or be scaled to distinguish intensities of events?	A. Unidimensionality vs. multidimensionality (Kegley, Salmore, and Rosen 1974) B. Methodological approaches to scaling and typology construction (Calhoun 1972)

IV. Source coverage considerations: which public sources should be coded, and how many different sources are adequate? (Burrows, Muzzio, and Spector 1974; Azar et al. 1972*b*)	A. Single vs. multiple sources
	B. Differential source coverage comparisons: relative saliency of source yields with respect to
	  (1) Coverage of particular actors,
	  (2) Mix or distribution across event types, and
	  (3) Magnitude (volume) of aggregate yield
	C. Comparative source related biases:
	  (1) Systematic
	  (2) Random
	  (3) Ethocentricism
	  (4) Sensationalism and concomitant overrepresentation of hostile events

V. Event data validity: to what extent do international events constitute a	A. Techniques of index construction B. Validation tests of indicator systems

Table III–1 (continued)

Problem	Related issues
meaningful operational measure or indicator of interstate behavior? VI. Event data reliability: to what extent are the data reproducible?	A. Procedures for calculating intercoder reliability coefficients B. Kinds of reliability, and their relative significance (1) Intercoder (2) Interproject (3) User reliability

Much has been learned, and prior investments in these efforts appear to survive rigorous appraisal. The benefits—methodological and substantive knowledge gained, students trained, the heuristic value of extant events data research—are substantial. But the time has come for a rigorous stock-taking and for the design of strategies that will build on cumulative investments of the past, that will maximize the payoff from future efforts, and that will—to use Bellman's words—increase our capacity "to make a system operate in a more desirable way."

The suitability of events data for the realization of these goals may be evaluated in the essays which follow.

Notes for Table III–2

* African Foreign Relations and International Conflict Analysis.
Source: Burgess and Lawton 1972, pp. 56–57.

ᵃ The standardized common and unique nation codes of the International Relations Archive, originally developed by Russett, Singer, and Small (1968), apply only to the twentieth century.

ᵇ Political groups (PG's) refer to groups in rebellion which have gained international recognition by at least one nation.

ᶜ Geographical areas (GA's) refer to such areas as the Soviet-Bloc or the West, and all actors and targets included in that area are thus coded under the same code. GA's included by Corson also encompass subnational units such as Alaska.

ᵈ When the conceptual equivalent of one of our criteria of comparison has been developed by a project, their label will be used to facilitate comparison.

ᵉ Henceforth recorded as DID.   ᶠ Henceforth recorded as SA/MT.

ᵍ Except for war.   ʰ Continuous domestic conflicts are recorded.

ⁱ In addition, data on the Taiwan Straits Crises and Berlin are available.

ʲ Data set does not presently cover this entire period, but project plans call for eventual coverage.

ᵏ For most of the time period under consideration, only the *New York Times* was employed.

ˡ In addition, Corson has employed a large number of diplomatic histories.

ᵐ Information is not presently available other than to indicate that multiple sources will be employed.

ⁿ For the Department of State's operational traffic, differentiation is made as to whether a cable or a formal report constituted the original source.

TABLE III-2

Events Data Projects Summarized

EVENTS DATA PROJECTS / CRITERIA OF COMPARISON	World Event Interaction Survey (WEIS)	Dimensionality of Nations Project (DON)	Conflict and Cooperation in East-West Crises	Conflict and Peace Data Bank (COPDAB)	Middle East Cooperation and Conflict Analysis (MECCA)	Middle East Project	AFRICA*	Comparative Research on the Events of Nations (CREON)	Foreign Relations Indicator Project (FRIP)	Situational Analysis Project (SAP)	Leng-Singer Events Data Typology
Number of Actors	160	Varies, approximately 107 actors	25	44	7	6	32	35	4	23	Unknown
Standardized Nation Codes	Yes	No	Yes	No	No	No	Yes	Yes	No	Not applicable[a]	Yes
Types of Actors and Targets	Nations, IGOs, and Political Groups[b]	Nations, IGOs, PGs, and Colonies	Nations, IGOs Alliances, & Geographical Areas[c]	Nations, IGOs, PGs, and GA	Nations, IGOs, and PGs	Nations	Nations, IGOs PGs, and Alliances	Nations, NGOs IGOS, and Alliances	Nations	Nations, and PGs	Nations, IGOs, and PGs
Types of Targets	Direct	Direct	Direct	Direct and Implied	Direct	Direct	Direct	Direct and Indirect	Direct	Direct and Indirect	Direct and Indirect
Collective Nature of the Act	No	No	Yes	Yes	No	No	Yes	Yes	No	No	Yes
Identification of Actor's Agent	No	Yes	No	No	No	No	Yes	Yes	Yes	Yes	Yes
Setting	No	Context[d]	No	No	No	No	Yes	Channel	Instrument	No	No
Multiple Interactions	Disaggregates into Dyads[e]	DID	DID	DID plus one Descriptor	DID	DID	Single Actors with Multiple Targets[f]	SA/MT	Not applicable	DID	SA/MT
Continuous or Discrete Actions	Discrete	Discrete[g]	Continuous and Discrete	Discrete	Discrete	Discrete[h]	Discrete	Discrete	Discrete	Continuous and Discrete	Continuous and Discrete
Sequence Numbers	Yes	No	Yes	No	No	No	Yes	Yes	Yes	Yes	Yes

Time Frame	1966-1969[i]	1910,1935, 1950,1955, 1960, and 1962-1968	1945-1965	1945-1969	1961-1967	1949-1967	1957-1969	1959-1968 (random quarters)	1971	1870-1890	1815-1965[l]
Scaling or Categorization	Categorizes	Categorizes	Scales	Scales	Categorizes	Categorizes	Categorizes	Categorizes	Categorizes	Scales	Categorizes
Type of Scale	Not applicable	Not applicable	Ratio	Interval	Not applicable	Not applicable	Not applicable	Not applicable	Not applicable	Interval	Not applicable
Descriptive Deck	Yes	No	Yes	Issue Area	No	No	No	Yes	Yes	Master List	No
Unique Codes	Conflict Arena	Revisions	Resource Referred to	Activity	Comment	Comment	Regime, Proximity, Goals	Affect, Specificity	Effect of Policy on US Goals	None	Media of Action
Resource Area	No	No	Yes	No	No	No	Yes	Yes	CASP Categories	No	Medium
Number of Sources	3[k]	1	3[l]	17	9	4	17	1	1	8	Multiple[m]
Source Comparisons	Yes	No	No	Yes	Yes	No	Yes	No	No	Yes	No
Source Identification Numbers	Yes	Yes	Yes	Yes	Yes	Yes	Yes	No	No[n]	Yes	Action Numbers
Reliability Measures	Yes (.83)	Yes (.75)	No	Yes (.82)	No	Yes (.79)	No	Yes (.92)	Yes (.54)	Yes (.92)	Yes (.95)
Types of Data Collected	No	Attributes, and Domestic Conflicts	Attributes and Domestic Events	Perceptions Transactions Attributes	Domestic Conflict	Domestic Conflict	No	National Attributes Data	Domestic Events	No	War, IGO, Alliance, and Attribute Data
Source of Observation[c]	24,25,32	32	15,32,40	5,7,9,10, 12,15,17 20,21,26, 28-30,33, 38,40[p]	11,13,15, 16,27,29, 31,32,33	17,21, 29,33	1,2,3,4,8, 14,15-17 21,33	15	34	6,18-19 22-23, 36-37,39	Unknown

3

Evaluating Events Data: Problems of Conception, Reliability, and Validity

PHILIP M. BURGESS and RAYMOND W. LAWTON

One of the major achievements of the 1960's was the establishment of a large-scale data base by students of international relations. The international relations archive now includes a new class of data—events data—devised to support substantive studies of foreign policy, international interaction, and patterns of international conflict and cooperation, and methodological studies designed to improve sociopolitical monitoring and forecasting capabilities.

Enormous effort has been devoted to events data research. Since 1960, over 160 papers have been published or otherwise circulated in a variety of forms and sources—occasional papers, scholarly journals, anthologies, and symposia. Yet of these papers and research reports, fewer than a score have been available through easily accessible channels of scientific information exchange. Indeed, to the extent that events data research is known and its products available, much is owed to Charles McClelland, who has been generous in the circulation of papers from the WEIS (World Event/Interaction Survey) project and in the early and continuing distribution of the WEIS data through the facilities and net-

An earlier version of this chapter appeared under the title *Indicators of International Behavior: An Assessment of Events Data Research*, Sage Professional Papers in International Studies, Vol. 1, No. 02–010. Copyright © 1972 by Sage Publications, Inc., Beverly Hills, Calif. Portions of the text and some notes have been deleted. Reprinted by permission of the authors and publisher.

work of the International Relations Archive (IRA) of the Inter-University Consortium for Political Research (ICPR), and to Edward Azar (now at the University of North Carolina), who sponsored three annual events data conferences at Michigan State University. In this chapter, an effort will be made to identify critical issues of theory and method that are contained in fugitive reports and monographs.

The Conception and Measurement of Events

Burrowes and Spector (1970) have offered a profile of the typical events data user, a characterization which can also serve to indicate both the scope of events data research and the type of associated intellectual activities. The typical user

is a quantifier armed with statistical or mathematical techniques. He is a comparativist, positivistic in orientation, with a commitment to general or middle-range theory. Not primarily interested in idiosyncratic inquiry, he is not prepared to devote a large part of his active professional life to discovering all there is to know about a particular historical situation. When he uses the single case study, he does so for exploratory purposes and casts his problem in general terms. Ultimately, he seeks to discover and test descriptive generalizations, explanatory propositions or predictive statements using data drawn from a large number of historical cases. (P. 2)

Events data researchers have developed concepts, methodologies, data, and empirical findings that are applicable to analyses pitched at the level of the international system (i.e., interaction analysis) or to comparative studies of foreign policy (i.e., action analysis) among the several events research projects.

Events data have a number of antecedents and parallels worth noting. Events data research has methodological roots in content analysis—that is, the systematic study of written and verbal communications for propaganda analysis and media reports (Angell, Dunham, and Singer 1964; Namenwirth and Brewer 1966; George 1960; Lasswell 1942), for the analysis of diplomatic documents (North et al. 1963; Holsti, Brody, and North 1969b; Holsti 1968), and for reducing data generated in simulated environments (Zinnes 1966; Hermann and Hermann 1963). Events data are also linked to measurement innovations in sociometry and small-group research—for example, Robert Bales' (1950) Inter-action Process Analysis, designed to facilitate the systematic and unobtrusive observation of an individual's initiatives and reactions toward others in a small-group context. The Bales technique uses twelve categories (such as subject shows tension, shows solidarity, gives advice) to measure certain properties of the interaction among members of a group in order to generate system-level measures of control, tension management, and integration; these properties include the direction of the interaction (positive or negative) and its instrumental or expressive character. Not only does events data research extend the more established and familiar methodological techniques noted above, but its development also parallels the increasing attention given by students of domestic political systems to the invention of indicator systems designed to support program planning and evaluation, assess political performance, forecast social and political conditions, and measure the quality of life. These systems supplement more conventional, largely economic indicators of societal growth, stability, and cleavage.

In the most general sense, *events data* refers to words and deeds—verbal and physical actions and reactions—that international actors—statesmen, national elites, intergovernmental organizations, and nongovernmental international organizations direct toward their domestic or external environments.

In order to understand more fully what is meant by the phrase *event-interaction,* we must first consider the concept of an "event." Riker (1957) has postulated that reality is composed of a continuous stream of actions and motion, which man orders into discrete events by the imposition of analytical boundaries. These boundaries, and hence the length or type of event contained therein, are arbitrary and artificial. Thus, an event can be most profitably characterized as a subjectively differentiated and discrete portion of motion or action as determined by the observer. An event-interaction, therefore, represents the application of the concept of a discrete event to the ongoing process of communication among nations.

In order to characterize interactions among entities that make up the international system, McClelland (1968b) has posited an exchange theory of international relations, in which international behavior is viewed as the result of the great flow of events among the nations making up the international system. These flows, he notes, are subject to minor and major disturbances and are composed of "transactions" and "event-interactions." Transactions are routine, aggregated, nonpolitical flows such as mail, trade, or travel patterns. Transaction data are typically used as measures of behavior for studying intersocietal processes such as integration (Deutsch et al. 1957; Cobb and Elder 1970) and are used in the earlier events data work in comparative politics (Gurr 1968; Feierabend 1966a, 1966b). Event-interactions are turbulent, public, political flows such as threats, protests, and demands. Events are major disturbances, above the level of routine, which find their way into the public press; and they are dealt with by political rather than administrative actors. The major control system (i.e., the higher levels of national government) can act to reduce or amplify the disturbing events in the interaction stream.[1]

In other words, events data are seen as important indicators of international behavior that serve to expand the scope and content of more traditional and familiar measures—budgetary allocations (defense expenditures), international transactions (tourism, trade, and mail flows), participation measures (diplomatic outposts and intergovernmental organization memberships), and political behavior (manifested by alliance affiliations and votes in international bodies). Events data bring to the international data archive measures of regulatory or control behavior that are consequences of political decision-making rather than of administrative routine.

The Problem of Reliability

A great deal of energy has been devoted to documenting problems encountered and routines used to apply coding schemes to the public press, and methods for estimating and controlling reliability vary considerably among the projects. We will distinguish between two kinds of reliability: (a) intracoder and intercoder reliability and (b) interproject reliability.

Considerable resources have been devoted to the careful training of coders to ensure acceptable levels of intra- and intercoder reliability. The graduation from training to actual coding usually occurs only after a given level of coding accuracy is achieved. Coders are often supervised and frequently have samples of their work cross-checked. This process is used in both the categorization schemes and in the scaling approaches documented below. Azar (1970a), for example, has designed reliability experiments that juxtapose results obtained from student coders with results obtained from Middle-East specialists—with encouraging results. Rummel personally coded twenty-five daily issues of the

---

[1] Bernard Cohen (1963) has elaborated the process by which events become newsworthy and dominate the agendas of the policymaker as well as the attention of opinion makers and the general public.

New York Times (*NYT*), which then constituted his criterion set, *S*. Three assistants, X, Y, Z, then coded the same issues of the *New York Times*. An error measure, *E*, was constructed and was applied as follows to determine the reliability of coder X.

$$E = \frac{a}{a + b + (c - b, \text{ only if } c > b)}$$

where

a = number of cells identically coded in *S* and in the code sheets of assistant X for specific *NYT* (measures agreement);
b = number of cells coded in *S* that are not identically coded by assistant X (measures error of omission);
c = number of cells coded by assistant X for which *S* does not contain codes (measures error of commission).

E was then computed for Y and Z in the same way. The error measure varied between 0 and 1, with 1 indicating perfect intercoder agreement and 0 indicating complete disagreement. The average intercoder reliability score, *E*, was 0.56. Rummel notes that *E* may be interpreted as a squared correlation coefficient, thus producing a correlation coefficient of 0.75 (Rummel 1966).[2]

Much less knowledge exists regarding interproject reliability. Experiments designed to compare results from coders in different projects using the same coding scheme have been rare. In one such check, involving the WEIS coding scheme, Sigler (1972) compared the results obtained by his coders at Macalester College employing the WEIS coding scheme with those obtained by McClelland's own coders. Agreement scores were computed for total volume of event types and for agreement on discrete events. For the first comparison, of the total volume of event types, Sigler found a product-moment correlation of 0.95 between the Macalester coders and the WEIS project coders. When discrete event agreement scores were computed, however, the coefficient dropped to 0.42. Further investigation into the low intercoder agreement on unique

---

[2] Rummel and Azar have applied the most demanding measures to the assessment of coding reliability. Though other projects report generally acceptable coder reliability scores, readers of original source papers should examine the reliability methods used on a case-by-case basis, for some projects have reported coder reliability estimates without carefully explicating the methods of estimation from which the scores were derived. Further discussion of criteria for assessing general event coding schemes can be found in Phillips (1972).

events, in contrast to the high agreement achieved on volume, revealed that the WEIS project had based its data collection effort on the city edition of the *New York Times* while Sigler had used the microfilm copy of the *New York Times*, which is the late city edition. On the basis of his comparison, Sigler concluded that although the two editions of the *New York Times* do differ significantly in the unique events reported, they do seem, on the whole, to be reasonably similar in the volume of event types reported. These findings have tended to increase confidence in the WEIS event classification scheme and to alert researchers to the sensitivity of some analysis designs to source variations. For example, designs using pattern correlation would probably not be affected by the Sigler discovery, but designs using stochastic models might well yield results that are largely an artifact of the source used (Ezekiel and Fox 1959).

The Problem of Validity

Assessing the validity of events data requires us to consider those situations in which the assumptions of the events data model are or are not met. For example, the conceptualization and measurement of events assumes that most of the major control efforts of governments are public. If important aspects of the major control actions are not public and do not appear in the public press, then the validity of the events data model can be called into question. Another fundamental assumption of events data research is that coding rules are sufficiently inclusive to capture the essential information contained in a message.

Event coding rules often exclude or underreport the actions of a third country or of intergovernmental or nongovernmental organizations on the behalf of members of an interacting dyad. Though the recording of third-country or nonnational actors is primarily determined by the theoretical or empirical purposes of the researcher, this problem is in part a function of the lesser coverage given nonnational actors by the press. To the extent that empirical or theoretical interests include nonnational actors or multilateral actions, several events data collections are progressively less useful. It is often economically feasible, however, for researchers to apply a project's coding rules in an *ad hoc* fashion to more specialized sources and thereby augment available data to suit their own needs.

One of the first findings reported from the WEIS project (McClelland and Hoggard 1969) indicated that the twenty most active nations accounted for 70 percent of all events reported. The uneven (or skewed) distribution of events among nations thus presents the events data analyst with several problems, not the least of which is the fact that in any analysis pitched at the global level, a number of nations will have to be excluded, owing to unrecorded behavior or insufficient data. By aggregating time into larger units (say, from days into weeks or months), however, the analyst can reduce this problem somewhat. Also, press attention to developed nations and the events data researchers' tendency to rely on English-language sources may tend to overrepresent certain nations in subsequent analyses.

Events data collections exclude whatever effects perceptual distortion may play in the interpretation of event-interactions among decision-makers and assume, instead, an objective perception. Communications are judged by the manifest intent of the sender (as determined by the coder via the coding rules) and not by the receiver's perception of the sender's intent (Newcomb 1974, p. 3). The assumption of a neutrally or objectively perceived stimulus is entirely different from and provides interesting contrast to the perspective employed by the Stanford group in their 1914 crisis and Cuban missile crisis studies (Holsti, Brody, and North 1969a; Holsti, North, and Brody 1968; Zinnes 1968; Holsti 1969). The perceptual evaluation of communications received by the decision-makers was, in fact, one of the major research questions explored by the studies. The importance of perceptual distortion by decision-makers has also been forcefully argued by the Sprouts (1969) and has constituted a basic assumption of the decision model underlying *The American Voter* (Campbell et al. 1960) and of the foreign policy decision-making paradigm of Snyder, Bruck, and Sapin (1954). Osgood, Choucri, and Mitchell (1974) have attempted to discover if there exists an upper ceiling above which the perceptual distortions of the decision-makers become less relevant to behavioral responses than to actual stimuli. Propositions were tested in a two-step mediated response model (S-r; s-R) at the height of the Sino-Indian border conflict. Scaled multiple-source events were coded and perceptual data extracted from a machine content analysis of documents employing the General Inquirer System. The findings, though somewhat ambiguous owing to the lack of data measuring Chinese perceptions, led the authors to conclude that while the 1914 crisis studies overstressed perceptions, the data indicated that the 1914 crisis studies should not have overstressed "objective" acts.[3]

[3] The best predictor of China's level of violence was China's own perception of its strength, whereas the best predictors for India were Chinese actions (Osgood, Choucri, and Mitchell 1974).

Thus, if a model is employed that posits perceptions as a mediating factor, events data as they are presently collected are not likely to be a profitable source of data.

Research results have been reported with days, weeks, months, quarters, years, or years as time units. Most events data have been collected over the period since World War II, with most occurring after 1960. Extended longitudinal analysis and generalizations to other international systems are correspondingly limited at present. Several events data projects are, however, seeking to extend their data sets to include longer time periods.

Dependence upon the public press as the initial collector of raw data for events data sets is not without difficulties, as national public presses tend to overreport their own country's actions (Sigler 1972). Because of the political preferences and idiosyncracies of their editors and wire services, their paper's news/profit ratio, and the size of the paper's independent news-gathering apparatus, newspapers will differ in the number and type of events reported (Azar 1970a). Employing multiple sources or establishing the error tendencies, scope, and biases of a newspaper would seem to constitute minimal prerequisites for events data projects desiring high correspondence between concepts and data.

Events data have been collected primarily on the basis of an implicit or explicit unidimensional conflict-cooperation dimension, with some projects adding resource area in an attempt to be more multidimensional. WEIS, for instance, is unidimensional, concerned primarily with political conflict; Corson, however, is able to deal with the economic and cultural, as well as political, dimensions of conflict. The uni- or multidimensional nature of the data set is particularly important if one is seeking to map the international system. If only the political dimension of conflict-cooperation is being measured, then one should not be surprised to find a unidimensionality in the factors that are associated with it.

Validity: Source Coverage

Although the events data movement has been built around McClelland's distinction between an event and a transaction, in practice it is not always clear where the borderline between an event and a transaction lies. Conceptually and operationally, reliance upon public sources of information provides the crucial distinction between events and transactions. Events cross a threshold, emerge from the ordinary flow of transactions, and become both public and political. This basic point of agreement among the projects is not, however, without its problems;

for it leaves unanswered the issue of the source—that is, the channels through which public issues may be raised, views exchanged, and control exercised. Consider, for example, the fact that the *New York Times* does not report as many interactions among the Persian Gulf sheikdoms as does the *Times* (London). Then consider the interactions that would be recorded if researchers consulted oil industry publications, information brochures of the sheikdoms, the First National Bank of New York, and the several histories of the Trucial Coast. In short, because of the multitude of specialized publications, each covering a geographical or issue area, or engaging in propaganda, we can soon find ourselves hard-pressed to distinguish between an event and a transaction. Events reported in semipublic or specialized journals or in commercial house organs would seem to be beyond the conceptual boundaries of an event —in turn raising such questions as what *public* is; what the meaning of *missing data* is, given the operational, if not the conceptual, definition of an event; and how criteria are to be developed that will permit a continued distinction between routine transactions and nonroutine event-interactions.

When issues related to "exhaustive" event coverage are raised, one is reminded of the old puzzle: does a tree falling in a forest make noise if no one hears it? The answer is either yes or no, depending on how the problem is conceptualized. And because events data researchers (1) have varying purposes and (2) have not, with only few exceptions, clearly explicated their theoretical purposes, this issue of exhaustive coverage and of the need for multiple sources cannot be answered abstractly. In the meantime, efforts to deal with these problems are in progress—including comparisons of event yields from diplomatic cable traffic with yields from public sources (Lanphier 1972), McGowan's (1974) effort to develop Bayesian estimators, and Burrowes' comparison of yields generated from major global and regional news sources (Burrowes, Muzzio, and Spector 1974).

Thus, it should not be surprising to find that the number and type of sources felt necessary to obtain valid event yields vary considerably among the various projects. McClelland's WEIS project has, until recently, relied on a single data source, the *New York Times*. Most of the other projects have consulted multiple data sources.

Hermann (1971) has argued for the necessity of consulting multiple sources:

We acknowledge with McClelland and McGowan that knowledge of foreign policy activity is almost exclusively from secondary sources, *but we seek to avoid letting the source define what comprises an event.* The definition of an event can be thought of as analogous to a box or some other container. The data sources provide the stream of filtered information that serves as the content of the container. We depend upon the data sources to determine what we put in the boxes, but we need not be dependent upon them to determine the nature of our conceptual containers. (p. 15; emphasis added)

Compelling as this argument is, however, it is not altogether clear what supplementary criteria are being invoked to design the "conceptual containers." Those criteria would most likely be theoretical or problem-oriented. Hence, one of the ironies is that the problem-oriented and often *ad hoc* events data studies may be on stronger methodological grounds than the project work, owing to the multiple applications inherent in most collaborative project efforts, where theoretical elaborations have been lacking and problem definitions too broad to provide unambiguous criteria for source selection.

The WEIS project has supported several methodological studies to determine differences in news coverage among different sources, concluding that, globally and regionally, the *New York Times* yields the same approximate volume of interactions as, and often will have greater coverage than, some regional sources (McClelland and Hoggard 1969; Hoggard 1970). Azar (1970*a*) examined regional source coverage for the Middle East, with the result that WEIS findings were repeated for volume, but not for intensity scores. In addition, Azar noted that the overlap in reported events between the *New York Times* and the next most important source, the *Middle East Journal,* was only 10 percent, and that these two sources differed in the patterns of conflict and cooperation reported.

Burrowes, Muzzio, and Spector (1971) conducted an even more extensive source comparison for the Middle East. They compared nine global and regional news sources, searching for overlap in reported events and for the frequency of unique events (events reported in only one source). The sources were then rank-ordered in terms of the different combinations of sources which reported the most events with the least overlap; the event source with the highest yield was *Cahiers,* followed by the *Middle East Journal,* the *Times* (London), and the *New York Times.* Ranking the sources in terms of their percentage of the total yield of events produced the following order: *Cahiers, New York Times, New York Times Index, Middle East Journal,* and *Times* (London). In both comparisons, *Deadline Data, Facts on File, Keesing's Contemporary Archives,* and the *Asian Recorder* were found to have mar-

ginal yields as sources of events data. Though this study focused only on
the Middle East, its conclusion—that a minimal prerequisite for events
data projects is a thorough investigation and comparison of the strengths,
weaknesses, and yield patterns of their candidate sources—appears warranted. This kind of sensitivity testing should precede a commitment to
a single source or an *a priori* commitment to multiple sources.

Gamson and Modigliani (1971) undertook precisely the same type of
sensitivity testing advocated by Burrowes in their attempt to monitor
the daily interactions between the Soviet and Western coalitions between
1946 and 1963. Because a daily analysis of the front-page headlines of
the *New York Times* provided their sole source of data on U.S.-Soviet
interactions, they compared the *Times* with other major newspapers in
order to determine if their dependence on it would unduly bias their
picture of U.S.-Soviet interactions. They found that the *New York Times*
appears to be in substantial agreement with the *Times of India* and the
Manchester Guardian as to the composition of U.S.-Soviet interactions
(Gamson and Modigliani 1971, p. 165). Armed with the finding that
the three newspapers did not significantly differ in the composition of
reported events and that the *New York Times* recorded 97 percent of
all events recorded in a seven-paper comparison, they concluded that the
New York Times constituted an acceptable source upon which to base
their investigation.

The Foreign Relations Indicators Project (FRIP) of the Department
of State supplies the only systematic evidence we have of the difference
between the number and type of events reported in the public press
and those found in official diplomatic traffic–telegrams, airgrams, diplomatic notes, memoranda of conversations, informal letters, and some
press materials. The reliance of FRIP upon such decidedly nonpublic
sources represents a distinct departure from the public sources relied
upon in the events data model advanced by McClelland and others.
It is not easy, however, to argue against cable traffic as a source for
observing international control efforts—a central feature of the original
conceptual definition of an event-interaction.

The FRIP project coded events for two different six-month cross
sections. Some idea of the quantum difference between the volume of
data produced by the FRIP project and the volume produced by other
events data collections can be established by comparing the adjusted
total events yields of FRIP and WEIS. Comparison can be achieved by
multiplying the FRIP nation average per month (1,250 events) by the

145 nations and forty-eight months covered by WEIS. Judged by these standards, the WEIS events data pool (20,000 events) is but 0.23 percent of the 8,700,000 events which the FRIP extrapolation would yield.

The distinction between an event and a transaction, however, is based upon the event's appearance in the public press; and while the FRIP data set is not presently available for inspection, it would not seem unreasonable to suspect that Department of State records include large numbers of routine transaction data. Support, albeit weak, for this assertion can be garnered from the fact that during the escalation among the great powers in the 1914 crisis, five thousand messages were exchanged (Zinnes 1968). It does not seem at all unreasonable, therefore, to argue that a data source which can produce an equivalent number of messages for four Latin American countries (Ecuador, Guatemala, Panama, and Venezuela) during a reasonably normal period must certainly be measuring something other than the "turbulent, public, political" exchanges we now call events.[4]

It is clear that the important question is not simply that of determining whether one should employ single- or multiple-source coverage, but rather, that of determining conceptually or theoretically what the trade-off point between exhaustive event coverage and ordinary transactions is for a particular researcher or events project. The location of this cut-off point will, in practice, be influenced by the resource investment required for each additional source. The desire to increase the number of events in order to increase the analytical options available may tend to create incentives to include sources that report the most items, rather than publications which are closer to a researcher's conception of an event. For, utilizing McClelland's conception of an event, if national decision-makers or attentive publics do not "see" an event or if the event does not cross their generalized attention threshold, it is not at all apparent why the more specialized, lower attention threshold of others should be substituted in its place. Further elaboration and specification of the threshold level would seem to be a high-priority item for events data researchers.

Measurement routines for coding the content or subject of the event interaction vary considerably among the events data projects; indeed, the

4 Further support for this proposition stems from Gary Hoggard's comparison of the *Times* (London) and the *Indian White Papers*, in which he reports that a large number of routine events (e.g., reports on broken windows) are included with reports of major events, such as the armed Chinese intrusions on the Indian border.

projects may be divided between those that categorize and those that scale events.[5] Categorization involves placing events into nominal categories, such as threat, request, accuse, or comment. WEIS employs twenty-two general and sixty-three specific nominal categories—a basic coding scheme that has been adopted by several other events projects and one whose categories may be used in alternative combinations consistent with unique research designs. Scaling, by contrast, involves identifying the content of an event and then measuring it along a given dimension by assigning a number to indicate its position on a given continuum. Azar, Corson, and Rosecrance have measured the intensity of an event along a conflict-cooperation dimension. In more general terms, scaling can be best understood as a standardized set of operations using a standardized numerical scale for transforming mininal data, such as protests, accusations, and threats, into ordinal-, interval-, or ratio-level data. The most common scaling procedures involve the use of judges to order items in terms of their increasing level of violence or cooperation (Torgerson 1967).

Events scaling, in particular, originated out of the earlier efforts of the Stanford group in scaling perceptions (Moses et al. 1967). Typically, the scaling procedure involves the use of judges to rank a large number of phenotypic events (e.g., nation A withdraws its ambassador from nation B) from least to most conflictual. Judges, most commonly college students, first determine the number of categories or markers necessary to characterize a given range of behavior.[6] The ranked phenotypic events are then each assigned to an ordered category and given that

[5] McClelland's WEIS, Rummel's Dimensionality of Nations (DON) project, Burrowe's Middle East Cooperation and Conflict Analysis (MECCA) project, the Hermann-Salmore-East Comparative Research on the Events of Nations (CREON) project, McGowan's African project, Lanphier's FRIP, Wilkenfeld's Middle East project, and the Leng-Singer project categorize events; Azar, Corson, and Rosecrance scale events.

[6] The use of markers to form a scale on which to measure events is rather simple and straightforward. First, judges rank a small number of phenotypic events which have been selected because they cover a wide range of internation behavior. This set of cards thus forms the set of "marker" cards. Next, another group of judges is given a larger set of phenotypic events (including the set of marker cards) and is instructed to rank them. Each phenotypic event card is then given a score equivalent to the number of marker cards which it exceeds. Validation of the scale formed by the marker points occurs when the dispersion and mean are calculated for each phenotypic event. The greater the agreement between the judges—i.e., low dispersion around the mean—the more confidence a researcher may have in the resulting scale. The purpose of a marker card, thus, is to serve as an indicator or signpost for each category on a given scale. The use of interjudge agreement to rank or scale markers and events is based upon Torgerson's law of comparative judgement (Torgerson 1967, pp. 159–60).

particular intensity score. Thus, for example, the 32-point interval scale developed by Rosecrance requires coders to code information, such as actor-initiator and target, and then to measure the intensity of each extracted event along the scale.[7] Rosecrance reports that high intercoder reliability scores ($r > 0.94$) have been obtained.

Overall, assessment of the reliability and validity problems faced by the events data projects suggests that the projects score highest on reliability. It should be recognized, however, that the testing and interpretation of reliability is an easily handled, routine problem. Validity, on the other hand, must be assessed according to the individual needs and purposes of the researcher and is ultimately dependent on the conceptual and theoretical baggage he brings to event data analysis and interpretation. If clear theoretical standards are lacking, criteria may be derived from the empirical problem itself. To the extent that a researcher stresses perception, intergovernmental and nongovernmental organizations, and underdeveloped nations, several events data pools will probably yield low validity scores. If, on the other hand, a researcher does not need the preceding considerations or extant coding conventions, then a given events data set may provide a more adequate base for research. Validity assessment must ultimately be decided with reference to the analyst's research requirements.

While much has been learned from the research reviewed above about events data and related methodological and data generation problems, the theoretical superstructure of most major events data source papers is weak, implicit, or *ad hoc*. Clearly, further development of events data research will demand closer attention to the theoretical or problem-oriented issues about which events data are to inform us.

---

[7] The Situational Analysis Project's 32-point Corkeley scale ranges from "unlimited use of nuclear weapons" (scale value, 1.01) to the "establishment of political federation" (scale value, 99.6). Other points include "ultimatum" (16.3), "warning" (32.5), "start negotiations" (60.3), and "arms control agreement" (82.9).

4

Problems in the Measurement and Analysis of International Events

RICHARD A. BRODY

American students of international politics are now focusing on the exchange of actions (activities, behaviors) between nations to a degree that contrasts sharply with the emphasis on attitudes, cognitions, and perceptions that emerged from the "behavioral revolution" of the early 1950's. The substantial interest in action data is testimony to the belief that what nations do to and with each other is one important means of explaining how they see and act toward each other. Put differently, increased attention is being paid to the "stimulus" in seeking explanations of "responses" within and from the "organism."

Two general classes of data are considered to comprise the set of international behaviors; these have been styled *transactions* and *event-interactions* by Charles McClelland (McClelland and Hoggard 1969, p. 713). This essay will focus on the latter, and more specifically, on a cluster of issues concerning how we may deal with such data. In the first instance we face the choice of treating each event as unique or as a member of a class of actions. In addition we may choose to consider either the manifest or the latent content of the action. Finally, we face the problems of quantification and dimensionality.

This chapter originally appeared in Edward E. Azar, Richard A. Brody, and Charles A. McClelland, eds., *International Events Interaction Analysis: Some Research Considerations*, Sage Professional Papers in International Studies, Vol. 1, No. 02–001, pp. 45–58. Copyright © 1972 by Sage Publications, Inc., Beverly Hills, Calif. Reprinted by permission of the author and publisher.

Given the range of choices and the considerable range of research problems into which these data enter, it would be quite surprising if an all-purpose way of dealing with events data were found. Why should we expect the same way of handling events data to be of equal use in a psychodynamic theory which focuses on, say, compulsivity and in a "stimulus-response" theory focusing on the links between frustration and aggression? In the former, since our theory of personality leads us to expect a decision-maker to act compulsively under certain circumstances, our scheme for classifying events has to be sufficiently comprehensive to permit the circumstances which make up the events to be concatenated in a variety of ways. This, in turn, will permit determining whether a particular concatenation of circumstances is linked to a pattern of compulsive response. The classification requirements of the frustration-aggression hypothesis, in our other example, are less stringent. Because the categories stated in the theory are broader, fewer discriminations have to be made in the data. The discriminations which are made are of degree (levels of aggression) and not of kind. Hypotheses of this type require measurement within classes of actions.

Illustrated in these examples are the two main approaches to typifying international event-interactions. We find, on the one hand, systems that offer a vast array of categories of actions. McClelland and Hoggard (1969, pp. 714–15), for example, distinguish seven types of action derived from twenty-two classes, which were, in turn, derived from sixty-three subclasses of event-interactions. A classification scheme as rich as this offers the possibility of investigating whether responses are related to types of actions irrespective of their context or whether it is the pattern or configuration of inputs (i.e., the input of the context of other inputs) that is systematically linked to a response category. Missing from this approach, as it is currently handled, is specific attention to the effects of the intensity of the action.

Concentration on the intensity of one or another class of action has been the dominant feature of the second main approach to event-interaction. Moses and associates (1967), for example, offer four alternate unidimensional scales which distinguish thirty levels of international conflict-cooperation. Data coded on these scales can be used in testing propositions which link responses to intensities of an input and some past "norm." Typically, these scales are designed to index one or, at most, two dimensions. While there is no reason in principle for such parsimony, in practice the focus on intensity has been narrow.

Fortunately, we are not being asked to choose one approach or the other. For the time being, we do not know enough to be able to choose scientifically between these alternative approaches. If we are careful (and lucky) we will steer our course between an approach in which overdifferentiation makes comparison impossible and one in which inappropriate parsimony stretches or chops reality.

Leaving aside this discussion of the differences between systematic approaches to the study of events, let us consider their similarities. Both approaches emphasize latent as distinguished from manifest content; both seek systems that are cross-situationally general. Both the multifaceted approach, which emphasizes frequency, and the unidimensional approach, which emphasizes intensity, seek nomothetic categories of action.

The Uses of Events Data

Even if the dimensionality of events is unsettled, the uses to which such data can be put can still be essayed. Let us consider two generic and interrelated uses: operational definitions for hypothesis testing and analytic diagnosing.

Four types of concepts can be defined operationally through the use of measured events. Thus far, event measurement tools have been used primarily to characterize stimuli and responses. They have also been used, however, to define such state variables as the level of conflict or cooperation or the level of violence existent during a period of time. State variables are intervening variables, or the familiar "initial conditions" of J. S. Mill's *Logic;* they enter propositions as delimitors on the generality of laws—for instance, "when the general level of conflict is high, decision-makers will tend to overperceive the hostility of a given stimulus."

Closely related to state variables are situational variables, such as *crisis,* which can be and have been defined in terms of the frequency or intensity of events. Thus, Gary Hoggard (1969) identifies *crisis* by contrasting the flow of events during periods of unusually high activity with flows during normal periods. Such as operational definition has the virtue of being free of mentalistic tautologies (e.g., a crisis is a situation experienced as a crisis by a decision-maker).

Finally, event measurement data can be used to define sequence pattern variables, such as *détente* or *rapprochement.* Upon close examination, such terms have fairly specific implications for the distributions of data through time. *Rapprochement* has been defined as the "reestablishment of good relations between states" and *détente,* as "the cession of strained relations between states" (Elliott and Summerskill 1957, pp. 251, 86). If we use a measure of good relations between states (such as the one suggested by Moses and his associates), we can anticipate how a pattern of action might look under these two concepts. Figures III–1 and II–2 depict hypothetical data under conditions of rapprochement and détente, respectively.

FIGURE III–1

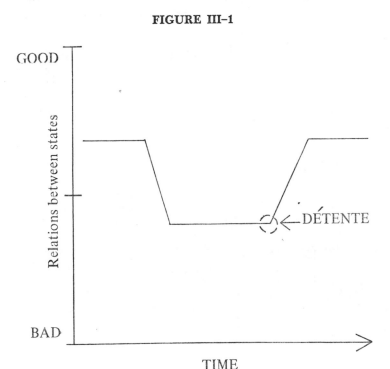

These idealizations of the two concepts show how more basic operational techniques can be used to define complex concepts. But the application of techniques for measuring the quality of relations to the search for the patterned sequence, such as that represented by the Elliott and Summerskill definition of *rapprochement,* raises two fundamental questions of research design: (1) How far back in time do we begin our search? (2) How much change is necessary in order for us to feel comfortable arguing that relations in two periods are different?

The first question takes on significance if we believe that the pre-détente pattern of relations has explanatory value. I know of no general answer to the question, but two classes of arbitrary answers suggest themselves—an arbitrary date and an arbitrary criterion. The former is justified if we are testing an assertion of the form "a rapprochement pattern occurred between such and such dates"—for example, "the post-October 1962 détente capped off a rapprochement in Soviet-American relations that had been building for thirty years," or "the Vietnam conflict aborted the rapprochement that otherwise would have resulted from

FIGURE III–2

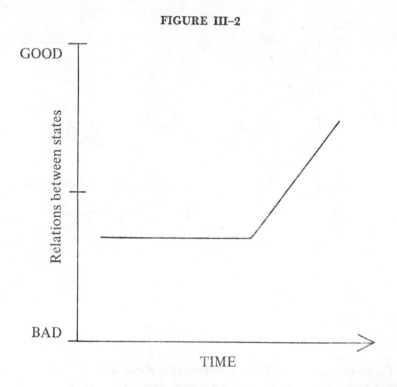

the Cuban missile crisis." Since we can always test an assertion in its own terms, there is no difficulty with the dates as given. When we are not testing a time-referred hypothesis, we will need some reasonable (albeit arbitrary) criterion for deciding when to begin data gathering. If it is practical, we can go back to the beginning of formal or official relations—1917 and 1933 in the case of the Soviet-American dyad—or to the point when normal relations can be said to have been established.

To illustrate the problem involved in the second question, let us consider some hypothetical distributions (Figure III–3). If we found a pattern like the one depicted in Figure III–3a, would it be proper to call it a rapprochement? That is one way of asking if the relations in time period 7 are different from the relations in periods 2 through 5. What about the wildly fluctuating data illustrated in Figure III–3b? Surely in this case it would depend on our time scale: if our time periods are generations, we might be willing to speak of the relationship depicted as alternating between deep conflict and rapprochement under some Kaplan-like "rule" that neither nation can afford to destroy relations with the other permanently. If our time periods were days, we might consider throwing away our instrument. Assuming that we agree that Figure III–3c represents *rapprochement,* with which of the infinitude of graphs depicted in Figure III–3 do we draw our definitional line?

That concepts operationally defined in terms of measured or counted event-interactions can enter many interesting hypotheses is hardly debatable. Any proposition which includes inputs, outputs, actions, reactions, stimulus, or response among its variables or initial conditions can be cast in terms of measured event-interactions. In many hypotheses (especially those of the unmediated stimulus-response variety) no other types of measurement need be used. But events data also can be combined with other forms of data to explore more complex theories.

These data can also be used in a diagnostic mode—they can be employed to inform the researcher when other (more costly) research techniques can be fruitfully brought to bear. Consider, for example, the question of when to employ content analysis in studying the impact of perceptions on actions. Since content analyses are expensive to conduct, it is desirable to be able to focus resources on especially critical periods (i.e., periods in which perceptions are most apt to affect actions). Such periods can be indicated by points of inflection (turning points) on a trend in relations between two states; by generating such trends, by indicating points of inflection, event-interaction data can indicate time periods in which content analyses can be most economically employed.

Other authors have dealt with a variety of approaches to the classification or measurement of events; there is no need to review them here. But two methodological problems which are common to all approaches —the unit of analysis and the dimensionality of action—are worth considering.

RICHARD A. BRODY

FIGURE III–3

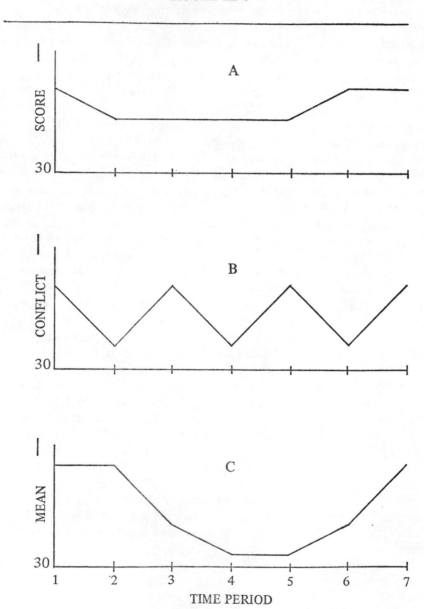

Units of Analysis

Although we speak of "event-interactions," typically the unit of analysis is a single act by a nation-state. The *act* is what is classified or measured. The prototypic unit retrieved from a data source (newspaper files) is a sentence of the form "Nation A does x to or with nation B," and x is the unit of analysis—x is classified or measured, counted, and aggregated with other x's within some unit of time. Syntactically, the act is a predicate and it will take all modifiers applicable to predicates. Thus, x can be complex or simple, general or delimited in time, space, or pace.

However complex the act that can be accommodated in this format, this approach does not permit distinguishing between identical acts emanating from different sources—nation A's x is indistinguishable from nation B's x if $x_a = x_b$. While this restriction is entailed in the act as the unit of analysis thus conceived, if need not be a serious restriction. Whatever we deem relevant to the differences between nations should circumscribe the behavioral repertoire of a nation such that two different nations will not have coextensive repertoires.

This still leaves open the question of whether acts from the area of shared repertoire but representing different levels of effort for nations A and B should be considered the same. The answer lies with the classification scheme. If level of effort is a feature of that scheme, acts which represent different levels of effort for the nations producing them will not be classed together. If level of effort (or any other feature) is not part of the classification system *and* if it is material to the nature of the act, it will be a source of systematic error variance that can be discovered through the analysis of the residuals or by some other appropriate technique.

Not so easily dealt with is the assumption of independence of acts which is entailed in considering the act as the unit of analysis. Treated this way, x is not conditional upon prior x's from either nation A or nation B. It is assumed to be statistically independent, this is to say, it is treated as if knowledge of the t_{th} x (x_t) gives us no information about the next x (x_{t+1}).

Explicating this assumption may make the act as unit of analysis appear ludicrous; this is neither my intention nor is it a warranted conclusion. Since most of us would agree that x_{t+1} is not independent of x_t, what are the effects of this conditionality (i.e., autocorrelation)? From the point of view of statistical analysis, the effect is an absolute and total prohibition against tests of significance based on independent probability models for any score, mean, and so on. It directs our attention to different scores, change scores, or other measures which are independent of the trend. In general, it urges caution upon us when we use these data in any but a descriptive mode; further, it urges serious consideration of other units of analysis.

Since we are dealing with the behavior of one nation toward another, it might be reasonable to consider sequences of action as our basic unit. Sociologists studying interpersonal violence are employing two-stage sequences to increase their understanding of the escalation of aggression (Toch 1969, p. 34).[1] The statistical properties of such sequences are not clear to me, but formally they bear a resemblance to interaction process models, such as the Richardson equations.

There is room for experimentation with respect to units of analysis. We may expect task-specific units to emerge from this experimentation. Projecting a guess, if we are concerned with escalation of crisis (such as, for example, McClelland's 1961 studies of Berlin and Quemoy-Matsu), compound units may be required. I offer this guess because situations like this are managed by leaders who may consider the other nation's range of action in selecting their own moves. Thus, the other nation's response may signal, or appear to signal, intentions in context of the sequence which they would not when considered per se.

If we are dealing with the perceptions of those less directly attending to the other nation's actions, the act as unit may prove to be a reasonable way to handle the data. In comparing public opinion trends with trends in Soviet behavior (Richman 1969), for example, it may be safe to ignore the contribution that American actions make to Soviet behavior.

Acts singly and aggregated, and acts in sequence, do not exhaust the potential units of analysis: discrepancies from trends, ranges on dimensions, or most prominent act in a period also might be useful candidates. I can only conclude that much investigation of the question of unit remains to be done.

---

[1] In studying the escalation of violent interpersonal encounters between police and citizens, Toch (1969) came to the conclusion that the citizen's response to the policeman's opening move so affected the nature of the policeman's second move that it would be misleading to treat the act as a unit of analysis. Toch's unit of study is a two-move sequence, i.e., A moves and B counters. This sequence predicts A's second action better than either A's first act or B's response alone.

The Dimensionality of Acts

We can come to the same conclusion about the question of dimensionality but let us arrive there *a posteriori*. An empirical as well as a theoretical case can be made against unidimensionality. But how do these cases fare upon examination?

Empirically, our suspicions are aroused when repeated study shows higher interjudge variation in coding acts at the cooperative than at the conflict end of conflict-cooperation continua. One source of this variation could be greater dimensional complexity for cooperative behavior. The case against unidimensionality is strengthened by Rummel's (1967*a*, pp. 196–206) and Hannah's (1968) findings on dyadic international behavior, although most of the variables entering the factors, which form the coordinates of their multidimensional space, are transactions rather than event-interactions. But the issue is beclouded by a study specifically addressed to the question of the dimensionality of event-interactions, McClelland and Hoggard (1969).

McClelland and Hoggard claim to have identified six independent dimensions of event-interactions, but reservations about their interpretation of their findings seem warranted. They discovered one massive factor on which 80 percent of the variables are loaded ($FL \geq 0.50$). This factor accounts for six times the variance accounted for by the second factor (56.9) and twenty times the variance accounted for by the sixth factor (McClelland and Hoggard 1969, p. 718). It is tempting to identify their first factor as a conflict-cooperation dimension, but variables generally thought to be associated with these (presumably) polar concepts are all positively associated with the factor. For example, both "reward" (extending economic aid) and "deny" (deny policy, action) are action categories having positive factor scores of 0.95 on this dimension. Thus, a nation ranking high on this dimension would, in the same period, engage in much giving of aid, much denying of aid, and other kinds of actions based on requests. Spelled out in this way, the dimension is not unreasonable:[2] it indexes a nation's level of participation in the international system.

The finding is a specification and detailing of these authors' report

[2] McClelland and Hoggard (1969, p. 717) interpret their first factor as "routine international behavior." This is semantically at odds with their definition of event-interactions as "nonroutine" (p. 713). The first factor appears to be a "participation" dimension. It would be instructive to correlate national factor scores on this dimension with scores for these same nations on Rummel's participation factor.

that 80 percent of their coded interactions were produced by 22 percent of the 153 countries examined (McClelland and Hoggard 1969, p. 716). It is thus an extension into international relations of the oft-confirmed social-psychological finding that those who rank high on one type of interaction rank high on all types. But this still leaves unanswered the question of whether conflict and cooperation as directed behaviors are negatively correlated—that is, at opposite poles on one dimension—or independent—that is, on two different dimensions. The question is unanswered by their research because they did not address it with the proper unit of analysis. In order to test these two constructions of the relationship between conflict and cooperation, behavior directed in a specific dyad must be the unit of analysis. The unidimensional hypothesis does not argue that a nation specializes in behavior at one end of the scale or the other; rather, it argues that in its relations with another nation, one mode of acting or the other will be characteristic.

The second factor identified by McClelland and Hoggard, if it is real (Lawley and Maxwell 1963), would tend to indicate that some nations are specialists in verbal conflict behavior. Knowledge of nations' propensities for this type of behavior may prove useful in explaining anomalies arising from aggregating verbal and physical acts.

If the operation of one social-psychological principle leads to the expectation that other such principles also operate, then the McClelland-Hoggard study would lead us to expect a verdict for multidimensional event-interactions.

Most theories of interpersonal behavior classify, or expect perceivers who are parties to the interaction to classify, behavior in terms of the intersection of several independent dimensions. There is, moreover, an extraordinary level of agreement on the number and nature of the co-ordinates of interpersonal behavior space. Two fundamental axes appear in study after study—power and affection. Bales (1968), Heider (1958), Leary (1957), Osgood, Suci, and Tannenbaum (1957), and W. A. Scott (1965) are among the psychologists who code interpersonal behavior on these axes. Couch (1960) has shown that the same experimental data coded with several of these schemes leads to the same conclusions.

Consider Leary's report (1957, p. 64), for example: "All [generic interpersonal trends surveyed] had some reference to a power or affiliation factor. When dominance-submission was taken as the vertical axis and hostility-affection as the horizontal, all of the other generic interpersonal factors could be expressed as combinations of these four nodal points." In the Leary scheme one of the axes lying at a 45-degree angle to the power and affiliation dimensions is cooperation-aggression; in other words, cooperation-aggression is the joint product of the two principal axes. This construction would argue that we cooperate with the good and strong and aggress against the bad and weak. This conclusion is also reached by Scott (1965, pp. 83–84) and was found to be true of the communication of verbal hostility, in a simulated international situation, by Brody, Benham, and Milstein (1967).

This line of argument leads us to conclude that treating international event-interactions as unidimensional is appropriate for certain classes of dyads (those which fall in two quadrants of the power-affiliation space) and appropriate for other classes of dyads (those falling in the other two quadrants) but that *the* dimension will have to be different for different types of dyads (Price 1968). In other words, if we bring to bear such considerations as the attributes of the nations interacting and their role vis-à-vis each other in the international social structure, it may not be unwarranted to code the event-interactions between them along a single dimension.

Part IV

Analyzing Foreign Policy Behavior

Introduction:
Patterns and Determinants
of External Conduct

ROBERT M. ROOD

The scientific analysis of foreign policy involves a search for patterns of foreign policy behavior and for those factors which are associated with, or account for, variations in those patterns. The investigator begins with some pretheoretical hunches from which he formulates explicit hypotheses. These are tested to arrive at generalizations which can be used to build theories. In turn, new hypotheses are derived from the impact of these generalizations upon the original pretheoretical ideas. The three articles in this section give examples of hypotheses which link independent and dependent variables. Wittkopf uses a diachronic, or longitudinal, research design to test whether or not there has been a progressively declining trend in the political success of the United States in the United Nations (Chapter 7). Hermann and East both use synchronic, or cross-sectional, research designs to examine whether size or wealth have effects upon foreign policy behavior (Chapters 5 and 6). Hermann tests the hypothesis that less-developed states tend to engage in more multilateral acts than do developed states, while East investigates the question of whether smaller nations have lower levels of participation in world affairs than do larger nations. The range and diversity of these variables and hypotheses is considerable, because the selection of variables and the statement of hypotheses always reflect an existential choice by the investigator of a problem he personally finds challenging and worthy of examination.

An hypothesis can be constructed in a number of ways. Propositions about the behavior of states can be generated by intuition and insights which result from probing specific aspects of foreign policy. Another fruitful way to arrive at hypotheses is to search the literature on a given topic and to inventory the propositions one finds. One may also formulate hypotheses through the application of formal, deductive logic to a specific problem area. Once hypotheses are stated that suggest criteria by which appropriate indicators can be established for observed variables, analytical tests are applied in order to judge the validity of the relationship. The investigator must then observe, classify, compare, analyze, and generalize about foreign policy behavior in order to test those hypotheses of substantive interest to him. The previous section of this book emphasizes the observational procedures employed to gather events data as indicators of foreign policy behavior. In this essay, the remaining four processes are illustrated with references to the articles in this section and to a selected bibliography.

Classification

Because comparison is a form of analysis which requires examining the relative order of magnitudes of units within a given class, foreign policy acts must be classified before they may be compared. Only then can the magnitude of each state's behavior be compared with that of other states within each separate type. The objects of a given class are compared in terms of the degree to which they possess the attribute represented by the type.

Three forms of typology may be distinguished: definitional, *ad hoc,* and empirical (Kegley 1973, pp. 37–39). Most typologies of foreign policy behavior are either definitional or ad hoc. Both represent the analyst's *a priori,* pretheoretical conceptions about the nature of interstate behavior. The primary feature which distinguishes ad hoc typologies from definitional typologies is that the former have readily identifiable empirical referents by which observed behavior can be assigned to a class and then be counted. Definitional typologies classify external behavior in such categories as "interventionist," "status quo," and "expansionist," and are often found in international relations textbooks, as well as in diplomatic discourse. They are often abstract, providing no criteria for observation, and lend themselves to polemics rather than to reasoned inquiry. In contrast, most ad hoc typologies are devised as coding schemes for various data-gathering projects, especially those used in gathering events data. Several of the following articles make use of ad hoc typologies to classify behavior, so that frequency counts may be made of each type of behavior. Hermann classifies behavior by the type of target, the type of decisional unit, the type of skill or resource used in formulating policy, the degree of conflict and/or cooperation of the behavior, and the degree of commitment. East classifies behavior by whether it is conflictual or cooperative, by whether it is verbal or non-verbal, by number of targets, by the specificity of problem and targets, by the involvement of economic bureaucracies, and by types of skills or resources used. Wittkopf is interested in how successful the United States and the Soviet Union have been in the United Nations. Each of these typologies allows the investigator to assign an act to a given class. To say whether an act is conflictual or cooperative, for example, the investigator must be provided with clear criteria by which he can assign an observed act to either of the two classes. For example an investigator may have observed that the United States has mobilized military units in response to Soviet actions in the Middle East. This event clearly involves some element of hostility, including the implication that the United States may resort to force if necessary. Thus, this particular action can be classified as a conflictual act. Similarly, an observation that the United States has granted aid to Israel can be categorized as a cooperative type of behavior. As these illustrations of the variety of types that may be employed suggest, an act may be classified in numerous ways, depending on the specific research interests of the investigator.

There have been several attempts at building empirically based typologies—that is, typologies which allow the investigator to describe and find the major distinguishing features of behavior but which are themselves based on the results of empirical observation. Empirical typologies allow the investigator to differentiate between classes on the basis of observed characteristics rather than on the basis of assumed, a priori differences, as is the case with definitional and ad hoc typologies. An analytic device such as factor analysis allows one to delineate the independent dimensions or classes of behavior and to cluster or assign the ad hoc types to broader categories. Examples of types of foreign policy behavior described by empirical typologies are the three classes of foreign policy behavior found by Rummel (1963) and Tanter (1966) — diplomatic conflict, belligerency, and war—as well as the two types identified by Kegley (1973) —affect and participation. Examination and comparison of these two typologies, along with others which have been delineated,[1] suggest that participation or involvement in international relations and cooperation-conflict behavior constitute the basic types, or classes, of foreign policy behavior (Kegley, Salmore, and Rosen 1974). This suggests, in turn, that a degree of patterned consistency exists in types of interstate behavior.

Comparison

Once behavior has been classified, nations can be compared within each class. That is, some operation is performed by which each nation's behavior is ordered according to its relative magnitude on each type (e.g., by assigning each state's behavior to an ordinal category such as high, medium, or low, or by assigning it a numerical value). Perhaps the most frequently used method is a simple count of the number of times a state has engaged in a particular type of behavior within a given time period. The actors are then compared in terms of the frequencies. For example, Hermann and East aggregate type of behavior by type of nation, which allows them to compare the behavior of classes of states.

Alternatives to simple frequency counts are the use of an index constructed to measure some dimension of behavior or the use of some scaling procedure to measure the intensity of behavior. Wittkopf, for example, measures the political success of the United States and the Soviet Union with the use of a support level (SL) index. The SL index shows whether a member of a voting body votes with the majority proportionately more or less than he would if his votes had been cast randomly. This index, calculated for both the Soviet Union and the United States, gives an indication of how often each was in the majority, and serves as an indicator of their respective degrees of political success in the United Nations. If the investigator compares behavior within a class derived by factor analysis, as do Rummel (1963) and Tanter (1966), then he may use factor scores as indices for comparing the behavior of each nation in terms of each dimension or factor.[2] Another

[1] Other attempts at deriving empirical typologies of foreign policy behavior include McClelland and Hoggard (1969), McGowan (1973b), Munton (1973), and Salmore and Munton (1974).

[2] Factor analysis is an analytical technique which delineates classes, or factors, on the basis of shared variance and from which factor scores can be derived. Factor scores provide a composite indicator of the weight, or intensity, of the behavior represented by each of the classes or factors for each of the behaving units or nation-states (Rummel 1967b, 1970).

approach is the use of judges to assign intensity scores based on a continuum, such as a conflict/cooperation continuum, in order to derive a composite intensity score for each separate event (Moses et al. 1967; Azar et al. 1972a).

Once a value locating the relative position of each nation within each class has been determined, the investigator may compare these positions, or ranks, for each nation within a given class. He can compare the position of a single nation at several different points in time, or of two or more nations at particular points in time, or of classes of nations at particular points in time.

Analysis

The purpose of analysis is to test hypotheses about the patterns and determinants of foreign policy behavior in order to arrive at empirical generalizations. In making an analysis, the investigator seeks to determine whether foreign policy behavior varies systematically with changes in an explanatory, or independent, variable. Questions may be raised about whether variations in the characteristics of individual decision-makers, in societal and political characteristics, or in characteristics of the international system are systematically related to variations in the patterns of foreign policy behavior; and the problem of which of these variations—in man, the state, or the international system—is the principle determinant of variation in foreign policy behavior is a question that has intrigued a number of scholars (Waltz 1954; Singer 1969b). The argument for each of these has its strengths and weaknesses, and ultimately the investigator must choose the level at which he wishes to search for explanation. The discussion of analyses which follows is intended to provide suggestions about the variety of hypotheses which have been tested at each level and which require further empirical testing.

Individual variables

A number of scholars have examined the effects individual decision-makers have on foreign policy behavior.[3] These attempts have utilized one of three approaches. One method has been to examine the effects of personality on foreign policy behavior. For example, Barber (1973)

---

[3] Greenstein (1969) addresses himself to the problems of ascertaining the relationship between personality factors and politics, while de Rivera (1968) discusses the psychological factors affecting foreign policy.

examined, categorized, and compared the behavior of presidents on the basis of the personality characteristics which they manifested during times of crisis. In an innovative research procedure, Margaret Hermann (1972) measured personality traits of chiefs of state by systematically content analyzing their speeches and then relating these traits to foreign policy behavior. Her findings suggest that foreign policy leadership is related to sentiments of nationalism, to degree of dogmatism, to cognitive simplicity, and to an existential belief in the ability to control events. Perhaps more typical of attempts to link personality traits to foreign policy behavior is the psychological biography; in this mode the investigator intensively studies a single individual and relates personality factors to major events in the individual's life. As an example, the Georges' (1956) study of Woodrow Wilson found that Wilson's attitude toward his father resulted in episodic compulsive rigidity, which in turn contributed to several crucial defeats at various points in his career, the most notable being his fight with the Senate over ratification of the Treaty of Versailles and entry into the League of Nations.

A second approach to the analysis of individual variables is used by those who examine the effects of perception on foreign policy decision-making. A comparison of the crisis immediately preceding the outbreak of World War I with the Cuban Missile Crisis indicates that in the former dispute, both parties significantly misperceived each other's actions and intentions, whereas during the Cuban Missile Crisis, each side correctly perceived the actions and intentions of its opponent (Zinnes 1968; Holsti, North, and Brody 1968; Holsti, Brody, and North 1969a). In a separate examination of the 1914 crisis, Zinnes, Zinnes, and McClure (1972) found that the actions of the decision-makers on both sides were influenced not only by their perceptions of their opponents but also by their perceptions of their own past actions.

Finally, others have attempted to determine whether the individual characteristics or the role characteristics of foreign policy leaders have more influence on their decisions and actions. Stassen (1972), for example, attempted to determine whether a role model or a cognitive balance model better explained the actions of foreign policy officials. In a study of the responses of U.S. senators to various secretaries of state, Rosenau (1968c) found that role variables appeared to be more important than individual variables. Generally, most studies have suggested that the role held serves to mold the personality and behavior of the individual occupying that role.

Most of the research designs employed in the examination of personality characteristics or perceptions of decision-makers tend to be case studies, either of individuals or of a particular occurrence. Margaret Hermann's (1972) study of the personality traits of heads of state is a major exception. Thus, in the absence of multiple case studies examining a common dimension or problem, generalizations have limited utility. The comparison of the actions of various presidents or of senatorial reactions to secretaries of state provide examples of a variant on the case study approach which can provide valid generalizations about the behavior of a particular state over time, but the case study of one or several actors acting at a particular time produces generalizations which are valid only for that time period and which serve only to suggest new hypotheses to be tested in other contexts.

Societal and Governmental Variables

Instead of focusing upon the characteristics of individual decision-makers, some researchers have sought to explain variations in the behavior of states by examining variations in the characteristics of the nation.[4] Spurred by Rosenau's (1966) contention that size, wealth, and political accountability were crucial variables affecting foreign policy, a number of scholars have attempted to determine whether these variables, when they are dichotomized as large/small, rich/poor, and open/closed states, affect foreign policy behavior. In a cross-sectional study, Salmore and Hermann (1969) found that size and wealth appeared to be the most potent variables in producing differences in foreign policy. Chapters 5 and 6 in this volume are also representative of research in this area.

The relationship between variations in national political characteristics, such as whether the nation is a democracy or dictatorship, and variations in foreign policy behavior is another possible area of investigation. In an application of the most-similar type of concomitant variation design, Waltz (1967) compared the conduct and formulation of foreign policy in two democratic political systems, the British parliamentary system and the American presidential system.

A somewhat different area of investigation is an examination of the relationship between domestic political conflict and foreign conflict behavior. Propositions drawn from the sociological writings of George Simmel and Lewis Coser suggest that nations will attempt to mitigate the level of domestic instability by engaging in and diverting attention

[4] See the volume edited by Wilkenfeld (1973a) for a selection of articles dealing with the relationship of nation-level variables to foreign policy behavior.

to foreign conflict. Early cross-sectional, intersocietal surveys by Rummel (1963) and Tanter (1966) found little relationship between domestic and foreign conflict. Employing the same data set in a series of studies, Wilkenfeld (1968, 1969, 1972) demonstrated that if the hypothesis is tested separately for polyarchic, centrist, and personalist types of regimes, the hypothesis is confirmed for certain types of regimes and for certain classes of conflict, especially when allowing for time lags.

Most of the research designs used to investigate the relationship between societal and political characteristics are either of the concomitant variation type or of the intersocietal survey type. As such, the generalizations arrived at are applicable to a wider range of phenomena than those arrived at through the case study. Thus, we can usually have more confidence in generalizations arrived at in this area of research than those found on the individual level thus far. Generalizations from cross-sectional research are limited to the time frame defined by the study, and causal inferences drawn from cross-sectional studies are tenuous at best.

Systemic Variables

The investigator may also go beyond the boundaries of the nation-state and search for variations in its environment which may serve to explain foreign policy behavior. Such variations may exist in the actions of other states, in the degree of polarity, in the degree of military imbalance in the system, or in the geographic distribution and propinquity of the nations involved. A case in point is East and Gregg's (1967) analysis demonstrating that nations' actions are systematically related to their international situation. Many of the investigations of this aspect of foreign policy behavior have concentrated on the behavior of other states as explanatory factors. Gamson and Modigliani (1971) have analyzed the behavior between the United States and the Soviet Union for the period of the Cold War, focusing on the hypothesis that the actions of either party will be reciprocated in the actions of the other. Weede (1970) confirmed the hypothesis that geographical propinquity is likely to lead to more aggressive behavior. In an examination of factors relating to conflict behavior in the Middle East, Milstein (1972) found that the basic interactions between states are more crucial factors in their behavior than are either military imbalance or levels of foreign aid coming into the conflict system.

Research into systemic factors lends itself to either longitudinal or cross-sectional research designs. Milstein's (1972) study is cross-sectional, with the behavior of other nations lagged in order to introduce a time element, while Gamson and Modigliani's (1971) study is longitudinal. With the exception of global studies that analyze the effects of geographical factors or situational variables, most of the research designs are of the regional type. The behavior of nations in a geographic area, such as the Middle East, or in behavioral groupings, such as those engaged in a significant amount of interaction (e.g., the United States and the Soviet Union during the Cold War), is analyzed in the regional type of design.

Generalization

The generalizations which emerge from empirical analyses serve as building blocks for explanatory and predictive theories of foreign policy behavior. Confidence can be placed only in those which are the products of replicated research and which thus represent a cumulative set of findings.

Perhaps the area of investigation which presents the most difficulties is the relationship between characteristics of individual decision-makers and foreign policy behavior. Personality factors must be extrapolated from secondary sources rather than from direct observation of the individual, making inference difficult and of questionable validity. The gathering of data on the perceptions of decision-makers is also difficult, requiring the processing of enormous quantities of information. The whole question of obtaining reliable information on the characteristics of individuals presents the investigator with problems of such magnitude that little systematic research has been done in this area. The findings that are available are scattered and offer little evidence for the development of generalizations because the observations have been of behavior in a single case. There has been little replication, and none of the findings can be considered the cumulative result of several investigations.

Much the same can be said of the attempts to search for explanations of foreign policy behavior outside the nation-state, either in the behavior of others or in systemic factors. Although there are many studies which analyze interactions between states, most are limited to a study of the exchanges leading to a specific event, such as the Suez Crisis of 1956 (Azar 1972) and the 1967 Sino-Indian border war (Smoker 1969), or to the study of broader historical phenomena, such as the Cold War (Gamson and Modigliani 1971). These all follow the regional type of research design and have broader generalizability than case studies. Although events data is adaptable to longitudinal analysis on a limited basis, much of it has been gathered for the purpose of analyzing behavior on a cross-national basis. Until more data is gathered and scaled for longitudinal analysis, progress in developing empirical generalizations in this area of investigation will be slow.

Two areas in the study of foreign policy presently show evidence of replicated research and emergent sets of cumulative findings: (1) the relationship of size, wealth, and political accountability to foreign policy behavior; and (2) the relationship of domestic instability to foreign conflict behavior. In a series of published and unpublished reports, a number of generalizations have emerged. First, the effects of size, wealth, and accountability are not interactive, as suspected; instead, each separately affects different aspects of foreign behavior. Domestic conflict has no discernible effects on foreign policy behavior when states are undifferentiated according to type of political system. When states are classified according to political type, there is a clear relationship between types of domestic conflict and certain classes of foreign policy behavior.

There are many generalizations which can be culled from a myriad of empirical studies, but they have not been replicated and they do not represent a cumulative set of findings.[5] Yet many such propositions deserve further replicative research. Thus, there are few generalizations in the comparative study of foreign policy behavior in which we can place confidence. If we are to have nomological explanations of foreign policy output, then as investigators we must continue to push forward the frontiers of knowledge about foreign policy behavior and its determinants and to expand the number of empirical generalizations in which we have confidence.

[5] For compendia of research findings in international relations and foreign policy, see Jones and Singer (1972) and McGowan and Shapiro (1973).

5

Comparing the
Foreign Policy Events of Nations

CHARLES F. HERMANN

This chapter deals with initial efforts to collect machine-readable data on foreign policy actions for a sample of thirty-five nations.[1] Three assumptions underlie both the chapter and the research it describes.

First, despite years of study, there exist few ways of conceptualizing foreign policy activities that allow one to classify the entire range of national foreign policy actions in order to allow reliable comparisons between nations. Why should anyone want to classify foreign policy behavior? It would be difficult for a brokerage firm to work effectively in stocks without descriptive statistics about the performance across time not only of the entire market but also of particular industries and given companies. Similarly, an insurance company needs actuarial data on people, information on the frequency of various kinds of accidents, and so on. Such numerical data record human behavior and are vital to the industries that use them. This chapter assumes that establishing such patterns could be at least as beneficial in increasing our understanding of foreign policy and in improving the quality of foreign policy analysis.

An earlier version of this essay was presented at the 66th Annual Meeting of the American Political Science Association, 9–12 September 1970, in Los Angeles. The present version was written specifically for this volume.

[1] The Comparative Research on the Events of Nations (CREON) project, which is its basis, is supported by grants from the National Science Foundation (GS–40356) and the Mershon Center at Ohio State University.

Second, given the desirability of mapping the entire spectrum of foreign policy for a variety of nations, one must assume that "soft" data are better than no operational data at all for large areas of foreign policy activity. Soft data are not readily available in standardized, countable units, as are U.N. votes, trade statistics, or amounts of military assistance, which represent only a small component of the entire foreign policy activity of most nations. What is needed is a means of measuring behavior ranging from a diplomatic note of congratulations on the anniversary of a nation's independence to acts of massive violence against the people or property of another country. One unit that lends itself to such comprehensive coding is the discrete foreign policy act, or what has been called events data. With careful definition, events can encompass not only "soft," or normal, data but also "hard," or quantifiable data. Only such an inclusive unit will allow us to map the complete spectrum of foreign policy activity.

Third, given the assumption that any foreign policy activity can be broken down into discrete events, how shall we group, or classify, foreign policy activities to comprise a national profile? The search described in this chapter assumes that some fragments of theory exist that require better description of the empirical universe of foreign policy events before they can be developed further or replaced.

The present research draws upon three theoretical frameworks in constructing a definition of foreign policy actions and in selecting the properties of these actions to be coded. The first of these is decision-making, which was brought to the attention of students of politics by men like Lasswell (1956), Simon (1957), and Snyder, Bruck, and Sapin (1962), but whose subsequent development has proceeded largely outside of political science in such fields as organizational behavior, social psychology, and economics. Though not all decisions lead to action, those behaviors which are conscious and deliberate result from decision processes undertaken by one or more individuals who must be treated as actors. Decision-making gives prominence to the organizational context in which the actor operates.

The second theoretical perspective underscores the importance of this organizational setting in foreign policy. It has been emphasized in the recent writings of men like Neustadt (1970), George (1972), Hilsman (1967), Halperin (1972), and Allison (1971), who stress that foreign policy actions are not exclusively the product of the decision-makers' perceptions of the environment external to their society, but also reflect their struggle as members of competing bureaucratic organizations within the government, each with different objectives and perspectives.

Finally, Rosenau (1966) has called attention to certain basic qualities of nations—political accountability, economic development, and physical size—which may serve as parameters affecting the potency of certain kinds of variables in explaining foreign policy actions.[2]

The research effort described below is guided by these related theoretical perspectives. The ultimate actors are individual, authoritative decision-makers or their representatives. Efforts are made to identify the positions or roles these actors occupy and to ascertain whether large bureaucratic organizations are involved in the event. Rosenau's genotypes figure prominently in the interpretation of the data. The ultimate aim is to show that events data can be found in public sources with sufficient regularity to allow the use of these theoretical perspectives for the comparative study of foreign policy.

Using Events Data

One of the tasks in using events data is to define the foreign policy event in which a specific action is embedded. "Event" is an arbitrary, analytical concept which imposes boundaries on a continuous stream of international activities. The particular collection of events data used in this chapter, taken from the Comparative Research on the Events of Nations project (CREON), consists of foreign policy activities of thirty-five countries for one randomly selected quarter in each of the years from 1959 to 1968. Although the data set ultimately will draw on multiple sources, the present events are those reported in a single source —*Deadline Data on World Affairs*. Table IV-1 lists the nations included in the study and the number of foreign events initiated by each in the thirty months for which data were collected.

Table IV-1 also indicates the eight nation-types which Rosenau (1966) formed by dichotomizing three fundamental variables—political accountability (open/closed), economic development (developed/less developed), and size (large/small). Rosenau suggests that the nature of a nation's foreign policy is conditioned by these variables, which, in static analysis, can be regarded as parameters. In contrast to the early work of Rummel (1968), Tanter (1966), Gurr (1968), and Feierabend and

---

[2] Rosenau's (1966) article on pretheories and his subsequent writing on comparative foreign policy deal with more than nation-types, or what he calls genotypes. Although some other aspects of his conceptualization have been influential in our research and data collection strategy, they are not dealt with in this essay.

TABLE IV-1

CREON Event Frequencies for 35 Nations Classified into Rosenau Genotypes

(Total Number of Events = 11,617)

Developed nations

Large Open		Large Closed		Small Open		Small Closed	
France	845	Spain	172	Belgium	386	Cuba	326
Italy	430	USSR	968	Canada	393	East Germany	165
Japan	272			Chile	208		
USA	1,859			Iceland	177		
West Germany	539			Israel	321		
				New Zealand	207		
				Norway	236		
				Switzerland	71		
				Uruguay	148		
				Venezuela	224		
Total	3,945	Total	1,140	Total	2,371	Total	491

Less developed nations

Large Open		Large Closed		Small Open		Small Closed	
India	491	China	449	Costa Rica	173	Ghana	271
Turkey	312	Mexico	195	Kenya	98	Guinea	208
				Lebanon	160	Ivory Coast	170
				Philippines	214	Thailand	163
				Tunisia	271	Yugoslavia	257
				Uganda	159		
				Zambia	79		
Total	803	Total	644	Total	1,154	Total	1,069

Sources: Attribute data for this table were collected and archived by the Comparative Analysis of Policy Environments (CAPE) at Ohio State University and are outlined in Burgess 1970a and 1970b.

Note: Nations are classified according to discriminant function analysis (see n. 5, chap. 5). Values after each nation refer to the total number of events currently in the data set for that nation. The following indicator variables for 1963 were used to construct the scale by which nations were classified: *for economic development*, (1) GNP/capita, (2) energy consumption/capita, (3) agricultural workers as percentage of total economically active population, (4) newspapers/1,000 population, (5) radios/1,000 population, (6) urban primacy, and (7) ratio of population from age 5–19 enrolled in primary and secondary schools; *for size*, (1) total population, (2) total GNP, (3) total land area, and (4) total KWH; *for political accountability*, (1) freedom of the press (revised), (2) competitiveness in election for head of government, (3) horizontal power distribution, and (4) representative character of regime. In each case the indicator first mentioned was used as the primary variable for establishing alternative points of partition

Feierabend (1966*b*) —who seek to find relationships between selected behaviors for all nations (e.g., political instability and conflict) — Rosenau contends that many relationships involving foreign policy behavior will be obscured unless nations are differentiated into some subgroups, such as the nation-types.[3] The method used to assign nations to each of the eight genotypes was discriminant analysis developed for this problem by Burgess (1970*b*) and others.[4]

Descriptive Findings on the Components of Events

As Table IV-1 indicates, there are enormous inequalities between nations with respect to the number of events initiated by any given nation.[5] At one extreme, Switzerland averaged fewer than two and one-half events per month; whereas the United States initiated an average of almost sixty-two events per month. Undoubtedly, substantial differences occur between nations in the frequency with which they initiate actions, but the small number for some states in the CREON data raises the possibility that the difference is due partially to unequal coverage by the data source. The confounding of actual differences in the initiation of events with source differences in coverage makes it difficult to conclude with confidence what variables might account for the following differences in number of events reported for each of the nation-types:

Eleven large countries initiated 6,532 events (mean 593.8) ;
twenty-four small countries initiated 5,085 events (mean 211.9) .

[3] Of course, there are other groupings of nations besides the one proposed by Rosenau. For example, one might cluster nations according to some concept of region, as has been done by Russett (1967) .

[4] Discriminant function analysis provides a technique for grouping entities (in this case, nations) when multiple indicators of a single concept are employed. First, one indicator (the primary variable) is used to establish alternative cutting points for partitioning the derived scale. Then, an analysis is performed that minimizes the number of misclassifications and maximizes the distance on the scale between groups. The indicators used by Burgess (1970*b*) for physical size and economic development and by Gary Hoggard for political accountability are listed in the note in Table IV-1. Mexico has been assigned to a different group from the one originally determined by Burgess and Hoggard as a result of calculations by Salmore (1972) . It is possible, of course, to treat size, development, and accountability as continuous rather than dichotomous variables and analyze the effect of gradual increments in each variable. Although there is merit in performing such analysis, it would not follow the Rosenau (1966) scheme presented in this chapter.

[5] The exact number of events in the CREON data set may vary slightly from one published report to another during the present period of data cleaning. The version of the CREON data used here has been designated as 2.03.

Twenty-four open countries initiated 8,273 events (mean 344.7);
eleven closed countries initiated 3,344 events (mean 304.0).

Nineteen developed countries initiated 7,947 events (mean 418.3);
sixteen underdeveloped countries initiated 3,670 events (mean 229.4).

These breakdowns tend to conform to my prior expectation that
western data sources will underreport the activities of relatively small
as compared to large nations, open as compared to closed societies, and
developed as compared to less-developed countries. It should be noted,
however, that the mean difference between open and closed systems is
not very substantial.

In addition to total frequencies of actions, a few findings should be
reported on the other components of an event as the term has been defined. Every event was required to have one or more direct targets.
Ninety percent (10,443) of all the events had only one direct target,
with little variation occurring when events for the nations were grouped
under each of the three dichotomized genotypic variables. For example,
89 percent of all events initiated by open countries had one target, as
compared to 92 percent for closed countries. This was the largest difference. If this initial pattern of findings is substantiated, it would suggest that decision-makers usually seek to address one target at a time, no
matter how many other entities the actor attempts to affect indirectly
by his action.[6] Events were also required to have indirect objects of influence; 61 percent (7,046) had one or more explicitly mentioned indirect objects that were entities other than those classified as direct
targets. In other words, in three out of every five events, the actor addressed one entity but sought to influence someone else in addition to
the immediate recipient of his action. As with direct targets, none of the
three genotypic dichotomies differentiated between nations that had
separate indirect objects and those that did not. The largest difference
between nation-types was 3 percent: 60 percent of all events in open
nations and 63 percent of all events in closed nations had separate
objects.

The absence of differences between nations with respect to the number of targets and indirect objects is in marked contrast to the results on
governmental participation in multilaterally-initiated actions. Sixty-five

[6] The percentage of events with a single direct target includes those in which the
target was an international body such as the U.N. General Assembly. If such targets
were separated into their separate member governments, the number of single target
events would be substantially reduced.

percent of all actions in our sample were undertaken by two or more governments[7] with the nation-type division as follows: large, 53 percent, vs. small, 80 percent; developed, 61 percent, vs. less developed, 74 percent; open, 69 percent, vs. closed, 55 percent. In small or less-developed countries, governments may collaborate to add to the authority of their actions. Governmental decision-makers in open societies may engage in more collaborative efforts out of a conviction that consensus-building is a desirable tactic.

One additional finding on the components of events concerns the nature of the direct target and indirect object. For all countries 39 percent of the direct targets and 71 percent of the indirect objects were other governments. Six percent of the direct targets, but less than 1 percent of the indirect objects, were domestic entities within the actor's own country. The percentages of direct targets and indirect objects that consisted of external, nonnational entities (e.g., political parties and officials of international organization) were 55 percent and 29 percent, respectively.

Classification by nation-type revealed no substantial differences in kinds of indirect objects. Nation-types, or genotypes, do affect the distribution of direct targets, however, as indicated in Table IV-2. Almost 48 percent of all direct targets of events from large nations were other governments, as contrasted with only 27 percent for small nations. Similarly, events initiated by developed nations had proportionately more direct targets that were other governments than did events initiated by less-developed nations, and governments in closed societies addressed other governments as targets proportionately more than did those in open societies. In comparison, small, less-developed, and open nations initiated more events having as targets external, nonnational actors—most likely, alliances or international organizations. This pattern may suggest differences in the world view of governments in different types of nations. Governments in large or developed countries may believe that their foreign affairs require the attention of other national governments. These national targets, at least individually, seem less relevant to small or less-developed nations either because such com-

---

[7] The CREON definition of an event stipulates that no event may have more than one national government as the actor. Therefore, a joint communiqué by the foreign ministers of Japan and New Zealand would be considered two events—one for each nation. The assumption is that each government must make its own separate decision as to whether it will be a party to a collaborative undertaking. For each event, however, a record is kept as to whether it involved a joint initiative, and it is that variable which is being used at this point in the text.

TABLE IV-2

Relationship between Kinds of Direct Targets and Rosenau Genotypes
(Total Number of Direct Targets = 13,669)

Direct targets	Large	Small	Developed	Less developed	Open	Closed	All genotypes
Other governments	3,681 (47.9%)	1,618 (27.0%)	3,839 (41.1%)	1,460 (33.7%)	3,655 (37.1%)	1,644 (43.1%)	5,299 (39.0%)
External, nonnational	3,367 (43.8%)	4,129 (68.9%)	4,887 (52.3%)	2,609 (60.2%)	5,712 (57.9%)	1,784 (46.8%)	7,496 (55.0%)
Domestic	631 (8.2%)	243 (4.1%)	611 (6.5%)	263 (6.1%)	492 (5.0%)	382 (10.0%)	874 (6.0%)

munication is an inefficient use of their limited resources or because they believe that individual governments are less likely to be responsive. The proportionately smaller attention given external, nongovernmental actors by governments in closed societies, as compared to open societies, may reflect the former's minority position in many international political and financial bodies. Table IV-2 also reveals that governments in large as compared to small nations and those in closed as compared to open systems have twice as many foreign events in which domestic targets are mentioned. In both large and closed systems the problem of internal control may account for the observed attention to domestic groups.

Types of Foreign Policy Behavior

The CREON data provide several distinctive ways of describing and measuring foreign policy behavior on a cross-national basis.[8] One involves the use of a series of items which are combined to form scales representing predetermined attributes of behavior that the investigators judged to be of potential theoretical significance. Variables have been included for scales on (1) the intensity of a government's commitment in terms of energy and resources present in the action; (2) the specificity with which the action is defined with respect to the problem it addresses and the target; (3) the affect (hostility-friendliness) of the actor toward the direct target; and (4) the duration of the event. An alternative approach to scale construction uses statistical reduction and aggregation techniques, such as factor analysis, to identify underlying dimensions of behavior. Scales formed in this manner may or may not reflect those concepts which the researcher regarded as basic to his theoretical interests. At the time of this writing, the CREON project is still in the early stages of scale construction using both of these approaches.

Still another procedure for event classification involves simple nominal categories. For example, data have been collected on various kinds of threats and promises, various uses of military force, and various ways by which a state yields control over its territory, citizens, or their property. (The latter type of action ranges from commercial air rights to acts of total surrender.) Inspection of 11,617 events suggests that proportionately few actions involve transfers (513 events), military force (825), or restrictions on sovereignty (368). Of course, the significance of any

---

[8] Alternative types of policy classification, including the two reported in this section, are described in C. F. Hermann (1972).

TABLE IV-3

Revised WEIS Scheme for Categorizing Foreign Policy Event Actions

Direction of action	Verbal			Nonverbal
	Evaluation	Desire	Intent	Deed

Conflictive	*Category 1*
	Deny
	Accuse
	Comment (Neg.)
		Category 3
		Demand
		Protest
		Propose (Neg.)
		Request (Neg.)
			Category 5
			Threaten
			Warn
			Reject
			Intend (Neg.)
				Category 7
				Use force
				Demonstrate
				Increase
				  military
				  capability
				Aid oppo-
				  nent
				Reduce
				  relationship
				Seize
				Expel
				Subvert

Neutral or cooperative	*Category 2*
	Comment (Pos.)
	Approve
		Category 4
		Request (Pos.)
		Propose (Pos.)
		Negotiate
			Category 6
			Intend (Pos.)
			Offer
			Promise
			Agree
				Category 8
				Yield
				Grant
				Decrease
				  military
				  capability
				Consult
				Carry out
				  agreement
				Reward
				Increase re-
				  lationship

	Increasing commitment to action from left to right			*Action*

Note: The actions are those of the actor toward the first direct target, unless the actor and direct target are in the same country, in which case the action is that of the actor toward the most affected foreign indirect object. The original WEIS categories were developed by Charles McClelland and associates at the University of Southern California. The present eight-fold classification was prepared by Walter Corson. The individual categories in their present form were revised by Maurice A. East, Walter Corson, Patrick McGowan, Stephen Salmore, and Charles F. Hermann.

type of action in foreign policy does not necessarily correspond to the frequency with which it appears. The relatively infrequent occurrence of some classes of behaviors, however, reinforces one assumption of this essay; namely, that students of foreign policy tend either to overlook or to be unfamiliar with the most frequent activities undertaken in foreign affairs. By concentrating on the behaviors that we regard as in some way important—such as political crises, military engagements, or trade agreements—we lose perspective on the scope and distribution of external activities conducted by governments. It may well be that these little-recognized foreign activities make certain types of "significant" actions more or less likely.

One of the most elaborate sets of nominal categories in the CREON data is derived from the World Event/Interaction Survey (WEIS). Every event is assigned to one (and only one) of the thirty-five categories, grouped into eight clusters, as shown in Table IV-3. The categories in the upper half of Table IV-3 include all hostile or conflictual behavior, while those in the bottom half incorporate neutral and friendly, or cooperative, behavior. Furthermore, from left to right, the eight categories in the table represent an increasing disposition toward physical action and thus offer a crude measure of commitment.

Table IV-4 presents some preliminary results with the data for all thirty months when actions are grouped into the eight broad categories just described. The first column of that table gives the frequency and percentage of actions in each category for all nations in the CREON data set. The largest proportion of actions in this column (27 percent) appears in the category consisting of friendly or neutral evaluations of some aspect of the actor's external environment (category 2). In fact, this lowest level of neutral or affirmative commitment ranks first in every column in Table IV-4; that is, the highest percentage of events for every type of nation represented in the table falls into this category. Similarly, the second highest ranking category not only for all nations but also for each of the separate nation-types involves expressions by the actor of a desire for neutral or favorable actions by others (category 4). The third highest percentage for all nations (14 percent) is category 6, which consists of expressions by the actor of his own intention to take neutral or favorable action in the future. (In other columns of the table, category 6 is ranked or is tied for third or fourth rank.)

Using this information, if we look back at Table IV-3, we discover that the three categories with the largest proportion of events fall in the lower half of this table and move sequentially from left to right through

TABLE IV–4

CREON Events Distributed by Nation-Types and Categories of Action

Categories of action	All nations	Type of nation					
		Large	Small	Developed	Less developed	Open	Closed
1. Hostile evaluation of external situation	1,453 (13%)	1,044 (16%)	409 (8%)	1,052 (13%)	401 (11%)	876 (11%)	577 (17%)
2. Neutral/coop. evaluation of external situation	3,137 (27%)	1,659 (25%)	1,478 (29%)	2,076 (26%)	1,061 (29%)	2,329 (28%)	808 (24%)
3. Desires others act in way unfavorable to target	461 (4%)	281 (4%)	180 (4%)	253 (3%)	208 (6%)	226 (3%)	235 (7%)
4. Desires others act in way neutral or favorable to target	2,376 (21%)	1,136 (17%)	1,240 (24%)	1,546 (19%)	830 (23%)	1,738 (21%)	638 (19%)
5. Actor's intended unfavorable action to target	738 (6%)	497 (8%)	241 (5%)	548 (7%)	190 (5%)	465 (6%)	273 (8%)
6. Actor's intended neutral or favorable action to target	1,669 (14%)	971 (15%)	698 (14%)	1,225 (15%)	444 (12%)	1,297 (16%)	372 (11%)
7. Deeds hostile to target	313 (3%)	180 (3%)	133 (3%)	236 (3%)	77 (2%)	226 (3%)	87 (2%)
8. Deeds neutral or friendly to target	1,442 (12%)	747 (11%)	695 (14%)	1,004 (13%)	438 (12%)	1,090 (13%)	352 (11%)
Total N	11,589	6,515	5,074	7,930	3,659	8,257	3,332

the three types of verbal behavior. The higher commitment in a neutral or friendly mode, as represented by category 8, ranks fifth for all nations, but ranks third or fourth for some individual nation-types. The category that ranks fourth for all nations and interrupts the progression of ranks across the bottom of Table IV-3 is hostile evaluation of the external situation (category 1). Behaviors in this category are judged to represent the least degree of commitment that can be associated with a hostile action. At all but the highest levels of positive commitment, the overall pattern suggests that nations initiate more neutral or friendly behavior than they do any kind of hostile or conflictual behavior. The least common type of behavior for all nations—and for every nation-type—is conflictual deeds (category 7), which is the highest level of hostile commitment. In sum, the first column of Table IV-4 suggests that nations typically keep their hostile behavior confined to low intensity.

One of the striking characteristics about the remaining columns of Table IV-4 is the rather small percentage differences between pairs of nation-types. The largest percentage difference (eight percentage points) appears between large and small nations on hostile evaluation of the situation (category 1). Governments of large nations have a higher proportion of negative evaluations. Policymakers in large states may feel more secure from reprisals for making negative evaluations of the international situation. The second largest percentage difference (category 4) indicates that governments of small states, more than those of large states, express the desire for affirmative action by others. This last finding is consistent with our general characterization of small states as devoting much of their external effort to seeking aid.

The same explanation might apply to the finding that governments of less-developed countries make proportionately more statements urging positive action by others (category 4) than do the governments of developed countries. In fact, less-developed countries generally seem more concerned with seeking action by others, regardless of whether they urge neutral, favorable, or unfavorable action (categories 3 and 4) with respect to the target. If we combine categories 3 and 4, all such events account for 29 percent in less-developed nations as compared to 22 percent for developed nations.

Turning to the last pair of nation-types in Table IV-4—open and closed systems—we find two differences of five percentage points or more. Governments of closed nations more frequently make hostile evaluations of their external environment than do those in open systems (category 1). Moreover, governments of open systems as compared to those of closed systems have a larger proportion of their events in category 6 (neutral or favorable declarations of their own future action toward the target). As suggested by the first six categories for these nation-types, some sort of paranoia regarding the external world may be inherent in most closed systems, leading them to talk more negatively and less favorably about foreign affairs. It should be noted, however, that in the

CREON data this pattern does not carry over into physical deeds. Open nations appear to be slightly more active in both categories of physical deeds (7 and 8), including those which are hostile to the target.

Conclusions

It must be emphasized again that the findings in this essay should be regarded as tentative, although suggestive. Before we can place confidence in them, we must seek answers to further questions, including the following:

1. Would the pattern of results be sustained if additional data sources were added to the present one and coverage were extended to include all months between 1959 and 1968?
2. With respect to the variables in the CREON data, what is the variability among nations in the same nation-type? Are only a subset of nations within each type accounting for the observed patterns?
3. How stable is the pattern of process and actions with respect to different targets or with different samples of initiating states?
4. To what extent are the observed differences in the three Rosenau genotypic variables independent? For example, if one controls for accountability and size, are there differences between developed and less-developed countries?
5. How stable are the patterns across time? If one divided the data into smaller time intervals, would the same pattern exist in most time periods?

Regardless of whether the answers to these questions substantiate the findings in this particular study, they will strengthen our understanding of foreign policy by providing a means of empirically investigating pretheories of foreign affairs such as those described at the outset of this essay. As these theoretical frameworks are modified and improved, they become the keys to better explanation and forecasting.

6

Size and Foreign Policy Behavior: A Test of Two Models

MAURICE A. EAST

Recently, the concept of size as a factor affecting foreign policy has received an increasing amount of attention. One manifestation of this concern is the renewed interest in the foreign policy behavior of small states.[1] In his pretheory of foreign policy, Rosenau (1966) includes size as one of three "genotypic" variables alleged to exert a major influence on foreign policy. Several empirical studies have also shown size to be an important factor underlying variations in the international behavior of nation-states (see Rummel 1969c; Sawyer 1967; and Salmore and Hermann 1969).

The focus of this study is on the similarities and differences in the foreign policy behavior of small and large states. After discussing several models of such behavior, we will then use data generated by the Comparative Research on the Events of Nations (CREON) project to assess their validity.

This chapter is an abridged version of an article which first appeared in *World Politics* 25 (July 1973):556–76. Copyright © 1973 by Princeton University Press. Reprinted by permission of the author and publisher. The style of the footnotes and the bibliography have been altered for this volume.

[1] Recent books focusing on small states and foreign policy behavior include Vital (1971), Schou and Brundtland (1971), Rapoport (1971), and Sveics (1970).

The Models

The literature describing differences in the foreign policy behavior of small and large states is far from consistent;[2] however, a generally perceived model of small-state behavior in foreign affairs can be abstracted. This conventional model generally assumes that small states are characterized by one or more of the following: (1) small land area, (2) small total population, (3) small productive capacity, and (4) a low level of military capabilities. According to this model, the foreign policy behavior of small states is expected to exhibit the following patterns:

1. Low levels of overall participation in world affairs;
2. High levels of activity in intergovernmental organizations (IGO's);
3. High levels of support for international legal norms;
4. Avoidance of the use of force as a technique of statecraft;
5. Avoidance of behavior which tends to alienate the more powerful states in the system;
6. A narrow functional and geographic range of concern in foreign policy activities;
7. Frequent invocation of moral and legal norms in diplomatic interactions.[3]

Underlying the attribution of these behavior patterns to small states, there seems to be a major implicit assumption: small-state behavior is the result of the same general processes of decision-making as those found in larger states. For example, the above patterns correspond quite closely to what might emerge from the application of a rational-actor model of foreign policy to the situation facing any state with limited resources and a limited international potential.[4] In virtually every pattern indicated above, small states exhibit a low-profile posture, minimizing their perceived risks and their expenditure of scarce resources such as manpower, military capabilities, and hard currency. In addition, it is often assumed in the literature that the foreign policy actions of small states are the results of decisions arrived at by a decisional unit which has

[2] For an excellent discussion of the inconsistencies in the literature regarding the relationship between power and aggressiveness, see Salmore (1972, pp. 40–68).

[3] The abstraction of these foreign policy behavior patterns is based on wide reading in the general literature of international politics and foreign policy. Among the more revealing sources are Morgenthau (1967), Aron (1966), Organski (1968), and Liska (1968).

[4] In this instance, the term *rational* is used to imply the minimizing of costs and the maximizing of impact by operating under the same assumptions and rules that might apply in a large, developed state.

been monitoring world affairs relatively closely, operates from an adequate information base, and has a long-range policy perspective.[5] Paraphrasing Rothstein (1968, p. 2), the conventional model assumes that small states are simply large states writ small.

If one assumes, however, that there are fundamental differences between the foreign policy processes of large and small states, it is possible to construct a plausible alternative model of small-state behavior. Starting with the definitional characteristics of small states, one might assume that the total amount of resources available for allocation by the political system of a small state is relatively small. Even though the demands made upon the political systems of small states may also be proportionally smaller than those in large states, one may also assume that in small states fewer resources will be available for redistribution anywhere in the system after meeting all the minimal requirements for the maintenance of essential structures. Moreover, the cost of governing peoples has increased dramatically in the post–World War II era.[6] The result of all these factors is that, compared to large states, small states have a smaller proportion of an already small resource base to devote to foreign policy.

If these assumptions are correct, one can hypothesize that there are likely to be important differences between large and small states in processes of foreign policy decision-making. With fewer resources available for allocation to the foreign-affairs sector, the size and capacity of the organization charged with the primary responsibility for foreign policy are likely to be small. This means that there will be fewer persons involved in monitoring international events and executing decisions. Consequently, small states may be unable to cope with the total range of international issues facing them. Certain functional and geographic areas will be emphasized, while others are ignored. Moreover, this reduced organizational capacity in foreign affairs means that small states will be less active overall, and differentially active in various areas of policy.

A second consequence would be that small states are likely to be slower in perceiving events and developments in the international system. Because they have a smaller capacity to monitor the system, it is less likely that they will perceive various early warning signals indicating new developments and important policy shifts by other international actors.

[5] Although it would be difficult to point to an author who explicitly espouses these assumptions, much of the discussion of small states within a strategic perspective implies as much. There is discussion of strategic roles, long-range and short-range alliance objectives, and so on. See especially Liska (1968) throughout.

[6] For similar arguments, see Deutsch (1966) and Sprout and Sprout (1968).

Such difficulties, in turn, can have profound effects on foreign policy behavior. Conflicts often develop in stages. A state which becomes aware of a potentially troublesome situation in an early stage of development will have more opportunity to influence the outcome of the situation. Conversely, a state which perceives a conflict only at a later stage of development will have fewer alternatives to consider. Deutsch (1969, p. 60), for one, argues that "governments frequently . . . decide to go to war when they believe themselves to be constrained by the lack of any acceptable political alternative to war."[7] By the time small states perceive the signals, the situation may have reached a stage of development where definite, unambiguous high-risk behavior must be taken. A small state does not enjoy the luxury of engaging in early, low-level, ambiguous behavior when trying to take effective action in such situations.

The behavior predicted from the alternative model, then, runs counter to that predicted by the conventional model. According to the former, small-state activity is more likely to be at a higher level of intensity, less ambiguous, and frequently more hostile and threatening. The major difference between the two models of foreign policy behavior, therefore, concerns the degree to which small states engage in what can be considered high-risk behavior. The alternative model predicts more high-risk behavior for small states, while the conventional model predicts a more cautious, low-risk behavior pattern.

The assumption underlying the alternative model accounts for a third behavior pattern, one that is also predicted by the conventional model. Because of the relative lack of resources available for foreign affairs, the small state must seek methods of interaction that are less costly. Traditional bilateral diplomacy is a very expensive way of conducting affairs, and one that serves the interests of the large states well. Small states will rely more on other methods of interaction, such as multilateral diplomacy, international conferences, regional organizations, and multiple diplomatic representation.

Finally, there is an important difference between large and small states in their perception of the importance of various issues in world politics. Because internal demands on political decision-making are more acute in small states, owing to their lack of economic surplus and reduced total resource base, certain traditional issues in international politics are generally of little interest to small states. These are issues such as the Cold War, global prestige and influence, acquiring or main-

---

[7] The general communications-based model utilized here owes much to the work of Deutsch, although there are several points of disagreement between his position and mine. See Deutsch (1963) and Deutsch and Singer (1964).

taining alliances or spheres of influence, and territorial expansion. On the other hand, those international issues which are directly related to their economic growth and development will be most salient for small states (see O'Leary 1969; Good 1962).

To summarize: Both of the models of small-state foreign policy behavior that have been discussed allow one to make predictions about the behavior of small states in foreign policy. In several areas, the predictions of the two models are similar, but in one major area, relating to high-risk behavior, the models offer opposite predictions. In the analysis that follows, events data are used to identify differences between the foreign policy behavior patterns of large and small states, and to make some judgments about the relative validity of the two models. The events data analyzed here were generated by the CREON project and consist of 4,448 foreign policy events initiated by thirty-two nation-states during randomly selected quarters of each of the years from 1959 to 1968.[8]

The Analyses

The foreign policy event is the unit of analysis in this study. The strategy of analysis is to group events according to attributes of the initiating state in order to identify differences in foreign policy behavior between groups. Thus, the attributes of nation-states are the independent variables used to group events. The dependent variables include various aspects of the foreign policy event itself: whether the event was verbal or nonverbal behavior, conflictive or cooperative; whether the action was specific or ambiguous; and so on. These different measures of foreign policy behavior will be discussed more fully as they are introduced into the analyses below.

The results of the analyses are organized as follows. First, the distribution of events initiated by large and small nations is examined for important differences in levels of activity. Second, events are analyzed to determine whether small states tend to utilize low-cost techniques of statecraft. Third, substantive aspects of events are examined to determine the degree to which high- or low-risk behavior characterizes small states. Finally, there is an attempt to determine which issue areas of foreign policy are most important to large and small states.

[8] For a more complete description of the CREON project data set, see Hermann, Salmore, and East (1971). The exact time periods included are October–December 1959, April–June 1960, January–March 1961, October–December 1962, April–June 1963, July–September 1964, January–March 1965, July–September 1966, April–June 1967, and October–December 1968.

A secondary focus of these analyses is on the differences between small developed and small developing states. The argument is frequently made that there is a fundamental difference between the older small developed states (primarily Western European) and the newer small developing states (primarily in Africa, Asia, and Latin America).[9] In order to examine this argument empirically, all relationships between size and foreign policy behavior have been controlled for level of economic development. Only in those instances where the size relationship is significantly affected by development will the results of the three-variable analysis, controlling for development, be presented.

The groupings of nations according to size and development are those established by Burgess (1970b), who performed a discriminant analysis on 1963 data.[10] The distribution of the thirty-two states included in the CREON data set across the four groupings is as follows:

Small Developed	Small Developing	Large Developed	Large Developing
Belgium	Costa Rica	France	China
Chile	Ghana	Italy	India
Cuba	Guinea	Japan	Turkey
East Germany	Ivory Coast	Mexico	
Israel	Kenya	Spain	
New Zealand	Lebanon	U.S.S.R.	
Norway	Philippines	U.S.A.	
Switzerland	Thailand	West Germany	
Uruguay	Tunisia		
Venezuela	Yugoslavia		
	Zambia		

[9] Both Rothstein (1968) and Vital (1971) attempt to grapple with this problem but rather unsuccessfully. Rothstein's analysis of developing states is in a single chapter toward the end of the book and is not well integrated with the other sections, which deal almost exclusively with the older small developed states. Vital's work focuses on case studies of Czechoslovakia, Israel, and Finland, none of which fit the criteria for small developing states. Furthermore, Vital, in an earlier work, uses a different "rough upper limit" of population for developed countries from the one used for developing states (1967, p. 8). For economically advanced countries the upper limit of population is 10–15 million; for developing states it is 20–30 million.

[10] Discriminant analysis is a statistical technique for partitioning a linear combination of a set of variables so as to minimize the distance between the resulting groupings, taking into account the entire set of variables. In the final partitioning, large countries are those with populations above 23.7 million; developed countries are those with a gross national product per capita exceeding $401. See Burgess (1970b).

Level of International Activity

Both models of small-state foreign policy behavior predict that small states will participate in foreign affairs less frequently than large states. An analysis of the data with regard to number of foreign policy events initiated gives ample support to this proposition. The average number of events initiated and the median for each group is given in Table IV-5.

Large states initiate considerably more events than do small states, reflecting a higher level of international activity overall. Using a *t*-test for difference of means, large and small states show a significant difference at the $p = 0.05$ level. The difference between small developed and small developing states, however, is not significant at the same level. Nevertheless, the rank-ordering of groups of states indicates that size and development operate cumulatively with respect to international activity; that is, a small state with low economic development initiates fewer events than does a small state with high economic development.

With regard to level of overall international activity, the data tend to confirm the original proposition. Large states do exhibit a higher level of international activity than small states. The fact that the obvious is validated in this instance also tends to confer a degree of credibility on the data set. Furthermore, Table IV-5 indicates that size is more im-

TABLE IV-5

Mean and Median Number of Events Initiated by Groups of
Nation-States, 1959–68

Group	Mean	Median
All states (N = 32)	139	50
Large states (N = 11)	288[a]	196
Small states (N = 21)	55	43
Small developed states (N = 10)	65[b]	46
Small developing states (N = 11)	46	36

[a] The difference in means between large and small states is significant at the $p = 0.05$ level using a *t*-test; $t = 2.63$ with $df = 30$.

[b] The difference in means between small developed and small developing states is not significant at the $p = 0.05$ level; $t = 0.95$ with $df = 19$.

portant than development in accounting for differences in the level of international activity.[11]

Foreign Policy Techniques

It has been argued above that because of lack of resources, small states are more likely to employ various techniques of statecraft which will minimize the cost of carrying out their foreign policy. Several studies (Alger and Brams 1967; East 1969, pp. 128–46) have noted, for example, the tendency of small states to utilize intergovernmental organizations to a larger extent than do large states. It is possible to examine the degree to which states jointly initiate foreign policy events in order to test the hypothesis that small states are more likely to engage in joint foreign policy behavior because this allows two or more states to pool their resources to achieve greater influence.

Table IV-6 supports the hypothesis by showing that small states do initiate more joint behavior events than large states. The chi square value and the percentage differences are both quite large, and the magnitude of the relationship using the Goodman-Kruskal gamma is 0.38. Although it was not possible to separate out IGO events from all others, it should be noted that the third column of Table IV-7 includes events initiated by states as participants in IGO's. Thus, the evidence would

TABLE IV–6

Percentage of Events Initiated by Size and Number of
States Participating

	No. of participants			Total no.
	One	Two	Three	of events
Large states	65	30	4	3,153
Small states	46	40	14	1,135

Note: Chi square = 202.57; gamma = 0.38. For this and the remaining tables in this chapter, the significance level of the chi square value will be given only if it is below $p = 0.01$. The chi square values are likely to be large because of the large number of cases being analyzed.

[11] Although the thirty-two nations included in the data set are not a random sample of all nations, the choice of time periods for which data were collected is random by quarters. Therefore, there are certain inferential statistics in the tables presented here. In addition to the statistics given, it should be noted that a difference of four or more percentage points is statistically significant at the $p = 0.05$ level, given the size of the groups being compared.

seem to indicate that small states do initiate a greater proportion of their foreign policy events as joint undertakings, including events initiated in IGO's.

Another economical means of conducting foreign policy is to direct one's influence attempts at groups of states and at IGO's rather than at individual nations. Thus, it is hypothesized that many of the targets of small states' actions will be groups of states of IGO's. Table IV-7 presents these data. The major differences between large and small states appear in the first and last columns. Eighty-five percent of all large-state

TABLE IV-7

Percentage of Events Initiated by Size of Initiating State and Number of Targets

	No. of targets				IGO as target	Total no. of events
	One	Two to three	Four to ten	Eleven or more		
Large states	85	5	1	0	8	3,166
Small states	75	5	2	1	17	1,145

Chi square = 83.90; gamma = 0.30.

events have a single target, while only 75 percent of small-state events have one target. The difference in the frequency with which IGO's are the target of foreign policy events is also significant and in the predicted direction. Small states initiate 9 percent more events with an IGO as target.

There is a third type of foreign policy behavior which might also be considered low-cost. On the assumption that talking is a more economical form of behavior than action, the conventional model predicts that if foreign policy events are dichotomized into verbal and nonverbal behavior, small states will engage in more words and fewer deeds.

The alternative model offers a competing hypothesis, however. It assumes that small states are unable to maintain a high level of attention on foreign affairs. Furthermore, they often do not perceive developing situations until rather late. The result is that small states are unlikely to exhibit much of the verbal behavior that makes up much of international behavior. The action of small states, when it eventually comes, is more likely to be in the form of nonverbal behavior, or deeds. "Low-cost," verbal behavior is not likely to prove effective in influencing a situation which may just have come to the attention of a small state.

Thus, the competing hypothesis is that small states will exhibit relatively less verbal behavior and more nonverbal behavior than large states.

In this context, it should be noted that in coding events, verbal behavior always involves the actual commitment or utilization of resources. Using military force, granting a loan, buying or selling goods, and sending personnel or equipment are all examples of deeds.[12]

Table IV-8 clearly supports the hypothesis derived from the alternative model of small-state behavior. There is a statistically significant difference of 14 percent in the amount of verbal behavior exhibited by

TABLE IV–8

Percentage of Verbal and Nonverbal Behavior by Size

	Verbal (words)	Nonverbal (deeds)	Total no. of events
Large states	76	24	3,168
Small states	62	38	1,146

Chi square = 7.39.

large and small states, with small states generating less verbal behavior and more nonverbal behavior.

It is instructive to look at the effect of economic development on this relationship. Table IV-9 makes clear that size is more important than level of development in accounting for differences in the amount of nonverbal behavior. The percentage differences between small and large states are substantial, while the differences between levels of development *within* the size categories are either very small or virtually nonexistent.

The rankings of size and development groupings by percentage of nonverbal behavior events also support the alternative model. Developing states have fewer resources to devote to international affairs than developed states; thus, the cumulative effect of size and development on resources would predict an ordering in which small developing states ranked first, followed by small developed states. Both of these groups have fewer resources to expend than large states. This is precisely the rank-ordering of states found in Table IV-9.

[12] Under certain conditions, announcements of actions qualify as deeds rather than as verbal behavior. Generally, this is when the announcement is of an action that has already taken place, or when there are no conditional factors likely to intervene between the announcement and the action. See Hermann, Salmore, and East (1971).

TABLE IV–9

Percentage of Nonverbal Behavior by Size and Development

	Percentage	Total no. of events
Small developing states	40	501
Small developed states	37	645
Large developing states	24	774
Large developed states	24	2,394

High-Risk Behavior

The conventional model of small-state foreign policy behavior predicts that small states will exhibit behavior that produces the least amount of risk for them. Stanley Hoffman (1965) summarizes this point well: "At all times, the line separating smaller from larger powers has corresponded to two different attitudes toward risk. Small powers are forced, by their resources, their location, and the system, to be satisfied with establishing a hierarchy of risks and with attempting to minimize the risks they consider to be most serious" (p. 138). Such behavior is likely to include an unwillingness to engage in conflict or hostile behavior, a tendency to employ ambiguity to avoid alienating other states, and much cooperative verbal behavior. There would not be as much cooperative nonverbal behavior, since it is more costly.

The alternative model again presents competing hypotheses. First, small states are likely to exhibit more conflict behavior than large states, particularly nonverbal conflict behavior, because of the frequent need to take action of a definitive and often hostile nature. By the time a small state perceives the signals regarding a situation, that situation has frequently reached a stage where only definite, high-commitment action will be effective. Furthermore, it is possible that, before being perceived by the small state, the situation already may have deteriorated, in which case, only conflictual or hostile behavior is likely to be effective in changing the course of events. It is too late to utilize lower-level actions such as bargaining and negotiation.

Using the same general argument, the hypothesis derived from the alternative model is that small-state behavior will be less ambiguous and more specific than large-state behavior, precisely to avoid misunderstandings and misinterpretations. Ambiguity may reflect maneuvering and attempts at enhancing one's bargaining position when it occurs at an early stage in a conflict, but in the later stages, when a small state is likely to become involved, ambiguity can be misleading and dangerous to the state's position.

Let us examine these competing hypotheses, first with regard to conflictual and cooperative behavior, by analyzing the CREON data, which have been coded using a modified version of the World Event/Interaction Survey (WEIS) scheme for categorizing foreign policy interactions.[13] This modified coding scheme is organized into eight major categories of event-types, as shown in Table IV-3 (Chapter 5). The eight cells in the table represent three dimensions of foreign behavior: (1) verbal and nonverbal behavior, (2) conflict and cooperation, and (3) differing levels of commitment to action within the verbal behavior category. In the third dimension, it is assumed that evaluation statements symbolize the lowest level of commitment to action, statements of intent the highest level of commitment, and statements of desire an intermediate level of commitment.

The dimensions can be arrayed on an eight-point scale in the following manner:

1	2	3	4	5	6	7	8
Cooperation				Conflict			
Deeds	Intent	Desire	Evaluation	Evaluation	Desire	Intent	Deeds

This scale can be collapsed to form different variables. For example, the first and last types represent nonverbal behavior, while the rest are verbal; types 1 through 4 represent cooperative behavior; 5 through 8 represent conflict behavior.

The empirical relationship between size, development, and conflict behavior is a complex one. Nevertheless, the simple bivariate relationship will be examined first. The prediction from the conventional model was that small states would engage in less conflict behavior. By the same argument, the conventional model also predicts that developing states will engage in less conflict behavior. The alternative model, on the other hand, predicts that small states (and developing states, by

---

[13] On WEIS, see McClelland and Hoggard (1969). The revised scheme follows closely the work of Corson (1970).

TABLE IV–10

Percentage of Conflictive and Cooperative Behavior by Size

	Cooperation	Conflict	Total no. of events
Large states	63	37	3,168
Small states	69	31	1,146

Chi square = 16.76; gamma = 0.15.

the same logic) will exhibit more conflict behavior because of the perceived necessity of taking high-risk and often hostile action if they are to influence the direction of situations as they develop.

Tables IV-10 and IV-11 show the distribution of conflictive and cooperative actions by size and development. Note that both models, given these data, rate equally well: both yield one correct and one incorrect prediction. Small states exhibit 6 percent less conflict behavior than large states, and developing states exhibit 4 percent more conflict behavior than developed states. In both cases, the relationship is statistically significant above $p = 0.05$, but the magnitude of the relationship is relatively small. The relationship between size and conflict/cooperation is elaborated in a most interesting way not predicted by either model when controlling for level of development (Table IV-12). Large developing states have the highest percentage of conflict behavior, and small developing states have the lowest.[14]

TABLE IV–11

Percentage of Conflictive and Cooperative Behavior by Development

	Cooperation	Conflict	Total no. of events
Developed states	66	34	3,039
Developing states	62	38	1,275

Chi square = 6.04 (significant at the $p = 0.02$ level); gamma = 0.08.

[14] The findings presented in Table IV–12 correspond nicely to a status discrepancy model of international conflict; that is, those states whose status on one dimension (size) is incongruent with status on another dimension (development) are most likely to exhibit conflict behavior. Large developing and small developed states are the two status-discrepant types, and they rank first and second in percentage of conflict behavior. See Galtung (1964) and East (1972)

TABLE IV-12

Percentage of Conflictive Behavior by Size and Development

	Percentage	Total no. of events
Large developing states	49	774
Small developed states	38	645
Large developed states	33	2,394
Small developing states	22	501

It is now necessary to utilize the uncollapsed coding scheme to examine another set of competing hypotheses. As indicated above, the alternative model predicts that small states are more likely to exhibit nonverbal behavior and especially nonverbal conflict behavior. These predictions can be tested by referring to Table IV-13. The percentage of deeds, both cooperative and conflictual, is higher for small states, and small states do exhibit more conflictual nonverbal behavior than large states. Table IV-13 supports the alternative model of small-state foreign policy behavior. Several other aspects of Table IV-13 also lend support, at least indirectly, to the theoretical basis of the alternative model. As Table IV-13 shows, much international behavior consists of low-commitment verbal behavior. The model, however, predicted that, because of the lack of resources, small states would initiate fewer of these types of events than large states. In the revised coding scheme, this low-commitment verbal behavior is represented by the evaluative verbal categories. When the cooperative and conflictual evaluative events are combined, the small states initiate fewer evaluative events than do the large states.

The final aspect of high-risk behavior to be examined is the degree of specificity of foreign policy behavior. It will be recalled that the conventional model predicts that ambiguity (lack of specificity) will be a characteristic of the behavior of small states, who use it as a means to avoid alienating others. The alternative model, on the other hand, predicts that the behavior of small states will be *more* specific, as a way to avoid misunderstandings and misperceptions.

It is possible to test these two hypotheses, since the CREON project data set allows for the analysis of two dimensions of specificity: problem specificity and target specificity. A problem-specific event is one in

TABLE IV-13

Revised Foreign Policy Action Scheme by Size
(In Percentages)

	Cooperation				Conflict				Total no. of events
	Deeds	Intent	Desire	Evaluation	Evaluation	Desire	Intent	Deeds	
Large states	21	16	10	17	20	5	9	3	3,168
Small states	30	14	16	10	14	4	5	8	1,146

Chi square = 189.42.

which the target of the event understands clearly what the issue is and what the initiating state desires to accomplish as a result of the event action. An event has a specific target when it is clear what entities the actor is concerned about with regard to the issue at hand and/or what entities the actor wishes to influence by his action. The following is an example of an event which has both an unspecified problem and an ambiguous target: country A expresses its concern over recent developments in the South Pacific. Although specificity is clearly a matter of degree, for the present analysis the variable has been assigned a dichotomous yes or no.

As indicated in Table IV-14, the alternative model is supported with regard to both dimensions of specificity. Small states show 8 percent more specificity with regard to problems and 18 percent more with regard to targets. Development makes virtually no difference with regard to problem specificity. As for target specificity, the only difference occurs between large developed and large developing states, and as implied by the alternative model, large developed states show the least specificity of target. These are precisely the states which can most afford to be ambiguous.

TABLE IV-14

Specificity of Foreign Policy Events by Size and Development
(In Percentages)

| | Specificity of | |
	Problem	Target
Large states	70 ($N = 3,154$)[a]	64 ($N = 3,152$)[b]
Small states	78 ($N = 1,144$)	82 ($N = 1,144$)
Small developed states	79 ($N = 644$)[c]	82 ($N = 643$)[d]
Small developing states	78 ($N = 500$)	82 ($N = 501$)
Large developed states	71 ($N = 2,385$)	61 ($N = 2,382$)
Large developing states	68 ($N = 769$)	72 ($N = 770$)

[a] The chi square value for the 2×2 table of size and problem specificity is 14.33.
[b] The chi square value for size and target specificity is 55.86.
[c] The chi square value for the 4×2 table of state-types by problem specificity is 31.93.
[d] The chi square value for type of state and target specificity is 162.93.

Relative Importance of Foreign Policy Issues

Both the conventional and alternative models predict that small states will be interested in a narrower range of foreign policy issues than will large states. The alternative model further specifies that economic issues will be of great importance to small states. Certain aspects of this relationship can be examined with the aid of the CREON data. All events were coded on a series of dimensions designed to capture various aspects of the internal decision unit and decision processes involved in the event. For example, each event was coded according to the bureaucratic structures that were involved in the event.[15] In addition, each event was coded according to whether the primary skill or resource used in executing the event was economic, military, or diplomatic. By analyzing the relationship of size and development to each of these variables, it is possible to investigate, at least in an indirect manner, the relative importance of various foreign policy issues.

The prediction is that the economic bureaucracies (i.e., those agencies responsible for the economic aspects of the polity) of small states as well as of developing states will be involved in the execution of a higher proportion of foreign policy events than will the economic bureaucracies of large states. Table IV-15 indicates that this is in fact the case. When controlling for development, the data indicate that small states still have a higher proportion of events involving economic bureaucracies than do large states.[16] Small developing states have a higher proportion of such events than small developed states, as might be expected from the alternative model.

An examination of the data on the skill or resources utilized in executing events is even more revealing. The assumption underlying this variable is that different types of states will employ different techniques of statecraft in conducting their foreign policy. Some may rely heavily on diplomacy or other traditional means of influencing other states;

[15] Information on the bureaucratic structures involved in foreign policy events was available for 52 percent of all events. Given the nature of the source, *Deadline Data,* this degree of richness in the data exceeded the highest expectations of the most optimistic members of the project.

[16] It is not clear why large developing states have such a small proportion of events involving economic bureaucracies. Size again is the dominating factor, but the alternative model would predict that the large developing state would show more economically oriented activity. Also, it is of interest to note that in large developed states (the principal actors in international economic affairs), only 6 percent of the total foreign policy activity involves economic bureaucracies.

TABLE IV–15

Percentage of Events Involving Economic Bureaucracies, by
Size and Development

	Percentage	Total no. of events
Large states	5	1,365
Small states	18	901
Small developing states	22	416
Small developed states	16	485
Large developed states	6	1,079
Large developing states	1	286

some may rely more on economic, cultural, or even military techniques.[17] Table IV-16 shows the distribution of foreign policy events across the three skill, or resource, areas. As the alternative model predicts, small states initiate 15 percent more events involving economic resources than do large states. Again, the small developing states initiate the highest proportion of such events. Thus, the evidence does seem to indicate that economic bureaucracies and economic techniques of statecraft are more frequently involved or utilized in the foreign policy behavior of small states.

Finally, another look at Table IV-16 reveals several additional findings. Although the primary focus here has been on the role of economic factors in shaping foreign policy behavior, examination of the role of military and diplomatic resources shows that several hypotheses presented above are also supported by these data. For example, compared with large states, small states are shown to be involved in 6 percent more events utilizing military skills and resources and to initiate 23 percent fewer diplomatic events than large states. In both cases, these findings provide additional support for the alternative model of small-state foreign policy behavior.

[17] Given the conception of techniques of statecraft employed here, it is possible for a state to use economic aid as a technique of statecraft to secure military advantages. Similarly, military techniques—for instance, mobilizing troops—could be used to gain economic or diplomatic advantages.

The original coding used six skill or resource categories, but the distribution of events across categories was so skewed that three categories (containing only 3 percent of the events) were omitted. The omitted categories were political-legal, cultural, and ideological.

TABLE IV–16

Type of Skill or Resource Used in Initiating Events, by Size and Development
(In Percentages)

	Skill or resource			Total no. of events
	Economic	Military	Diplomatic	
Small states	25	11	59[a]	1,145
Large states	10	5	82	3,166
Small developed states	22	12	60[b]	644
Small developing states	28	10	57	501
Large developed states	12	5	81	2,392
Large developing states	5	5	85	774

Note: As indicated in n. 17 to the text, the percentages in this table do not add up to 100 because three categories have been omitted. The omitted categories account for about 3 percent of all events. The final column, however, lists the total number of events in all six categories.

[a] The chi square value for this 2 × 3 table is 240.25.
[b] The chi square value for this 4 × 3 table is 257.93.

Conclusions

This study has focused on the impact of size on the foreign policy behavior of states. A conventional model of small-state behavior was abstracted from the literature. This model is based on the defining characteristics of small size and the projection of a "rational" decision-making model into the situations that face small states. An alternative model was also presented, based to a large degree on a communications perspective: small states act as they do because their organizational capacity and ability to monitor international affairs adequately is limited, leading to a lack of information, an inability to perceive situations at an early stage, and a tendency to engage in high-commitment, high-risk types of behavior.

Foreign policy events data from the CREON project were used to test the hypotheses stemming from the two models. The general thrust of the data supports the alternative model. Small states do tend to minimize the costs of conducting foreign policy by initiating more joint actions and by directing influence attempts at joint- or multiple-actor targets. Contrary to the predictions of the conventional model, small states do not initiate as much verbal behavior as large states. This finding is consistent with the alternative model, in which it is assumed that small states do not have the capacity or the resources to engage in large amounts of low-level verbal behavior.

In terms of high-risk behavior, small states engage in much more nonverbal conflict behavior. Also, small states tend to avoid ambiguity in foreign policy behavior, exhibiting more specificity as to the issue at hand and the target being influenced. Both of these findings run counter to the conventional model's predictions that small states will tend to minimize risks.

Finally, the importance of economic factors in small-state foreign policy is demonstrated. The involvement of economic bureaucracies and the utilization of economic techniques of statecraft are more frequent in the foreign policy of small states than in that of large states.

Although the data at hand do give reason for believing that there are profound and significant differences in the behavior patterns of large and small states, such a belief cannot be sustained without considerably more research on foreign policy decision-making procedures in small and developing states. For example, it is important to determine whether the foreign ministries of small states do indeed perceive situations at later stages of development. Do small-state decision-makers perceive the sense of urgency and need for high-risk, high-commitment action that is posited by the model? These and other areas of research at the micro-level of the nation-state must be carried out before the alternative model can be fully accepted.

7

Soviet and American Political Success in the United Nations General Assembly, 1946-70

EUGENE WITTKOPF

In the early 1960's roll-call votes in the United Nations General Assembly were a widely used source of quantifiable information on the foreign policy behavior of nations. During the last decade, however, roll-call analyses have become increasingly rare, and other measures of foreign policy behavior have become more widely used. Events data, for example, have captured the imagination of an ever-larger coterie of scholars, and the events data movement promises to provide new insights into the behavior of nations through the use of information that has not previously been available.

There are good reasons why roll calls, as well as other data sources, have been replaced by events data as indicators of foreign policy. Roll-call votes do not provide information on the nuances of behavior that are so much a part of foreign policy. They do not provide information on why states vote in the way they do or on the intensity of their convictions on different issues. They do not provide information that would enable researchers to link the choices made by states to the various proponents or opponents of policy alternatives within a national society. They in no way exhaust all, and perhaps not even the most relevant, issues on the "international agenda" at any particular point in time. And even those issues that are simultaneously on the United Nations agenda and the international agenda will not necessarily be decided by roll calls.

These are compelling arguments for searching out new sources of information on foreign policy. And it is important to note that, at least conceptually, events data can provide much information roll calls cannot. At the same time, however, the advantages that were first seen in looking at voting behavior still seem appropriate: U.N. roll calls provide an easily accessible source of information about the positions that nearly all extant states take on a wide range of international issues within known institutional procedures and constraints. Additionally, we now have such information for more than a quarter of a century, which means we have an opportunity to analyze at least one aspect of states' foreign policy behavior longitudinally. By the end of 1972 nearly four thousand roll-call votes had been taken in the plenary meetings of the General Assembly and its seven main committees by between 55 and 132 states. This is an impressive array of information that deserves attention—not at the expense of interaction analysis or other types of analyses, but as a complement to them.

What follows is an analysis of the political success that the United States and Soviet Union have enjoyed in the U.N. General Assembly between 1946 and 1970 based on their roll-call voting behavior relative to all other members of the body.[1] The study is based on a session-by-session analysis of all 3,556 roll-call votes taken in the General Assembly between the first session (1946) and the twenty-fifth session (1970). (The one-vote nineteenth session has been excluded.) The number of yearly votes analyzed ranges from a high of 412 in the third session to a low of 77 in the eighteenth session. Although attention is concentrated primarily on the United States and the Soviet Union, the total number of actors on which the analysis is based also varies considerably, from a low of 55 in 1946 to a high of 127 in 1970.

The purpose of the study is descriptive, in the sense that it is designed only to characterize Soviet and American political success. This will be done with the aid of a few statistical measures, thereby fulfilling a second purpose of the study, namely, to demonstrate how quantitative techniques can facilitate the comparative analysis of foreign policy. Answering the question of what explains variations in each state's success from one assembly session to the next—that is, *why* states' political success varies—remains a separate, additional task.

---

[1] The data utilized in this chapter were made available by the Inter-University Consortium for Political Research and were originally collected by Charles Wrigley. Neither the original collector of the data nor the Consortium bears any responsibility for the analyses or interpretations presented here.

Measuring Political Success

The support level (SL) index developed by Steven J. Brams and Michael K. O'Leary (1970) has been chosen as a descriptive measure of Soviet and American political success in the General Assembly. The index measures the proportion of times that an individual assembly member votes with the majority or plurality across a set of roll calls, comparing this proportion with an expected value calculated on the basis of the proportion of all assembly members that support the majority or plurality. SL is a probabilistic measure calculated according to two criteria: the more frequently a member votes in support of the majority or plurality, the higher will be his SL score; and the fewer the number of members voting with the majority or plurality, the higher will be the score of those that did vote for the majority or plurality position. In other words, the SL index is a weighted measure that accounts for the size of the winning coalition on each roll call. Given the conceptual and empirical underpinnings of the SL index, it seems reasonable to interpret it as a measure of states' political success. This interpretation rests on a simple rational-actor assumption about states' voting behavior: all states will attempt to maximize the number of times they vote with the majority coalition in the General Assembly, for whatever reason, and all states will attempt to minimize the number of times they vote with the minority coalition.

The computational procedures used to derive SL scores for individual actors are quite straightforward. The SL for each member j across a set of roll calls is defined as

$$SL_j = \frac{A(S_j) - E(S_j)}{E(S_{j\epsilon})},$$

where $A(S_j)$ represents the actual number of roll calls on which member j votes with the majority or plurality, and

$$E(S_j) = \sum_{i=1}^{m} E(S_j)_i = \sum_{i=1}^{m} P(S_j)_i$$

represents the expected number of roll calls on which a randomly selected member, for all roll calls on which member j is present and voting (symbolized by m above the summation sign), votes with the majority or plurality (Brams and O'Leary 1970, p. 465). Throughout the subsequent analysis, all states that missed more than 40 percent of the roll calls in each assembly session are excluded from the calculation of SL scores.

Clearly, the critical value in the calculation of SL_j is the expected term, which is defined as the sum of the probabilities,

$$\sum_{i=1}^{m} P(S_j)_i,$$

that member j will agree with the majority or plurality across a set of roll calls, where m designates the entire set and i refers to each individual roll call. These probabilities are nothing more than the proportion of all members in a body that choose the majority or plurality option. An example will illustrate these points (Brams and O'Leary 1970, pp. 457, 465–66).

Assume we have a body of five voting members, each taking one of three voting options (yes [Y], no [N], and abstain [A]) on a total of five roll calls. The distribution of the votes in this hypothetical body might look as follows:

Roll call	Vote of members				
	1	2	3	4	5
1	Y	Y	N	Y	A
2	N	N	Y	A	A
3	Y	Y	Y	Y	A
4	N	N	Y	N	A
5	Y	Y	Y	Y	Y

On the first roll call the yeas comprise the majority. Since three of the five members chose the majority option, the probability that a randomly selected member will choose the majority option is 0.6 ($\frac{3}{5} = 0.6$). On the second vote both those casting nays and those abstaining comprise the plurality. Therefore, the probability that a randomly selected member will vote with the plurality on the second vote is 0.4 ($\frac{2}{5} = 0.4$). By the same logic, the probabilities for the three remaining votes are, respectively, 0.8, 0.6, and 1.0. Summing these probabilities yields $E(S_j) = 3.4$. This value can now be placed in the formula for calculating SL_j for each member of the voting body.

Across the entire set of roll calls, the first voting member actually agreed with the majority or plurality position on all five roll calls. Hence, the SL score for actor 1 is

$$SL_j = \frac{A(S_j) - E(S_j)}{E(S_j)} = \frac{5 - 3.4}{3.4} = 0.47.$$

This indicates that actor 1 was supportive of the winning coalition 47 percent more often than one would expect on the basis of the behavior of all five members in the body. Similarly, actors 2 and 4 were supportive of the winning side 47 percent more often than expected, while actors 3 and 5 were supportive of the winning side 41 percent less often than expected. Zero, then, indicates the point at which an individual actor agrees exactly as often with the majority as one would expect, and it becomes a baseline against which to assess the actual behavior of individual actors. This is true irrespective of the size of the body, which means we can easily use SL scores for comparative analyses of states' voting behavior in a body such as the General Assembly, which has grown appreciably over the past twenty-five years.

As Brams and O'Leary point out (1970, p. 466), the SL index will yield the same rank order of legislative members as would a measure based simply on the percentage of times that a member votes with the largest voting bloc.[2] The concept of "support" embodied in the SL index is, however, somewhat different than a simple percentage measure implies. In contrast to the latter, SL, because of the expected level it incorporates, would distinguish between support in bodies (or sessions) that tended to be closely divided and those characterized by large majorities on many roll calls. In those bodies that tended to be closely divided, the expected level of support would be low, so SL_j would be high for those members who lent their support on most roll calls. In voting bodies where roll calls tended toward unanimity, on the other hand, the expected level of support would be high, so even the most highly supportive members would not exceed the expected level by a wide margin, and their SL_j's would therefore be low. . . .

. . . For comparative purposes . . . SL_j would distinguish, by giving added weight to, a member of a closely divided body who tends to support "minimal" largest voting blocs from a member of a less closely divided body who tends to support large majorities. Thus, even though two voters might have the same "percentage agreement" scores in different voting bodies, our SL_j index credits the voter who tends to align himself with smaller pluralities in the closely-divided body with more "support."

[2] Percentages are used to analyze voting behavior in Hovet (1960) and Rowe (1969).

This bias in the operational concept well reflects the greater marginal importance a coalition leader normally would attribute to the member or members who "just make" the coalition a largest bloc (or a majority) than the members who join later and are superfluous to victory. Though we cannot determine in most voting situations the order in which members join a coalition prior to a ballot, it seems reasonable to assume that the "support" a plurality or majority of members receives from a voter is inversely related to its size: the more members a largest bloc contains, the less support that can be attributed to individual members of the bloc. (Brams and O'Leary 1970, p. 466)

Two points in this quotation deserve special emphasis since they are both related to the interpretation of the empirical results presented below. First, as the authors point out, SL gives the greatest weight to an actor when a coalition is a minimum winning coalition. This means that an actor can be in many majority coalitions, but if all of these are overwhelmingly large, his SL score will not indicate voting behavior supportive of the majority much more often than expected. If, on the other hand, an actor is in many majorities and most of these tend to be minimal in size (e.g., 51 percent in a situation with two voting options), SL will give considerably more weight to this actor's behavior than to the actor who was a member only of very large coalitions.

The second important point is that in most voting situations—especially in the General Assembly—we cannot be certain about the order in which members join a coalition preceding a vote. This also means that we cannot distinguish between leaders and followers, between those who are exercising influence in the pursuit of some goal and those who are being influenced. Because the SL index weights all actors' behavior in the same fashion, it is not a measure of leadership in a legislative body. This does not mean, however, that a determination of who is exercising influence within a voting body is unimportant. Indeed, the closing paragraphs of this essay contain some suggestions about how we might relate measures of political influence to states' SL scores. For the moment, however, it is important to remember that SL itself does not distinguish between the influencers and the influenced.

Soviet and American Political Success

We have operationally defined *political success,* based on the assumption of rational behavior, as voting behavior supportive of the winning coalition across a set of roll calls. What does this measure tell us about U.S. and Soviet behavior in the U.N. General Assembly during the last quarter of a century? One way to answer this question to is plot the SL scores for the United States and the Soviet Union, thus producing a graphic presentation of each actor's political success. This is done in Figure IV-1 where each point represents either the U.S. or Soviet SL score (identified on the vertical axis) in each assembly session (identified on the horizontal axis). The points have been connected with lines to highlight the movement over time in each actor's SL scores. Zero indicates the point at which the United States and the Soviet Union would have agreed as often with the majority as expected on the basis of the behavior of all assembly members in each session. Points lying above zero represent sessions in which the state agreed more often than expected (i.e., enjoyed a greater degree of political success), and points lying below zero represent agreement less often than expected (i.e., a

FIGURE IV-1

Soviet and American Support Level Scores, 1946–70

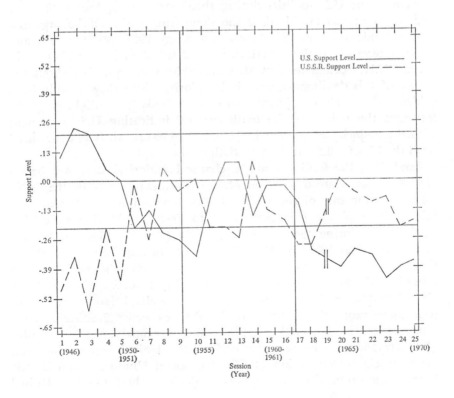

lesser degree of political success). In the First Assembly session, for example, the United States supported the majority position 10.9 percent more often than expected, while the Soviet Union supported the majority 48.1 percent less often than expected. Substantively, this points to the considerably greater degree of political success enjoyed by the United States in this early session, compared with the success of the Soviet Union.

Several features about Soviet and American political success in the General Assembly are apparent from Figure IV–1. One obvious feature is that there has been considerable variation in the success each actor has enjoyed over the last twenty-five years. It is particularly interesting to note that the United States, in eighteen of the twenty-four sessions, agreed with the majority less often than one would expect on the basis of the behavior of the entire body. Although this result might be expected for the sessions occurring in the 1960's (sessions 17–25), the low points for 1951–55 (sessions 6–10) certainly do not conform to conventional wisdom about U.N. politics during these early years. Presumably the United States was at this time the dominant power in the organization (Claude 1971, p. 129; Plano and Riggs 1967, pp. 156–57), and Soviet references to the American's "mechanical majority" abound in various U.N. documents. But SL scores raise some question about the nature of this dominant mechanical majority, since they provide little evidence that such a majority even existed. This is highlighted by the fact that the point for the tenth session, indicating U.S. agreement with the majority 33 percent less often than expected, is not surpassed until the SL of −0.37 in the twentieth session.

Paralleling the finding that "mechanical majority" may not be an entirely appropriate description of U.S. political success in the U.N., so, too, in the case of the Soviet Union, the notion of a "permanent minority"—a phrase frequently used to describe the Soviet position in the U.N. during the 1940's and 1950's (Claude 1971, pp. 127–28; Plano and Riggs 1967, pp. 156–57) —appears to require some qualification. In five of the fourteen sessions before 1960 the Soviet Union actually enjoyed a greater degree of political success than did the United States; in three of the five sessions Soviet behavior was somewhat more supportive of the majority than expected. Neither of these numbers is large. But neither are these findings consistent with the idea of a permanent Soviet minority vis-à-vis the United States. Moreover, since the eighteenth session (1963), the Soviet Union has consistently been more supportive of assembly majorities than has the United

States, although neither has been particularly prone to vote with the majority more often than expected.

In short, then, neither the United States nor the Soviet Union appears to have consistently been in either a topdog or an underdog position in the General Assembly relative to the other actor. Because this conclusion deviates so substantially from conventional wisdom, particularly as it pertains to the 1950's, one might well ask whether it is a consequence of the concept of support embodied in SL. The answer appears to be affirmative.

Earlier it was noted that SL attributes most support to actors that are in minimum winning coalitions and least support to actors that are members of very large majorities (as well as minorities). We might hypothesize, therefore, that the reason the SL scores indicate that American behavior was not supportive of the largest bloc(s) in the General Assembly during the 1950's was because the United States tended most frequently to be in overwhelmingly large majorities and because, on those issues where the body was closely divided, the United States voted with the winning coalition relatively infrequently. The converse, then, would hold for the Soviet Union. That is, we can hypothesize that the Soviet Union was in overwhelmingly large winning coalitions less often than the United States, but that it tended to be on the winning side relatively more frequently than the United States on those issues that were closely contested.

Some evidence drawn from the ninth and tenth sessions of the General Assembly supports these propositions. Of the twenty-four votes decided in the Ninth General Assembly by 75 percent or more of the members voting, the United States voted with the winning coalition 83 percent of the time, and the Soviet Union was on the winning side 71 percent of the time. But on those issues where the winning coalition was only between 51 and 60 percent of the voting body (fourteen votes), the United States was on the winning side only 7 percent of the time, while the Soviet Union was on the winning side 34 percent of the time. This pattern is somewhat reversed on those issues that commanded only a plurality (twenty votes). Here, the United States was in the dominant coalition half of the time, and the Soviet Union 39 percent of the time. During the Tenth General Assembly, the United States voted with the winning side 67 percent of the time when an issue was decided by a coalition comprising 75 percent or more of the voting members (thirty votes). Surprisingly, the Soviet Union was on the winning side in 90 percent of the votes. On the 51–60 percent splits (twenty-one votes), the United States was on the winning side 34 percent of the time, and the Soviet Union 52 percent of the time. Finally, on the twenty-eight votes that commanded only a plurality, the United States was in the dominant coalition on 39 percent of the votes, compared with 46 percent for the Soviet Union.

What these figures demonstrate is that the United States was indeed a member of the winning coalition relatively less often than the Soviet Union on those issues where the body as a whole was closely divided. Thus, if the United States did possess a "mechanical majority," in the sense of belonging to repeated majorities, it also appears to have been a majority that was mechanical in the sense of being largely ritualistic. It appears that in many cases when the chips were down, the United States was unable to muster a winning coalition, but that the Soviet Union was able to do so. Care must be taken with this assertion, however. Because SL in no way distinguishes between leaders and followers, it could be that on those issues where the assembly vote was narrowly divided—say 51 percent to 49 percent—the United States did not seek to influence the outcome of the issues because it did not perceive the issue as critical. Hence, more work is required before we can be certain that the United States did not possess a mechanical majority and that the Soviet Union was not a permanent minority. Both of these characterizations may be appropriate as the phrases are conventionally used; but the results of our analyses do rather seriously question the substantive significance of the terms.

Although neither overwhelming dominance nor persistent defeat seems to fully characterize Soviet and American political success in the General Assembly, Figure IV–1 does suggest that the position of one state relative to the majority can to some extent be described on the basis of the other's. Between the fifth and sixth sessions, for example, American political success declined and Soviet political success increased. Between the sixth and seventh sessions this pattern is reversed, with an American increase and a Soviet decrease; and between the seventh and eighth sessions the pattern reverts again to the earlier one. What these variations suggest is an inverse association between Soviet and American political success in the General Assembly.

To ascertain whether an inverse association is an accurate description, we can correlate the Soviet and American SL scores, using Pearson's product-moment correlations coefficient, designated r, to obtain a single number that describes the extent to which the two actors' political success covaries. The resulting calculation yields an $r = -0.66$ across the twenty-four sessions (i.e., $N = 24$). Since r varies only between $+1$ and -1, the correlation indicates that there is indeed a reasonably close inverse association between Soviet and American political success. More specifically, the standard interpretation of r is that, when squared, the coefficient measures the percentage of the variation in one variable that can be explained (i.e., accounted for) by knowledge of the other variable. Hence, the correlation indicates that 43 percent of the variation in American political success can be explained simply on the basis of knowledge about Soviet success or, conversely, that 43 percent of the variation in Soviet success can be explained by knowledge of American political success.

Further evidence of the close association between American and Soviet SL scores can be ascertained by testing the statistical significance of r. Statisticians have devised significance tests to determine the probability that a relationship between two or more variables is due to chance. In the case of $r = -0.66$ and $N = 24$, the level of significance is 0.001, indicating that the probability of a chance association is only one in 1,000. This test assumes that the variables correlated are normally distributed and that the data points (cases) have been selected at random. These assumptions have not been met here—indeed, they are seldom met in longitudinal or cross-national comparative foreign policy analyses. But had they been met, the test of statistical significance would provide additional support for the proposition that Soviet and American political successes in the General Assembly are inversely associated.[3]

Having determined that there is a close negative association between the American and Soviet SL scores, we should emphasize that much is left unexplained. An r^2 of 0.43 is a hefty correlation judged against many findings in quantitative political science and international relations research. But 43 percent accounted for still leaves 57 percent unexplained. The success that either the United States or the Soviet Union has enjoyed in the General Assembly does not, therefore, appear to be solely the consequence of the other actor's success. Since much of the time period examined includes the tight bipolar period of the international system, when Soviet successes were regarded as American losses and vice versa, the impression of a zero-sum condition as well as the

[3] Although the assumptions underlying significance tests are infrequently met in foreign policy analysis, many researchers use such tests as objective decision-rules for interpreting how closely two or more variables are related. Hence, significance tests are included in the remainder of the analyses reported here. For a discussion of the use of significance tests with nonsampled data, see Winch and Campbell (1969).

notions of a dominant mechanical majority and a permanent minority appear to be called into serious question, insofar as the General Assembly is concerned, by our simple, descriptive analysis.

A final aspect of Soviet and American political success that can be noted from Figure IV–1 is that, over time, the United States has enjoyed progressively less success in the General Assembly and the Soviet Union has enjoyed progressively more success. Both of these trends conform to conventional wisdom about assembly politics. Specifically, it is a frequent observation that as the United Nations has grown and changed in composition, becoming increasingly an organization of the have-not states in the international system, the United States has more frequently found itself out of step with majority sentiments in the world body. Conversely, the Soviet Union has aligned itself with the majority sentiments, thus escaping from its presumed position as a permanent minority (Plano and Riggs 1967, p. 157). To the extent that the have-nots, which now comprise the majority in the membership in the United Nations, use their numbers to control the content of the assembly agenda, future Soviet and American political success in the organization may very well emerge as a projection of the past. If, for example, the have-nots continue to press issues dealing with colonialism and economic development, and if the United States and the Soviet Union do not change their traditional positions on these issues, then simply as a consequence of the ability of the have-nots to control the agenda—or, conversely, the inability of either the United States or the Soviet Union to control it—the future is likely to be one of greater political success for the Soviet Union than for the United States.

Regression analysis can be used to describe precisely the extent to which American political success has declined and Soviet success has increased. As McGowan and O'Leary point out in Chapter 9 of this volume, regression is a statistical technique used to fit a straight line through a series of data points in such a way as to come as close to all points as possible. Hence, if we fit a line between the American and Soviet SL scores, using the scores as the dependent variables and time (defined as the number of the General Assembly session) as the independent variable, the slope of the line will yield a precise measure of the increase or decrease in each actor's level of political success over the past twenty-five years.

The relationship between time and American and Soviet SL scores is depicted graphically in Figures IV–2 and IV–3. The trend lines (regression lines) show quite clearly that American political success has indeed

FIGURE IV-2

Trend in American Support Level

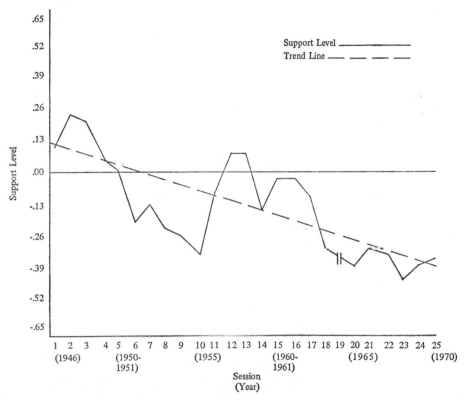

Support Level ————————
Trend Line —— — — —

declined over time and that Soviet political success has increased. Specified in terms of regression equations, the relationships shown in these two figures can be summarized as follows:

$$\text{American SL} = 0.126 - 0.020(\text{session}); \text{ and}$$

$$\text{Soviet SL} = -0.296 + 0.010(\text{session}).$$

The first number shown is the constant term, and the second is the regression coefficient, which measures the slope of the line. The sign preceding the regression coefficient indicates the direction of change over the twenty-four assembly sessions. A significance test applied to each of the regression coefficients shows them both to be statistically significant at the 0.05 level. Substantively, the equation for the United States

FIGURE IV-3

Trend in Soviet Support Level

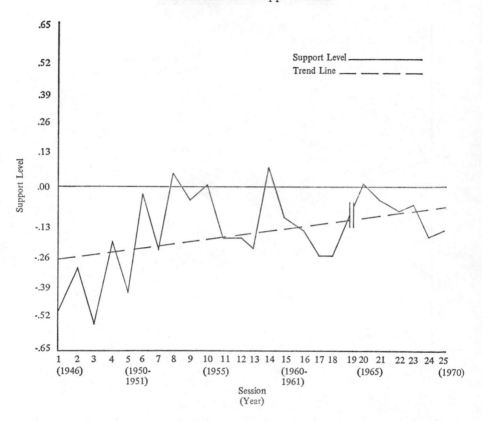

means that, beginning at the level of 12.6 percent, the SL scores decline, on the average, 2 percent per session. For the Soviet Union, the average increase is 1 percent per session.

For certain analytic purposes, it may prove useful to detrend the variables that are used to analyze foreign policy, since time may confound the analysis in the sense of obscuring the true relationship between two variables. Assume, for example, that we were attempting to explain American political success, and that for some theoretical reason we believe that the size of the Afro-Asian caucus in the General Assembly is an important predictor of American political success in the assembly. One way to analyze this proposition would be to correlate the number of Afro-Asian nations in the assembly in each session with the

American SL scores. The result is likely to be a strong negative correlation. We know this because (1) we know that the American SL scores have declined over time, and (2) we know that the number of Afro-Asian nations in the U.N. has increased over time. Unfortunately, however, because time is included in both variables analyzed, it may be time itself, rather than any relationship between the variables of substantive interest, that accounts for the high correlation. But until time is removed from the analysis, we cannot determine for certain what produced the high negative association.

The regression equations given above amount to prediction equations, with time as the predictive (independent) variable. Hence, we can use the equations to predict what the American and Soviet SL scores should be on the basis of the prediction equations (which assume a linear relationship between SL and time), and then measure the deviations of the actual SL scores from the predicted scores. The resulting scores are known as *residuals*. Residuals measure deviations of actual scores from a regression line—that is, variations in the dependent variable not accounted for by the independent variable. Because the independent variable in the above equations is time, the residuals would measure the variation in SL not accounted for by time alone. In other words, the residuals would amount to "detrended" SL scores, since they would measure only that variation that is not shared with (explained by) time.

The calculation of residuals, or detrended SL scores, is quite simple. All that needs to be done is to subtract the predicted SL_j for a particular session from the actual SL_j. In the case of the United States in the First General Assembly, for example, the actual SL score is 0.109. The predicted SL score, on the basis of the foregoing regression equation with time as the independent variable, is

$$0.126 - 0.020 \text{ (session)} = 0.126 - 0.020 \text{ (1)} = 0.106.$$

Subtracting the predicted SL from the actual SL yields 0.003, the detrended American SL score for the first session. By the same logic, the detrended SL score for the second session is 0.156, for the third session 0.149, for the fourth session 0.023, and so forth. Similar calculations can be made for the Soviet Union using the regression equation for the Soviet SL scores. The resulting detrended SL scores for both actors across the twenty-four sessions are shown graphically in Figure IV-4.

FIGURE IV-4

Soviet and American Support Level Scores with Trends Removed, 1946–70

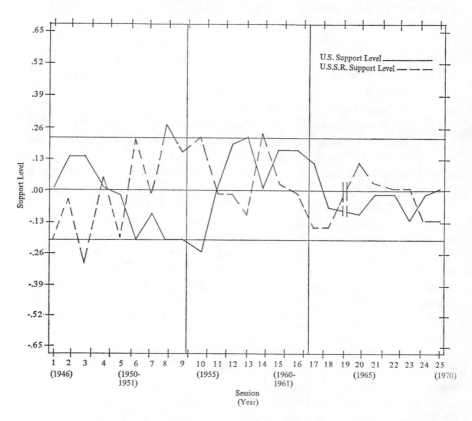

The most obvious feature of Figure IV–4 is that there is no apparent downturn or upturn over time in either actor's SL scores—which is exactly the purpose intended. On the other hand, the features noted previously about Soviet and American political success remain largely unchanged. Given the concept of support embodied in SL, the United States does not appear to have been the dominant power in the United Nations; the Soviet Union does not appear to have been a permanent minority, even in the 1940's and 1950's; and during the 1960's neither actor was particularly prone to vote with the majority more often than expected. Finally, Figure IV–4 again shows some interrelationship between Soviet and American political success, but not to the extent that one could describe their relative voting behavior vis-à-vis the majority as zero-sum. The correlation between the detrended SL scores for the two actors is $r = -0.56$ (compared with $r = -0.66$ before detrending). Thus, only 32 percent of the variation in each actor's SL scores is shared with the other actor—far from what one would expect if Soviet political success were entirely the mirror-image of American success, or vice versa.

Patterns of Political Success

Thus far attention has been confined exclusively to the United States and the Soviet Union. One might well ask with whom the United States and the Soviet Union have shared their success—or lack of it. We know that over time American political success has declined and Soviet political success has increased. To what extent are these trends shared with other actors in the United Nations? We also know that when the trends in American and Soviet success are removed, considerable variation still remains. To what extent are these variations shared with other groups of actors? Answering these questions begins to sound very much like explanatory analysis, a task beyond the purview of the present study. Neither of these questions, however, is specifically directed at the question of *why* political success varies. Instead, both are directed toward the task of describing the political groupings—majorities and minorities— of which the United States and the Soviet Union were a part when casting their ballots in the General Assembly.

Generating answers to the above questions might take a variety of different forms. One that seems particularly reasonable is to examine the extent to which Soviet and American political success has been shared with the members of the nine formal caucusing groups that exist in the General Assembly—the Soviet bloc, plus the Scandinavian, Benelux, Arab, Latin American, Commonwealth, Afro-Asian, European, and African caucusing groups. The first six of these groups have been operative since the First Assembly session; the Afro-Asian caucus became a formal group in the fifth session, the Western European caucus in the eleventh session, and the African caucus in the thirteenth session (Hovet 1960, pp. 103–5).

To ascertain whether Soviet and American political success has been shared with these political groupings, the SL scores for the members of each group were averaged, and the resulting average SL scores were

TABLE IV-17

Correlations between American and Soviet SL Scores and Average SL Scores for Nine General Assembly Caucusing Groups

Caucusing group	Correlation with			
	U.S. SL	Soviet SL	Detrended U.S. SL	Detrended Soviet SL
Soviet bloc	−0.68*	0.998*	−0.57*	0.999*
	(24)	(24)	(24)	(24)
Scandinavian	0.87*	−0.51*	0.75*	−0.34*
	(24)	(24)	(24)	(24)
Benelux	0.76*	−0.75*	0.77*	−0.71*
	(24)	(24)	(24)	(24)
Arab	−0.67*	0.64*	NA	NA
	(24)	(24)		
Latin American	0.51*	−0.56*	0.24	−0.44*
	(24)	(24)	(24)	(24)
Commonwealth	0.25	−0.44*	NA	NA
	(24)	(24)		
Afro-Asian	−0.48*	0.62*	NA	NA
	(20)	(20)		
Western European	0.93*	−0.47*	0.58*	−0.60*
	(14)	(14)	(14)	(14)
African	−0.73*	0.63*	−0.49	0.70*
	(12)	(11)	(12)	(12)

Note: The number in parentheses are the number of observations (sessions) on which the correlations are based. Correlations statistically significant at the 0.05 level are indicated by an asterisk. Correlations with the detrended American and Soviet SL scores are based on detrended average SL scores for the corresponding caucusing group. *NA* indicates not applicable, since the relationship between time and the average SL scores for the corresponding caucusing group is not statistically significant at the 0.05 level.

correlated with the American and Soviet scores.[4] The average scores for each caucusing group were also regressed on time. Using the same procedures previously described for the United States and the Soviet Union, the average SL scores were detrended for each group manifesting a relationship between time and scores statistically significant at the

[4] Caucusing group memberships were determined by the description in Plano and Riggs (1967, p. 149) and projected backward in time on the basis of the analysis in Hovet (1960, pp. 47–95). States joining the United Nations since publication of *Forging World Order*, by Plano and Riggs (1967), were assigned to what seemed the most appropriate political grouping, whether African, Afro-Asian, or both. The Soviet Union is a member of the Sovet bloc; the United States is not a member of any formal caucusing group.

0.05 level. The resulting detrended average SL scores were then correlated with the detrended U.S. and Soviet scores. The results of the correlation analyses are shown in Table IV–17.

The results contain few surprises. They demonstrate, for example, the extremely close association between Soviet political success and the voting behavior of the somewhat larger Soviet bloc (of which the Soviet Union is a part). They also demonstrate that Soviet success is inversely related to the success of those groups traditionally considered pro-Western in their foreign policy orientation, namely, the Scandinavian, Benelux, Latin America, Commonwealth, and Western European nations.[5] Conversely, Soviet success is positively related to the voting behavior of those groups composed primarily of developing nations outside of the Western Hemisphere—the Arab, Afro-Asian, and African caucusing groups. Two of these relationships, for the Arab and Afro-Asian groups, are depicted graphically in Figures IV–5 and IV–6. Since the average scores for neither of these groups is significantly related to time, we know that the associations shown in Table IV–17 are not solely the consequence of time.[6] Related to this point is the interesting finding that the convergence of Soviet and Arab behavior is not a particularly new phenomenon. On the contrary, the close association between Soviet and Arab behavior can be traced back to the earliest days of the United Nations. This says nothing, of course, about the exercise of political influence between or among these actors, but it does suggest that the close ties between the Soviet Union and Arab nations so much a part of international politics in the 1960's and 1970's may well have had their origin in an earlier period.

The groupings with which the United States has shared its political

[5] While the correlation between the Commonwealth and the Soviet SL scores is negative and between the Commonwealth and the United States SL scores is positive, in both cases the correlations are among the lowest of all associations shown in Table IV–17. The probable reason is that the composition of the Commonwealth has changed considerably over time. The group began as an association composed largely of developed, white, European-oriented governments. But as Britain granted independence to its colonies, the association increasingly encompassed developing, nonwhite nations whose governing elites had no direct ties, in terms of national origin, to the United Kingdom or other European states. No other caucusing group in the United Nations has undergone such a dramatic change in terms of the types of nations that it comprises.

[6] The correlations between the detrended Soviet SL scores and the Afro-Asian and Arab SL scores should therefore be approximately the same as the correlations shown in Table IV–17, which are based on the Soviet scores before detrending. This is in fact the case. The correlation between the Afro-Asian average SL scores and the detrended Soviet scores is 0.66; and the correlation between the Arab SL scores and the detrended Soviet scores is 0.59.

FIGURE IV–5

Soviet and Arab Support Level Scores, 1946–70

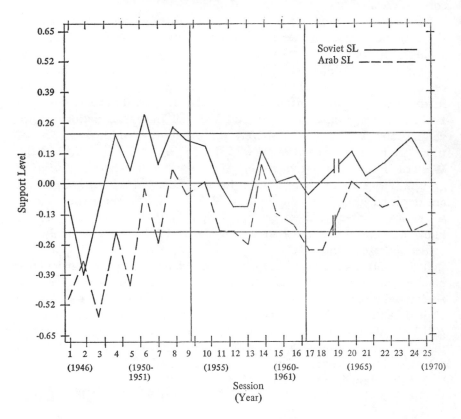

success, or lack of it, are exactly the opposite of those of the Soviet Union. Traditionally Western-oriented states have shared the same majority/minority status as has the United States, and developing nations have manifested the reverse pattern. Especially interesting is the very close association between American and Western European political success. The correlation based on SL scores before detrending suggests that the United States and the Western European caucus have experienced the same general downturn in their political success since the European caucus became a formal group in the Eleventh General Assembly. Figure IV–7 provides a dramatic illustration of this very close relationship. When the trends are removed from the SL scores, however, the association is considerably weaker, although there is still a

FIGURE IV–6

Soviet and Afro-Asian Support Level Scores, 1946–70

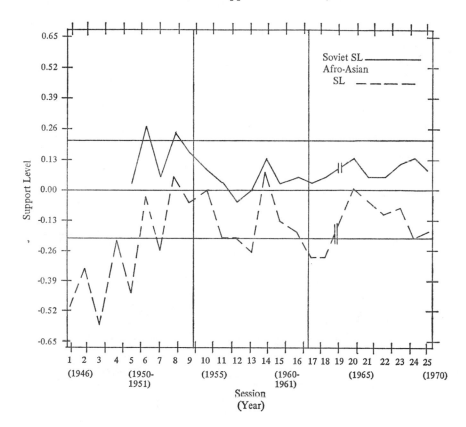

reasonably close relationship between American and Western European voting behavior vis-à-vis the majority.

Somewhat surprising is the rather low correlation between the United States and Latin American nations, as shown in Figure IV–8. In the early to middle 1950's, when U.S. political success turned downward rather dramatically, the Latin American caucus simply did not manifest this same behavior. Perhaps this difference reflects a propensity on the part of Latin American nations to vote with the winning coalition on closely divided votes more often than did the United States. Perhaps it also reflects in part the nature of the issues that were being decided in the assembly. It was during the 1950's that Latin American nations began

FIGURE IV-7

American and Western European Support Level Scores, 1946–70

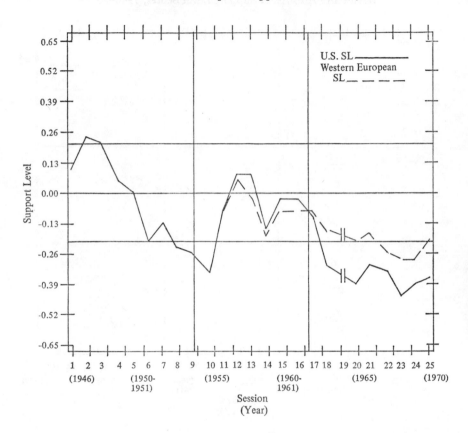

supporting issues that were very much akin to those that dominated U.N. politics in the 1960's.[7] What these data suggest is the need to examine issue-areas in order to explain fluctuations in states' political success. If the United States was out of step with assembly majorities on development and colonialism issues in the 1960's, perhaps the occurrence of the same types of issues earlier in the U.N.'s history can

---

[7] Some limited evidence in support of this presumption is provided in Alker and Russett (1965, pp. 63–64). See also Cornelius (1961) for a qualitative assessment of the divergence between American and Latin American voting behavior on such questions as trade, aid, and colonialism during the first ten years of the United Nations.

FIGURE IV-8

American and Latin American Support Level Scores, 1946–70

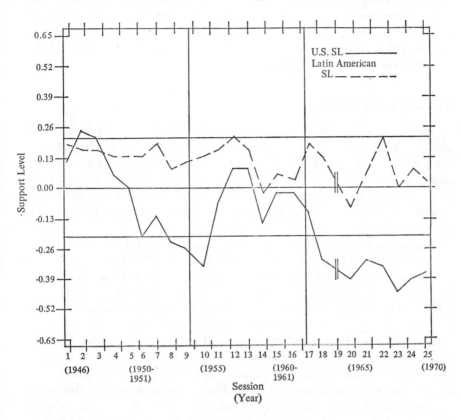

account for fluctuations in both Soviet and American political success across a much longer time period.

The similarity in American and Latin American voting behavior as compared with the majority appears to be confined largely to their sharing a general downturn in political success over the past twenty-five years. When the trends are removed, the correlation between the United States and the Latin American caucus is reduced to 0.24, suggesting that U.S. and Latin American behavior relative to the majority has in fact been quite dissimilar.

Politics make strange bedfellows, the cliché tells us. But this brief excursion into the question of who votes with whom also demonstrates that not all political alliances are so strange. In fact, the results of the preceding analysis are consistent with other related empirical studies (Rieselbach 1960; Russett 1966, 1967), as well as with more intuitive and impressionistic hunches about political bedfellows. Its value lies in part, then, not on the discovery of new and unexpected relationships, but rather on the fact that it has demonstrated the co-occurrence of voting behavior supportive of the majority systematically, empirically, and with considerable precision.

Toward Explanation

Precise measurement and description can be of value in itself. The ultimate goal of scientific inquiry into foreign policy is, however, a more exciting, if more difficult and often frustrating, task—that of building empirical theory about *why* states behave as they do. In attempting to explain why states' political success has varied from session to session in the General Assembly, one might pursue several alternative lines of inquiry.

Previous studies of voting behavior in the General Assembly have sought to relate voting outcomes to various political links between U.N. members outside of the organization (e.g., Alker and Russett 1965, pp. 218–52; Wittkopf 1973a; Clark, O'Leary, and Wittkopf 1971; and Alker 1969, pp. 163–69). Examples of such ties include alliance memberships, trading patterns, and foreign aid allocations. Most of these studies, however, have been cross-national rather than longitudinal in design. Consequently, they have been able to find considerable fluctuation in the variables used to explain states' voting behavior relative to one another or relative to underlying dimensions of behavior. But since few of these indicators are likely to vary much for a single actor over time, in contrast to the variations obtained cross-nationally, they are unlikely to be useful explanations of the kinds of fluctuations in states' political success that have been demonstrated in the preceding pages. Rather than searching for explanatory variables outside the United Nations, then, perhaps we should search for measures of nations' political influence within the world organization in order to explain voting behavior.

David A. Kay (1970, pp. 11–42) has argued that states' missions and delegations to the United Nations, formal caucusing groups in the assembly, limited membership organs of organization, negotiations among member states, and the process of presenting and finally voting on resolutions before the world body all represent instruments of influence in the sense that they are used to shape policy outcomes in the United Nations (Keohane 1967). One might therefore develop specific empirical measures of these various instruments of influence and correlate them with states' SL scores to ascertain whether fluctuations in the political success of nations can be accounted for by their use of these instruments. For example, one might correlate the number of permanent mission personnel or the size of a state's delegation to each annual meeting of the General Assembly with that state's SL scores to ascertain whether manpower committed to the organization can explain political success; or one might measure the covariation between a state's political success and the number of resolutions that it cosponsors with each of the formal caucusing groups in the General Assembly.[8]

An additional line of inquiry that seems particularly important would be an analysis of the various issues considered by the General Assembly. Earlier, it was suggested that the ability of certain states or groups of states to control the content of the General Assembly's agenda may have a significant impact on states' political success. This ability, in turn, is likely to be reflected in the types of issues that are brought before the General Assembly and decided by a roll-call vote. Not all fluctuations in the kinds of issues voted on will be a consequence of the ability of states to control the agenda; some variations may be caused by events occurring in the international system, over which the General Assembly itself has little control. To the extent that states take different positions on different issues, however, the proportion of items falling within different issue areas from one session of the General Assembly to the next may be an important determinant of states' voting behavior relative to the majority. It seems likely, for example, that one of the factors contributing to the downward trend in American political success is, as already noted, the increasing frequency with which decolonization, self-determination, and economic development issues have been brought before the General Assembly. By the same logic, therefore, the number of such issues coming before the assembly in particular sessions may also help account for the session-by-session fluctuations in American SL scores. In short, variations in the specific kinds of issues on which

[8] Some preliminary work in this direction has been done in my "Putting Politics Back into Easton" (Wittkopf 1973b). Unfortunately, the results of the analyses contained little encouragement. Because the analyses were confined to the United States, however, it remains to be seen whether more encouraging results can be obtained using other actors' SL scores as well as their personnel commitments and cosponsorship activity.

states must register some kind of position may help explain variations in their political success.[9]

The foregoing discussion amounts to a short agenda for additional research on the political success of member states of the United Nations. The discussion assumes that political success can, to some extent at least, be explained by factors internal to the organization. It assumes, in other words, that the United Nations can be treated as a political institution in its own right and that intra-organizational processes and influence patterns can provide fruitful explanations of political outcomes. This is not to say, however, that factors external to the organization should be ignored. Indeed, the United Nations itself is important only to the extent that it reflects and responds to the larger international system of which it is a part. If, however, we treat the United Nations as a self-contained political institution where politics are operative, we can move beyond the widespread tendency to analyze foreign policy outcomes as though they were environmentally determined—that is, determined by such nonpolitical factors as the size and level of development of the actors themselves.

Moreover, because the United Nations is an organization with known institutional procedures and constraints, it provides a setting in which we can talk meaningfully about foreign policy success. This contrasts sharply with other research settings, where foreign policy success is difficult to determine, both conceptually and empirically. Perhaps the lessons we learn by concentrating on the legislative processes of the United Nations could be transferred to other situations where the problems faced in describing and explaining political success are less tractable.

[9] Rowe (1969, pp. 247–51) demonstrates the utility of analyzing specific kinds of issues to distinguish between states' voting success. Rowe's overall findings regarding Soviet and American voting success in the General Assembly, however, differ rather substantially from the results reported here, particularly with respect to the longitudinal pattern of Soviet and American success vis-à-vis the majority. The difference in the results between the two studies probably lies in the different computational procedures employed and in the fact that Rowe analyzes only contested votes in the plenary sessions of the General Assembly.

Part V

Forecasting Foreign Policy Behavior

Introduction:
Research in the Predictive Mode

RICHARD A. SKINNER

The preceding pages have focused upon the stages involved in the scientific investigation of foreign policy behavior with an eye toward the construction of comprehensive theories. The emergence of a consensus concerning the means of inquiry appropriate to the study of foreign policy—the comparative method (Part II)—and the derivation of reliable indicators of that behavior—events data (Part III)—provide the foundation upon which empirical research can be conducted (Part IV). Yet, the history of science suggests that as a field of inquiry advances, it is increasingly justified not by the sophistication of its methodologies but by its ability to produce research for dealing with practical problems: "The high prestige that science enjoys today is no doubt attributable in large measure to the striking successes and the rapidly expanding reach of its applications. Many branches of empirical science have come to provide a basis for associated technologies, which put the results of scientific inquiry to practical use and which in turn often furnish pure or basic research with new data, new problems, and new tools for investigation" (Hempel 1966, p. 2). At the same time, researchers' concerns for practical affairs have been major stimuli for the development of scientific theories. Such theories offer the potential for reducing uncertainty and enhancing control over the world around us. Simply stated, the underlying rationale for the construction of empirical theories is that we are better able to predict the consequences of the actions we take when we are supplied with theoretically informed evidence. Even in our everyday lives, prediction is a pervasive need; without empirical knowledge, guesses and intuitions are necessarily required to organize our efforts toward a future we can only partially perceive and understand. The probabilities we attach to our predictions range from near certainty to sheer speculation. We can predict with near perfect accuracy the rising of the sun but must hedge our bets when forecasting the discovery of life somewhere in the universe. As Rothstein (1972, p. 177) has phrased the condition, "We are poor forecasters in contexts where the relevance of experience cannot be taken for granted."

In the world of the foreign policy practitioner, the need for prediction becomes paramount. The absence of a central authority for enforcing laws and the lack of universal norms relevant to the behavior of states ensure an uncertain, frequently chaotic environment with which the policymaker must contend in planning and deciding courses of action. The difficulties of anticipating events in such a system is made worse by the rate at which the conditions of yesterday and today are transformed.

The social scientist also needs a predictive capability. Prediction serves as a test of the validity of his models and theories; the closer the correspondence between predictive statements and empirical observations, the greater the researcher's confidence that his theory accurately reflects the real world. What distinguishes the predictive mode of the social scientist from the educated guesses of the practitioner is the former's reliance on systematic methodology and data to generate reliable and refutable knowledge. Forecasts and predictions resulting from this analytic process are therefore less dependent upon memory, imagination, and conjecture. While scientific predictions are not inherently more reliable than the practitioner's intuitions, they do afford the opportunity for assessment by the traditional and public standards of science, and not only by their accuracy.

Given the importance of predictions for the academic analyst and practitioner alike, it seems appropriate to ask whether the knowledge produced from data-based studies of foreign policy can be of use in forecasting the future. Can events data analyses of foreign policy be expected to generate the kinds of predictions which will permit a dialogue between analyst and practitioner? In Chapter 8, Professor Azar addresses these questions directly by framing his investigation in the "predictive mode" (McClelland 1969). The possibility of a meaningful dialogue between the student of foreign policy and the policymaker represents one important issue in the following discussion. Other issues examined in this section include the ways in which researchers have employed events data in predictive studies and the epistemological bases of explanation and prediction.

Events Data, Prediction, and Forecasting

Many of the pioneers of the events data movement made explicit commitments to developing reliable information systems capable of monitoring foreign policy behavior and providing the analyst with a "map" of the international system that would chart the flows and exchanges of events between nations (McClelland 1966, pp. 99–107). The value of such a map is that it describes empirically the structure of international political relationships and also provides not only the potential for a description of past and present but also a means for anticipating changes in the flow of events.[1]

Other events researchers have emphasized the use of these data for anticipating changes in the success of policymakers' efforts toward some declared national objective. Events data can be used to profile performance and alert the analyst to the need for "some intervention or change . . . in terms of a given goal, e.g., U.S. balance of payments surplus, international peace, free access to Berlin, economic growth in excess of population growth" (Bobrow 1972b, p. 222). This strategy— termed *engineering* (Bobrow 1972a, 1972b), or *design theory* (Burgess and Lawton 1972, pp. 71–76)—represents one of the points of similarity with the planning activities of the policymaker, since "the purpose of social indicators is not primarily to record historical events but to provide the basis of planning for future policies" (Bauer 1966, p. 19).[2]

Two assumptions underlie such endeavors. The first is that the past

[1] Events-based studies of crises are exemplary of this potential. McClelland's (1972) analysis of event interaction patterns during the Berlin Wall and Quemoy crises isolated the total quantity of action and the distribution of types of acts as especially useful variables for monitoring and identifying key changes in behavior. Azar (1972) introduced the concept of the "normal relations range" and demonstrated that it is possible to anticipate escalation and reduction cycles of crisis behavior by noting shifts in the intensity of cooperation and conflict between nations.

[2] See the volume edited by Choucri and Robinson (1974). Studies by Choucri (1973), Azar, Bennett, and Sloan (1973), and Hill and Ebrahimi (1970) provide excellent discussions of the various statistical techniques employed for forecasting interstate behavior. Soroos (1973) and Kent (1972) have outlined many of the key issues involved in peace research forecasting.

contains clues sufficient for the forecasting of the future. Efforts at short-term forecasting with events data (for one- to six-month intervals) indicate that this assumption is reasonable.[3] In keeping with the framework for policy analysis proposed by Rosenau in Part I of this volume, however, long-term forecasts (ten to fifty years) rely on a model which emphasizes the importance of "the configuration of national attributes and, by extension . . . , the relative distributions of national capabilities within the international system" (Choucri 1972, p. 240).

A second implicit assumption is that the policymaker can anticipate imminent occurrences, such as foreign policy crises, by monitoring behavioral regularities in order to identify deviations from those patterns. The monitoring systems currently employed to assess and anticipate changes in national economic performance, as well as strategic warning systems for defense against air attack, are examples of policymakers' uses of indicators for forecasting and planning. One such regularity in international relations is the "repetitive pattern of war" (Rosecrance 1973, pp. 4–7). Many events data researchers have engaged in forecasting efforts in the belief that this type of empirical work offers one way of confronting what they perceive as the preeminent issue of the field: the outbreak of violence between nations. Even in the absence of an exhaustive theory explaining why wars occur, the ability to forecast them would constitute a step of immense strategic and normative importance. Here again, one can envision a real possibility for interaction between basic research and policymaking.

Still others have stressed forecasting more as part of a process of empirical research designed to test models and theories. In this context, McClelland (1969, p. 18) has argued persuasively for research in the predictive mode: "This is a strategy of inquiry rather than an effort to produce working prediction approaches, at least at the present stage of work. Too often the testing of a hypothesis against empirical data leads nowhere but to some analytic result: the inquiry tends to be terminal. . . . The focus on prediction provides a vehicle for carrying out repeated observations on the same type of data." Thus, description and prediction assume a symbiotic relationship in research: descriptive models of past behavior patterns facilitate predictions of future actions, while predictive studies enable the researcher to validate his models and theories via tests of correspondence between predicted and observed values.

[3] The short-term forecast studies by Moore and Young (1969) and Hoggard (1969) are also important for introducing the student to some relatively simple techniques for generating forecasts of foreign policy behavior.

Some Conceptual Issues of Forecasting

The definitional problem is basic to an understanding of forecasting foreign policy behavior. What is meant by *prediction* and its related concepts? While terms do not have "true" meanings, the labels applied to concepts affect their capacity to communicate intended meanings. This is especially salient in scientific investigation, since researchers must have some measure of consensus among themselves on the meanings of the concepts they use in constructing theories and testing hypotheses. Young (1970, pp. 5–6) has suggested some distinctions in the usage of the terms *forecast, prediction,* and *projection:*

A forecast is a description of an event or trend which is expected to happen at some future time. It can be a result of intuition, prophecy, statistical analysis, or any other method of gaining insight. In science, however, a forecast is a result of the projection of at least one element of a predictive hypothesis. A projection provides an estimate of the value of a variable at some future time, the estimate being based upon the observed change in that variable during some past period. A prediction does not necessarily refer to the future at all, despite popular usage to the contrary. It involves only the form of the relationship between two or more variables, such as if variable "A" is present, variable "B" will be absent.

The distinction between a forecast and a prediction is important in light of the arguments among philosophers of social science about the logical equivalence of explanation and prediction (see Raymond, Part II of this volume). Forecasters of foreign policy behavior have usually adopted the position of the Sprouts (1961) that there are "some practical differences between explanation and prediction" (p. 66). They point to the abilities of election analysts to predict outcomes despite a general paucity of explanations as to why individuals vote the way they do. The point is illustrated by Singer (1969*b*, p. 22):

Despite the popular belief to the contrary, prediction demands less of one's model than does explanation or even description. For example, any informed layman can predict that pressure on the accelerator of a slowly moving car will increase its speed; that more or less of the moon will be visible tonight than last night; or that the normal human will flinch when confronted with an impending blow. These predictions do not require a particularly elegant or sophisticated model of the universe, but their explanation demands far more than most of us carry around in our minds. Likewise, we can predict with impressive reliability that any nation will respond to military attack in kind, but a description and understanding of the processes and factors leading to such a response are considerably more elusive, despite the gross simplicity of the acts themselves.

In short, this position assumes that while predictions and explanations have the same logical form ("Prediction is merely explanation in the future sense" [McGowan 1970c, p. 298]), it is possible to predict foreign policy behavior without providing an understanding of why particular conditions lead to certain effects.

Possibilities and Problems of a Dialogue

Even if the analyst can generate scientific forecasts of foreign policy behavior, the question remains as to whether or not these forecasts can contribute significantly to the performance of the policymaker. Both the foreign policy analyst and the practitioner are dependent upon prediction for organizing their activities and directing new efforts. Yet this similarity of needs has not been reflected in an ongoing discussion and exchange between the two. The academic environment and the world of the policymaker are profoundly different with respect to organizational goals and objectives, criteria for assessing and rewarding individual performance, and available resources (Bobrow 1971). Moreover, there exist within each strong divergences of style and method which can often frustrate dialogue.[4] For his part, the practitioner has been reluctant to enter into such a dialogue because he has usually accepted as axiomatic the notion that "the predictions that the social scientist can legitimately produce and the predictions that the practitioner needs are diametrically opposed" (Rothstein 1972, p. 160).

The basis for this assertion is the contrast between the types of knowledge and the kinds of predictions or forecasts the policymaker wants and those the academic analyst seeks. In the realm of strategic affairs, one critic of empirical efforts to forecast external behavior has argued that "strategic thinking relies upon nuance, grounded in empirical analysis and background knowledge, not in contextual regularities, except insofar as these form part of one's background knowledge. In the end, this is why . . . strategic analysis and planning depend only

---

[4] See Knorr and Rosenau (1969) for one of the best compilations of arguments between traditionalists and scientists in the field of international politics. Kissinger (1969) has noted some equally divergent leadership styles among foreign policy decision-makers.

indirectly and lightly upon the findings of quantitative behavioralism" (Chapman 1971, pp. 326–27). This point—suggestive of the remarks of many critics of inductive research on foreign policy[5]—is a reminder to the academic analyst not to lose sight of the purposes of inquiry. The discovery of empirical regularities should not be an end in itself but should provide the basis for further refinements which will, in turn, enhance his ability to forecast foreign policy behavior in a way that will meet the needs of the policymaker.

But if the analyst does produce reliable forecasts, other obstacles to a dialogue remain. Particularly troublesome for the social scientist is the policymaker's desire for predictions which describe a state of affairs as a certainty rather than as a probability. But social science predictions and forecasts are necessarily based on probability and "can deal effectively only with class phenomena and in terms of the probability of some specific kind of occurrence, given the presence of some set of specified conditions" (McClelland 1969, p. 2); as two other analysts have observed:

Social predictions are not designed to eliminate the need for an act of choice by the social practitioner: to assert that predictions cannot do what they are not capable of doing is a useless tautology. (Rothstein 1972, p. 164)

Forecasts cannot eliminate uncertainty; they can serve to reduce it, offering "a rough guide to 'inevitability, probability, reversibility, and plausibility' without prejudging desirability." (Wilcox 1971, p. 388)

Moreover, an insistence upon accuracy as the only criterion for assessing forecasts imposes severe constraints on the potential of the social scientist for sensitizing the policymaker to alternative ways of thinking about and thereby acting upon his environment (Millikan 1969).

A more positive result of a dialogue between the foreign policy analyst and the policymaker could be a concern for the kinds of analyses beneficial to both. The policymaker needs to know at what points in a

[5] Many scholars have reservations about a research strategy which is heavily inductive in its orientation. Oran Young (1972, pp. 198–99) has argued that such efforts are too often detrimental to the higher priority of constructing well-grounded theory. Russett (1972) has pointed out the problem of relying upon inductively derived patterns for forecasting purposes: "If we know empirically that A is associated with B, we may derive important policy benefits from predicting changes in B as a result of changes in A, without knowing *why*. But however exciting and important the discovery of high aggregate correlations may be, prediction without understanding is vulnerable to system changes; when we do not understand why two variables are related our predictions are vulnerable to shifts in the relationship" (p. 118).

situation active intervention can alter conditions toward a more favorable outcome. This objective requires of the analyst dynamic, causal models with explications of short- and long-term factors precipitating changes in foreign policy behavior. Present theories simply do not suffice in these respects, although there are promising signs that some researchers are moving in these directions. In particular, the use of events data represents a propitious avenue for inquiry in the search for short-term "manipulables" (Burgess and Lawton 1972, p. 72). Linking the conceptual framework of the comparative study of foreign policy to the forecasting enterprise is the next task: "Once a particular set of forecasted political relationships is generated, a second step is necessary. No matter what the propensity of a government might be, its actions will reflect its capacities. Technological and resource forecasts offer parameters within which political choices must be made, and suggest, therefore, what can *not* happen" (Wilcox 1971, p. 395). In this manner, analysts are able to move closer toward the development of a reliable methodology for forecasting foreign policy behavior. At the same time, the recognition of the dynamic quality of this behavior—the ways in which the sources of external behavior can vary across time—can help in redefining notions of causation in the study of foreign policy (Rosenau 1966, p. 41).

Any assessment of the issues raised here is necessarily preliminary. Efforts to generate forecasts of foreign policy behavior that satisfy both the criteria of scientific inquiry and the needs of policymakers are in a nascent state. But even though forecasting of that behavior cannot provide point predictions of future events, it can help in other ways in the planning of policy. Conversely, because such forecasts highlight new and promising areas of scientific investigation, they encourage refinements in existing models and theories and stimulate innovative treatments of an established body of data.

8

Behavioral Forecasts and Policymaking: An Events Data Approach

EDWARD E. AZAR

The production and consumption of knowledge can, to a certain extent, be compared to economic production and consumption; in both cases, the two activities are interrelated but clearly distinct.[1] The ways in which a consumer uses knowledge, like the ways he uses material goods, tend to be deeply influenced by the range, quality, and costs of the products offered him. Most of the research of the past decade on foreign policy forecasting has been basic, or pure, research, stimulated to develop in various directions by (1) the evolution of research techniques (computer-aided quantitative research, survey research, content analysis, social statistics, events research); (2) the availability and/or use of data bases and numerous case studies; and (3) advances in theoretical and operational conceptualization and a sharper emphasis on comparability.

Criteria for Evaluating Forecasts

The direct application of predictive knowledge has conventionally been a secondary goal. Of course, basic research can always have in-

[1] I wish to thank the Department of Political Science, the Institute for Research in Social Science, and the University Research Council of the University of North Carolina at Chapel Hill, and the National Science Foundation (#GS-366689) for their support.

direct relevance in that future policymakers (e.g., students) are exposed to it and may help create it. But most consumers of foreign policy research knowledge—whether academicians, government officials, or community groups—are interested in directly relevant knowledge, especially when it is derived from the analysis of good data and provides reasonable answers to their questions. They want valid forecasts.

Since there are many forecasting methods, how can one distinguish between forecasts which are valid and those which are not? The classical argument suggests that validity equals accuracy—technically, statistical significance. In other words, when a finding can be obtained, not by chance, but because certain data fit reasonably well into a structure defined by a model and arrived at through the use of appropriate statistical tools, then the forecast is valid. Or, if one can forecast the future in such a way that one's computations more or less duplicate real-world data, then the forecast is accurate or valid. Conversely, a forecast which does not duplicate real-world data is said to be inaccurate or invalid.

An alternative to this constraining rule can be based on the six criteria for valid forecasting established by Davis Bobrow (1973). Bobrow argues that accuracy, in the sense suggested above, does not constitute a valid forecast, for inaccurate forecasts may still have served a good purpose for individuals or groups, whether within or outside the governmental structure. For example, an unfulfilled projection of runaway inflation is surely more desirable for a nation than a forecast which comes true.

Bobrow's general criteria for valid forecasts include:

1. *Importance:* the extent to which actions taken in response to the forecast produce an outcome different from that which would otherwise have occurred.
2. *Utility:* the difference of direction between a forecasted outcome and the outcome which would otherwise have occurred. Warnings can have negative utility: for example, forecasts may be so awesome that they produce overwhelming fear and inaction.
3. *Timeliness:* being sufficiently ahead of its outcome so that if certain actions are taken, the forecasted future can be altered.
4. *Reduction of uncertainty:* the degree to which a forecast can state which alternative future is most likely (end-state forecasting) or the extent to which each of several actions would change the course set toward a forecasted future (contingency forecasting).

5. *Relevance:* the extent to which aspects of the futures treated have interest for the intended consumers. Relevance can be enhanced by changing either the forecast's content or the identity, interest, and so on of the users. For our purposes, the forecast should be relevant to policy: that is, it should aid in diagnosing and solving concrete, pressing foreign policy problems.

6. *Durability:* the extent to which a forecast is not vulnerable to invalidation by new information. Rather than being so all-encompassing as to be meaningless, a forecast may incorporate a structure for recalculation of new information.

To Bobrow's list, I would add two more criteria:

7. *Accessibility:* the extent to which the knowledge is present, readily usable, and intersubjectively transferable—with minimal understanding—to the concrete situation within which the consumer is acting. Different situations and roles (educator, administrator, official) call for different types of scientific findings which emphasize different aspects of the total set of knowledge.

8. *Cumulativeness:* the degree to which new knowledge takes into account and builds upon previous findings.

It may also be important to stress that Bobrow's criteria of "relevance" is directly related to the researcher's ability to raise the difficult questions which foreign-policy makers and the concerned citizen must consider, although the answers may not be available.

Not all aspects of a scientific research project are so new or so useful that its entire product will be directly useful for policymaking. In some instances, the data base generated by the researcher may be found partially useful. Or the researcher's method may be partially useful, if for nothing else than training persons engaged in policymaking in the use of new methods. In other instances, findings may have some direct use. Likewise, models and theories may be useful, if not in toto, then in their ability to pose questions, to surprise, and to affect the structure of other models or theories and the manner in which they explore reality.

The above criteria cut across the lines dividing one kind of basic research from another and one research technique or data base from another. To the consumer it often matters little whether a finding about, for example, foreign policy behavior of small states is based on aggregate data, events data, diplomatic history, or something else. What matters to him is whether a research finding can help in diagnosing what small nation A will do, or in suggesting or reinforcing certain courses of action. Unfortunately, there is at present a lack of "marketing" procedures—that is, the consumer cannot readily obtain foreign policy research findings or confirm their relevance or practical reliability. In this chapter I hope to show how foreign policy research can be used to forecast foreign policy behavior reliably and facilitate efficient foreign policy planning. First, however, we will explore some theories on forecasting and foreign policy behavior which will serve as background for our technique. The ideas presented here are not completely unknown to students of foreign policy, in or out of government. But these previously introduced ideas and some newly acquired ones are juxtaposed in a manner which, we hope, will be useful to the reader and to the foreign-policy maker who happens to come across them.

Academic Forecasting: Its Purposes, Nature, and Utility

The use of forecasting in social science research has had its opponents as well as its proponents and practitioners. Some, for example, have argued that this trend in international relations research is neither feasible nor even desirable, at least at the present. Some regard it as a potential threat to human liberty, and others feel it may be a self-defeating venture. A roundtable discussion on "The Nature and Limitations of Forecasting" held in 1966 by the American Academy of Arts and Sciences' Commission on the Year 2000, and reprinted in the Summer 1967 issue of *Daedalus* spotlights other somewhat pessimistic views. One participant, Lawrence Frank, doubted the validity of assuming causal relationships and "deterministic linear formulation" (p. 946). Harvey Perloff noted (p. 945) that a governmental decision or edict can upset the most meticulous forecast. Wilbert Moore felt that we lack the skills for creating genuine models from trend data and that "the best we can hope to do is predict the probability of a class of events" (p. 942). Herman Kahn (p. 947) doubted the feasibility of computer simulations.

Donald Schon (1967) holds a more pragmatically optimistic view. He reasons that decision-makers will continue to make plans, which may be based, at worst, on mere assumptions or, at best, on the most careful and reasonable forecasts that can be made (pp. 768–69). "All forecasts," he contends, "are used principally for planning" (p. 764). In general, those who feel that researchers in various disciplines should give first priority to forecasting probably outnumber the pessimists. Indeed, Igor Bestuzhev-Lada (1969, pp. 532–33) calls for—in fact, expects—the emergence of a new, separate science of forecasting, which he would call *prognostics*. As he has pointed out (p. 533), the country whose scientists can formulate a usable theory of forecasting will reap a tremendous payoff—a very effective weapon for scientific, economic, ideological, and political purposes.

But the fact is, arguments for and against forecasting have become largely academic. In the last twenty years, quantitative research in international relations and foreign policy has grown in such a way as to increase our capacity to forecast foreign policy behavior (see Alcock 1972; Newcombe and Wert 1972; Newcombe and Newcombe 1969; Richardson 1960; Smoker 1966; and Wright 1965). Methods, data bases, and models have proliferated. Recent developments have been aided by (1) growth in the quality and quantity of longitudinal data sets about the attributes and behavior of international actors, primarily nation-states; (2) continuous improvements and increasing sophistication in social science research methods, and (3) high-speed computers which can process many variables and large amounts of data.

The need for forecasting is probably as old as interpersonal and intergroup interactions themselves. This need stems from the individual and collective desire to reduce anxiety about the future, to plan for or anticipate the future, and to control the future. A forecast is thought to be capable of providing the actors involved with sufficient time to think out their alternatives and to work toward reducing future human and material costs.

Of course the precise nature of each case which could benefit from a forecast varies, and thus the reasons for a forecast vary. Bobrow (1973) has isolated seven purposes for forecasts:

1. *Social mobilization.* Some forecasts try to arouse and generate popular support for a certain course of action, usually by predicting either dire consequences or the loss of a golden opportunity. Unless the source and the forecast's proponents are seen as impartial, the course of action will gain little support.
2. *System replacement.* Some forecasts posit a future state of affairs radically different from and much more desirable for the majority

than the present one; the transition period is sketched in, but the timing of the outcome is left open.

3. *Warning.* Some forecasts spell out a specific negative and very costly event which will occur at a specific time and also describe the actions —usually costly and nonroutine—needed to avoid the event.

4. *Adaptive planning.* Some forecasts provide a contingency structure from the present to the projected end-point; each possible action is given a probable chain of events and an end-state, so that planners can view present actions in terms of future results.

5. *Group perquisites.* Some forecasts posit that success in steering toward a desirable future depends on money, authority, or some other commodity. The forecasts sound urgent, but few specifics (such as timing) are given, and they reappear regularly at allocation time.

6. *Efficient resource allocation.* Some forecasts predict specific results of specific mixes of hardware and programs to aid cost-benefit comparisons.

7. *Administrative control.* Some forecasts project goals which can be achieved by a specific time with specific resources, and subordinates understand that they will be held accountable for fulfilling them.

Nazli Choucri (1974) has evolved a somewhat different, more general typology. She identifies four types of forecasting goals: (1) understanding the unknown; (2) planning for the immediate future; (3) anticipating long-range futures; and (4) controlling future outcomes. We are concerned here with the second of these goals, the achievement of which is dependent upon developing forecasting methodologies for short periods of time and within relatively limited ranges of contingencies. Control and prevention of future outcomes that tend to increase inequalities among individuals, groups, and societies remains the ultimate goal of many social scientists—particularly this events researcher.

The literature on social forecasting suggests that there exist over a hundred methodologies for manipulating variables and projecting into the future (Bestuzhev-Lada 1969, p. 532). But the major methodologies, according to Choucri (1974), may be grouped under five headings (ranging from least to most systematic): (1) *normative projections,* such as the group-opinion Delphi survey method; (2) exploratory or *trend projections,* useful only for unchanging or slowly changing conditions; (3) *models,* either statistical or functional, Bayesian or Markovian; (4) *simulations;* and (5) *artificial intelligence,* a type of all-computer simulation.

In terms of the time-span covered by a projection, Rudolph Rummel (1969*b*, p. 2) defines two types of forecasts: the specific, or point, forecast and the trend forecast ("predictions about what the international system will be like in five, ten, or twenty-five years"). Long-range, or trend, forecasts tend to be made in the socioeconomic and politico-military areas. They require sophisticated models of social change including numerous variables. Long-range forecasting is common in major defense and foreign policy planning.

Although there is a clear bias toward long-range projections, we suggest that this tendency stems from the limited availability of social data and the worries of some forecasting practitioners about being proven wrong on short-range forecasts. It is our assumption that as short-range forecasting grows to overcome these obstacles, long-range projections will benefit substantially. Thus the forecasts in the latter part of this chapter have been made on a short-range (monthly) basis.

Of the purposes enumerated earlier by Bobrow, we shall specifically stress warning, and of the five approaches enumerated by Choucri, we shall use the model. Thus, we will emphasize in this study the forecasting of future hostile foreign policy acts between a pair of nations (a dyad), because standing as we do on the lower rungs of the forecasting ladder, hostile acts (which tend to be costly in human and material terms) are the easiest for us to isolate and project. We shall call this an early warning model of inter-nation hostilities. Research on crisis escalation and reduction (Azar 1970*b*, 1972) has made this task much simpler. Furthermore, there is a larger body of knowledge on conflict behavior than on any other inter-nation activities, and this body of knowledge has increased our confidence in the theoretical base used in forecasting. There are also sufficient conceptual schema for the description and explanation of foreign policy actions of nations, thus making our task of forecasting much easier. Discovering how a system of relationships is established and how a system functions in the future (i.e., knowing something about the mechanisms of change) is one of the forecaster's most difficult problems. The fact that some of these problems have been resolved by others, as we shall see in the following section, also simplifies our task.

As the reader will observe, the foreign policy models presented in the following section tend to be descriptive, explanatory, and at times, predictive, although prediction must be inferred in some cases. To carry out useful forecasts, the models must specify their predictive capability. Prescription is one criterion we shall examine scientifically.

Although foreign policy forecasting, and particularly early warning forecasting, is loaded with prescriptive overtones, we maintain that the findings generated from such research can serve as data for potential users.

Orientations in Foreign Policy Research

Foreign policy is a sequential, constantly unfolding set of actions. Its purposes relate to its sources (the process by which it is determined), which in turn relate to the forms through which it manifests itself (Rosenau 1969a). Operationally, we assume that the foreign policy of a nation manifests itself as that nation's overt external actions, reactions, and interactions (events). Students of foreign policy may differ on the theories, models, questions, and data sets they employ to study foreign policies of nation-states; however, virtually all of them focus on (1) the internal and/or external sources or determinants of foreign policy and (2) the forms of behavior which governmental agents use in selecting and implementing policies.

In the earlier chapters in this book, the reader was introduced to the many variables thought to determine or influence the overt behavior of nation-states toward one another. In a groundbreaking article, Rosenau (1966) suggested three principal internal variables: size, economic development, and political accountability. In subsequent research, Rummel (1972b) reached a similar conclusion; he found that size and the economic capability of nation-states are the major determinants of their external behavior. More recently, Robert C. North and Nazli Choucri (1968) have suggested that a nation's population size, technological level, and resource base are master variables in shaping its external behavior. Empirical comparative foreign policy research is beginning to determine the precise impact of each of these sources on the overall behavior of nation-states as well as on specific dyadic relationships. Rosenau and Hoggard (1976) have done some preliminary work in this area. They found that distance, degree of homogeneity, and similarity of military capacity do affect foreign policy behavior, but to a lesser extent than the variables of size, economic development, and political accountability.

But whatever the direct determinants of foreign policy, most analysts argue that a conscious or unconscious set of national goals underlines foreign policy behavior. The nature of national goals and interests has been the subject of much writing by foreign policy theorists.

Hans Morgenthau, for example, perceives two types of interests a state may have: those pertaining to the welfare of the state itself and those which several states may hold in common (Robinson 1969). An individual state has both primary and secondary interests, permanent and variable interests, and general (those affecting a large territory or long range in time) as well as specific (affecting a smaller time or space range) interests. International interests may be identical, complementary (the parties involved *can* find areas of agreement), or conflicting. National leaders consciously or unconsciously establish a hierarchy of interests and allocate available power accordingly. In deciding how, or whether, to conclude alliances with other nations, statesmen must estimate the weight and predict the duration of common interests. Thus, as Choucri (1974) has noted, good plans require good forecasts, and an alliance is after all actually a plan made by two or more nations.

Another writer, Arnold Wolfers (1969), sees three types of foreign policy goals a nation may have: self-extension, self-preservation, and self-abnegation. Self-extension means pursuit of a status not already enjoyed, such as more territory or freedom from foreign control. Self-preservation is a state's defense of its status quo—the pursuit of security. Self-abnegation means pursuit of supranational or international interests, though not necessarily to the exclusion of a state's own interests; Woodrow Wilson pursued a policy of self-abnegation in 1918, for example. Each goal can subsume a grand spectrum of behaviors, since the range of possible definitions of *self* is practically unlimited. The term can mean anything from a nation's physical territory to an abstract set of ideas and principles. In general, governments will seek only what they feel will be enough power to achieve a goal. Goals of self-abnegation usually cause a deemphasis of power. Goals of self-extension, however, rely greatly on power, though a nation may often cloak its goals of self-extension as self-preservation or even self-abnegation ("this use of power is for the salvation of mankind").

This common tactic of justifying self-serving actions by appealing to universal moral norms can be demonstrated to be completely untenable (Levi 1969). "Moral norms," states Levi (p. 194), "are qualifiers, not initiators or ends of behavior." In other words, treaties are signed, not to demonstrate reliability, but to protect territory, economic interests, and so on. Because moral norms are so broad, virtually any behavior can be given a moral justification, while virtually any behavior of an enemy can be "proved" to be immoral. Thus a set of moral norms will not—and does not—serve as a source of nations' behavior. National interests determine foreign policy actions, and in the words of Thucydides, *"Identity* of interests is the surest bond, whether between states or individuals."

Despite the promising work mentioned above, source analysis faces an avalanche of problems (Rosenau 1969a). How can one explain non-Western decision-making when most models have been based on the Western experience? How can one create a valid model without access to secret data? How can one avoid too many subcategories and create cohesive generalizations? How can one predict the future solely on the basis of past actions? In analyzing national capabilities, how can we decide on the most appropriate data (whether amounts of military equipment, size of population, extent of national unity, nuclear potential, degree of commitment), and how can we measure and weigh such intangibles as commitment? Events analysis also has its share of problems. How, for example, can we identify a satisfactory number of quality data sources? How can we assure the validity of inferences made from one medium of symbols to another and from one time-space to another? What mechanisms will best serve for communicating relevant findings to each potential user?

Very possibly, problems in both source analysis and events analysis can be resolved to some extent by mutual collaboration. Some events researchers who concentrate on foreign policy behavior have tended to emphasize, and at times study exclusively, conflictive situations such as mobilizations, boycotts, crises, and wars; the source researchers, by contrast, have tended to deal with the whole array of foreign policy acts—treaties, agreements, diplomatic relations, as well as conflictive acts—though with much less rigor until quite recently. The growing collaboration between students of both orientations, under the rubric of the comparative study of foreign policy and events research, is a major scientific development in that some of the artificial boundaries are fast disappearing. The problems under investigation and the theoretical base for studying these problems determine the boundaries of the method, the data, and the tools of analysis.

Foreign Policy Analysis Using Events Data: The Signal Accounting Model

National goals, interests, capabilities, and roots of power, as discussed in the previous section, help explain what motivates a nation to act and what supports a continuing course of action. Without sufficient economic or military capabilities, a supply of resources, or certain basic powers, a nation can hardly achieve even minimal objectives; indeed, it may not even consciously set goals. A great power or a nation with great military or economic capablities can afford to conduct a much more extensive foreign policy than a small power, which cannot satisfy even its domestic needs. Even if we know a nation's capabilities and goals, and the sources of each, we know only part of the story. In order to be able to forecast efficiently, we must develop useful models for describing, explaining, and ideally, projecting behavior profiles or characteristics. Therefore, in this section I will enlarge upon the signal accounting model (Azar 1970b), which allows one to describe how nation-states monitor and respond to each other.

In order for this partly revised model to work, we have to assume, first, that the parties in the interaction situation arc symmetrical in overall capabilities (both military and economic). Although there is nothing in this model which makes it inapplicable to neutral or co-operative situations, we think that it is most useful in treating con-flictive interactions. Therefore we will use it to forecast actions, reactions, and interactions (i.e., foreign policy acts) between conflicting dyads.

As we noted above, nation-states try to insure that they will achieve, at the very least, the foreign policy goals at the top of their priority lists. In order to do so, a nation considers its own preferences, costs, and available strategies, as well as its target's potential responses to each strategy, before taking action. Thus, decision-makers of one nation at-tempt to estimate the behavior of another in order to formulate policies and initiate actions which have the best chance of producing the desired response.

In his inventory of twelve modes of prediction in the social sciences, Daniel Bell asserts that an actor's forecast is based on his explanation or assessment of past experiences (Bell 1970, pp. 379–408). Hence, in formulating its estimates, a nation establishes the probabilities of pro-ducing desired responses in its opponent by the assessment of past be-havior in similar situations.

We will limit our discussion here, as mentioned previously, to short-range forecasts—profiles of the behavior of A toward B for a period of one month. In very pressing and highly tense conflict situations, such as border conflicts or crisis escalation, short-range forecasts are important because of their immediacy and potential cumulative effect on future developments; and nations have been shown to rely heavily on them (see Hermann 1969; Holsti, North, and Brody 1969*b;* McClelland 1961; Zinnes 1968). On the whole, these short-range predictions employ models which include only a few critical variables, such as costs, goals, and violent behavior.

In the signal accounting process we identify four stages in a conflict situation.

Stage 1: Perception and Assessment of Signals. Over a certain period of time, nation A receives an array of signals from nation B. The image which A has of B, his definition of the situation at hand, and the constraints produced by his priorities all have an influence in determining which signals he actually perceives and how important he considers them.

Following the reception of signals, nation A does three things. First, A assesses B's signals to determine their impact on his own priorities and on the probability of his being able to achieve them. Second, he weighs the costs he suffers by the signals' impact, objectively estimating the extent of the loss of matériel, territory, and personnel, and subjectively estimating how this loss influences the probability of achieving his objectives. Third, he assesses the violence content of the signals and the immediate threat presented by them.

An actor in a conflict situation tends to be interested not only in the level of violence, but also in any change in the level of violence. To nation A, the change in B's behavior indicates the probable direction of their future interactions (i.e., escalation, maintenance, or reduction of conflict); and, the extent of the change allows A to estimate the influence of that change on the strategic situation. Therefore, A tends to be interested in determining whether the impact of B's signals is so great that he must consider reordering his priorities, or else raise his expectations. A significant increase in A's cost may well affect what A can reasonably hope to achieve and might prevent him from responding as violently as he might wish. If his costs decrease, he may raise his level of expectations and increase or decrease his level of violence, depending upon whether he finds it useful to escalate or reduce the level of conflict.

Stage 2: Feed Forward Estimates. In conducting feed forward, nation A tries to ascertain how B rank-orders his preferences and how capable B is of achieving them. Second, A tries to estimate B's subjective cost analysis. Third, A examines B's past violent behavior in relation to that of the present to ascertain whether, assuming no other changes, the present level is likely to be maintained, decreased, or increased in the near future. On the basis of his perceptions of B's preference schedule, costs, and overt behavior, A formulates an estimate of B's probable future behavior.

Stage 3: Strategy Selection and Implementation. Nation A then assesses various strategies to direct toward nation B and selects an appropriate course of action. Nation A wants to select that strategy which gives him the best chance for achieving his objectives, as well as one that is so costly as to reduce B's chances of achieving his preferences. Obviously, A prefers to induce B to modify his objectives and behavior in a manner that is desirable to A. Secondly, A carries out a cost-benefit analysis for each strategy, estimating gains which would be derived from the employment of one strategy rather than another and the costs of producing those gains. The costs of pursuing one strategy should not be so great as to prevent A from responding properly to B's reaction if it were more violent and costly than expected. Therefore, A selects that strategy which he perceives would maximize his expectations and produce a desired response from B.

Nation A then carries out the selected strategy toward nation B. A critical assumption is made at this point. We assume that the output of nation A is a direct isomorphic actualization of the assessment, feed forward, and selection processes just described, and for the purpose of scientific theory may be analyzed as such.

Stage 4: Monitoring the Opponent's Response. Nation A monitors B's response (or possibly the lack of it). Nation B (now a sender of signals) makes his response by going through the stages described above. Thus, he perceives A's signals, assesses them, and responds.

In the above discussion of the four stages of the signal accounting model, a number of general conceptual assumptions were made. Several additional assumptions are necessary for the operationalization of the model:

1. Every event signal initiated by one nation-state and directed toward another has in fact been received by that target.

2. Assessment takes place within a certain image structure which does not change substantially during a relatively short conflict period. Thus, a nation assesses an event signal in relation to the present context and with a knowledge of what has already happened between it and its target.

3. Before selecting a particular strategy, an actor nation tries to project into the immediate future what its target is likely to do and what the actor itself might do.

4. An actor nation's overt output in the form of event signals is the result of the strategy selection process and is an indicator of that actor's policy toward its target.

Event signals, when aggregated, compose a profile of the foreign policy characteristics of A toward B at a specified time point. For example, an aggregated event signals profile may reveal that nation A is highly hostile toward nation B. The actual units of behavior of the disaggregated event signals (commonly referred to as tactics) are not the object of our forecasts in this chapter. There are a number of reasons for this decision. Our research experience has revealed that the most feasible and possibly most credible approach to forecasting foreign policy behavior using events data is forecasting policy characteristics or profiles in the aggregate (Azar 1973). Furthermore, by conducting studies on policy characteristics, or by developing policy profiles, one can make valid comparisons across actors and across time even though the disaggregated units of behavior vary because of somewhat different language used by various reporters.

What do we mean by a nation's foreign policy profile? At any specific time, the foreign policy behavior of nation A toward nation B is defined by (1) nation A's most hostile action toward nation B; (2) nation A's least hostile action toward nation B; and (3) nation A's relative hostility toward nation B (to be computed as the ratio of cooperation to hostile actions of A toward B). In generating profiles for this study, the most and least hostile actions of A toward B were taken to be those monthly events from A to B having the highest and lowest values based on the Azar 13-point scale (see the Appendix to this chapter). The relative hostility is measured in a more complicated manner according to the following procedure, which allows us to compare the relative amounts of hostility contained in the data and the changes in those amounts over time:

1. Divide the 13-point scale into two regions:
   (*a*) *Region I,* the less hostile end of the scale (points 1–6);
   (*b*) Scale point 7, the midpoint between the two regions;
   (*c*) *Region II,* the more hostile end of the scale (points 8–13).
2. Convert the scale points in each region as follows:

Region I			Region II		
13-point scale		Converted value	13-point scale		Converted value
1	=	+6	8	=	−1
2	=	+5	9	=	−2
3	=	+4	10	=	−3
4	=	+3	11	=	−4
5	=	+2	12	=	−5
6	=	+1	13	=	−6

3. Measure the amount of interaction between the members of the dyad by multiplying the intensity level (converted value above) by the number of events at that level (i.e., frequency) and then summing all these values for each of the two regions.

The results of step 3 are called dimensions of interaction (DI). Thus, for **Region I,**

$$DI = \sum_{+1}^{+6} f_j \cdot \ddot{y},$$

and for **Region II,**

$$DI = \sum_{-1}^{-6} f_j \cdot \ddot{y}.$$

The time interval can vary according to the researcher's interest. In this study, one month is the unit of time, and the DI's were computed using events data from the Conflict and Peace Data Bank (COPDAB).

The DI's from Region II are the more hostile quantities of dyadic interactions, and those from Region I are the more friendly quantities of dyadic interactions. Comparing the DI's from both regions by computing ratios of $DI_{Region\ I}/DI_{Region\ II}$ allows us to characterize the type of dyadic interaction during a given period of time. Thus, a friendlier interaction would yield friendly DI's (from Region I) in excess of hostile DI's (from Region II). A lack of interactions would be characterized by zero. Thus, for a relatively friendly interaction period, $R_f = DI_{R\ I}/DI_{R\ II} > 1$; for a relatively hostile interaction period, $R_h = DI_{R\ I}/DI_{R\ II} < 1$ and > 0; and for a period lacking interaction (an indifference period), $R_i = 0$.

The signal accounting model and the three foreign policy characteristics presented above allow us to identify the variables we use in the following regressions to make monthly projections or forecasts. The stepwise linear regression technique we employ below is entirely adequate for making monthly projections, particularly between nations which have relatively similar diplomatic-military capabilities, such as Egypt and Israel or the United States and U.S.S.R.

As a test of the model, we shall make monthly projections of the maximum, minimum, and relative hostile activities initiated by Israel toward Egypt and vice versa for a thirty-six-month period from 1955 to 1957, and by the Soviet Union toward the United States and vice versa for a thirty-six-month period from 1965 to 1967. We shall compare the projections generated by the model and those data from the real world (i.e., in COPDAB). These comparisons allow us to test the adequacy of the model and indicate how one might use events data to forecast foreign policy profiles.

The variables employed are as follows:

1. A's and B's most and least hostile acts during a specified month, t;
2. A's and B's most and least hostile acts at $t + 1$, i.e., the average for A and B of the most and least hostile acts from $t - 6$ to $t - 1$ (or at $t - 1$). This variable accounts for the fact that nations tend to employ memories of the past in their attempts to estimate their best possible responses. Memory at $t - 1$ is a moving average which decays as time increases, from t to $t + 1$, $t + 2$, . . . , $t + n$ (see Abelson 1963; Caspary 1968);
3. A's and B's cooperation DI_{RI}/hostile DI_{RII} at t;
4. A's and B's cooperation DI_{RI}/hostile DI_{RII} at $t + 1$; and

---

Note: The abbreviations and symbols listed below are used in Tables V-1 through V-4 on the pages following: F/H Ratio = Friendliness/Hostility Ratio = DI_F/DI_H

nd = no interaction

$+$ = friendlier interactions, or $R_f = DI_{R\ I}/DI_{R\ II} > 1$

$-$ = more hostile interactions, or $R_h = DI_{R\ I}/DI_{R\ II} < 1$ and > 0

$R_i = 0$ does not appear among the F/H ratios because a zero was replaced by the ratio preceding it.

TABLE V-1

Observed and Projected Maximum and Minimum Hostile Acts, and
Friendliness/Hostility Ratios: United States toward Soviet Union, 1965–67

Year	Month	Maximum Obs.	Maximum Proj.	Minimum Obs.	Minimum Proj.	F/H Ratio Obs.	F/H Ratio Proj.
1965	01	6	6	6	6	+	+
	02	6	6	6	4	+	+
	03	8	6	6	5	+	+
	04	8	7	8	5	−	−
	05	nd	7	nd	2	−	−
	06	nd	3	nd	2	−	−
	07	nd	5	nd	2	−	−
	08	8	5	8	4	−	+
	09	6	7	6	6	+	+
	10	8	6	8	5	−	+
	11	nd	7	nd	4	−	−
	12	6	4	4	5	+	+
Means		7	5.75	6.50	4.16	83% agreement	
1966	01	8	6	5	5	−	−
	02	8	7	4	4	+	+
	03	6	7	4	4	+	+
	04	8	6	6	5	+	+
	05	8	7	6	5	+	+
	06	8	7	6	5	+	+
	07	8	8	4	3	−	+
	08	9	8	5	3	+	+
	09	8	8	4	3	+	+
	10	6	7	4	3	+	+
	11	8	7	4	3	+	+
	12	6	7	4	4	+	+
Means		7.5	7.12	4.33	3.91	92% agreement	
1967	01	6	7	4	5	+	+
	02	8	7	4	6	+	+
	03	8	7	4	5	+	+
	04	8	7	3	5	+	+
	05	8	7	6	6	+	+
	06	8	9	4	5	+	+
	07	8	9	4	5	+	+
	08	11	8	4	5	+	+
	09	8	8	6	5	+	+
	10	8	8	4	4	+	+
	11	8	8	4	4	+	+
	12	6	7	4	4	+	+
Means		8	7.67	4.25	4.91	100% agreement	

TABLE V-2

Observed and Projected Maximum and Minimum Hostile Acts, and
Friendliness/Hostility Ratios: Soviet Union toward United States, 1965–67

Year	Month	Maximum Obs.	Maximum Proj.	Minimum Obs.	Minimum Proj.	F/H Ratio Obs.	F/H Ratio Proj.
1965	01	8	8	8	4	−	+
	02	8	8	6	6	−	−
	03	8	8	6	6	+	+
	04	8	8	6	6	+	+
	05	6	8	6	6	+	+
	06	8	7	8	6	−	+
	07	8	8	6	6	+	−
	08	8	8	6	6	−	−
	09	8	8	7	6	−	−
	10	8	8	8	7	−	−
	11	8	8	8	7	−	−
	12	8	8	6	6	+	−
Means		7.83	7.83	6.75	6.00	67% agreement	
1966	01	8	8	5	6	−	−
	02	8	8	4	5	−	−
	03	8	8	4	5	−	−
	04	8	8	4	5	−	−
	05	8	8	6	5	−	−
	06	8	8	5	6	+	+
	07	8	8	4	5	+	+
	08	8	8	5	5	−	−
	09	8	8	4	5	+	+
	10	8	8	4	4	+	+
	11	8	8	4	4	+	+
	12	8	8	4	4	+	+
Means		8	8	4.41	4.91	100% agreement	
1967	01	8	8	3	4	+	+
	02	8	8	4	4	+	+
	03	8	8	4	4	+	+
	04	8	8	3	4	+	+
	05	11	8	6	4	−	+
	06	10	10	5	5	−	+
	07	8	9	3	5	+	+
	08	8	8	4	4	+	+
	09	8	8	6	5	−	−
	10	8	8	4	5	+	+
	11	8	8	4	4	+	+
	12	8	8	4	4	+	+
Means		8.41	8.25	4.16	4.33	83% agreement	

TABLE V-3

Observed and Projected Maximum and Minimum Hostile Acts, and
Friendliness/Hostility Ratios: Egypt toward Israel, 1955–57

Year	Month	Maximum Obs.	Maximum Proj.	Minimum Obs.	Minimum Proj.	F/H Ratio Obs.	F/H Ratio Proj.
1955	01	8	10	4	5	—	—
	02	11	8	6	5	—	—
	03	12	11	6	5	—	—
	04	12	11	4	5	—	—
	05	12	11	4	5	—	—
	06	12	11	6	5	—	—
	07	8	10	4	5	+	—
	08	12	10	8	5	—	—
	09	12	11	4	6	—	—
	10	12	12	6	6	—	—
	11	12	12	6	6	—	—
	12	12	12	8	6	—	—
Means		11.25	10.75	5.50	5.33	92% *agreement*	
1956	01	12	11	4	6	—	—
	02	11	11	4	6	—	—
	03	12	11	4	5	—	—
	04	12	12	4	6	—	—
	05	12	12	4	6	—	—
	06	8	11	8	6	—	—
	07	11	10	4	5	—	—
	08	12	11	4	5	—	—
	09	12	11	4	5	—	—
	10	12	11	4	5	—	—
	11	12	12	4	5	—	—
	12	8	12	6	5	—	—
Means		11.17	11.25	4.5	5.42	100% *agreement*	
1957	01	8	10	4	6	—	—
	02	8	10	8	5	—	—
	03	9	8	6	6	—	—
	04	8	10	6	6	—	—
	05	8	10	8	6	—	—
	06	11	9	6	6	—	—
	07	8	10	4	6	+	+
	08	8	8	4	6	—	+
	09	8	8	8	5	—	—
	10	11	10	8	6	—	—
	11	8	9	8	6	—	—
	12	6	8	6	6	—	—
Means		8.42	9.12	6.33	5.83	92% *agreement*	

TABLE V-4

Observed and Projected Maximum and Minimum Hostile Acts, and
Friendliness/Hostility Ratios: Israel toward Egypt, 1955–57

Year	Month	Maximum Obs.	Maximum Proj.	Minimum Obs.	Minimum Proj.	F/H Ratio Obs.	F/H Ratio Proj.
1955	01	8	11	6	6	—	—
	02	12	11	6	6	—	—
	03	11	11	6	6	—	—
	04	12	11	4	6	—	—
	05	12	11	4	5	—	—
	06	8	11	6	5	—	—
	07	11	11	4	6	+	—
	08	11	9	4	5	—	—
	09	12	11	4	5	—	—
	10	12	11	4	5	—	—
	11	12	11	6	5	—	—
	12	11	11	6	6	—	—
Means		11	10.83	5	5.5	92% agreement	
1956	01	11	11	6	7	—	—
	02	11	12	8	6	—	—
	03	12	11	4	7	—	—
	04	12	12	4	5	—	—
	05	11	12	4	5	+	—
	06	11	12	8	5	—	—
	07	11	10	5	6	—	—
	08	11	11	8	5	—	—
	09	11	11	6	7	—	—
	10	13	11	6	6	—	—
	11	13	12	4	6	+	—
	12	11	11	4	5	+	+
Means		11.50	11.33	5.58	5.83	83% agreement	
1957	01	11	11	4	5	+	—
	02	8	11	4	5	+	—
	03	11	11	4	5	—	—
	04	11	11	6	5	—	—
	05	11	10	8	6	—	—
	06	11	10	6	6	—	—
	07	8	10	6	6	—	—
	08	8	9	8	6	—	—
	09	11	10	8	7	—	—
	10	8	9	6	6	—	—
	11	8	9	8	5	—	—
	12	6	8	6	6	—	—
Means		9.33	9.92	5.67	5.67	83% agreement	

5. A's and B's average of cooperation DI_{RI}/hostile DI_{RII} from $t-6$ to $t-1$, or memory of DI_F/DI_H at $t-1$.

The basic equations are:

$$A_{t+1}\begin{bmatrix} \text{Max} \\ \text{Min} \\ DI(F) \\ DI(H) \end{bmatrix} = xA_t + yA \, \text{mem}_{\text{at } t-1} + zB_t + \epsilon$$

$$B_{t+1}\begin{bmatrix} \text{Max} \\ \text{Min} \\ DI(F) \\ DI(H) \end{bmatrix} = x'B_t + y \, B \, \text{mem}_{\text{at } t-1} + z'A_t + \epsilon',$$

where x, y, z, x', y', z', ϵ, and ϵ' are constraints which we assume not to change for a period of one year. They are computed from regressions done on data from a twelve-month period preceding the twelve-month period we are concerned with; x, y, and z are the weights which A places on the behavior of itself and its target; x', y', and z' are weights which B places on its own behavior as well as on the behavior of its target.

Tables V–1 to V–4 are summaries of projected and observed maximum and minimum hostile acts and $DI_{Region\ I}/DI_{Region\ II}$ data. The maximum and minimum data are reported in terms of the 13-point scale. The comparisons made between observed and projected data are reported in simple percentage terms showing means and the amount of agreement between observed and projected data. We did not use any statistical measure of significance because we believe that such tests are irrelevant for our concerns and probably for similar time-series data.

Conclusion

Table V–5 summarizes the results of Tables V–1 through V–4. The high degree of agreement between the means of the observed monthly maximum hostile signals based on COPDAB's set and those projected from the model (based upon an actor's own behavior and memory of that behavior and the target's behavior) is very rewarding. The same overall agreement exists between the observed and projected minimum hostile signals for the entire six-year period and the four dyads under investigation. We are satisfied that dyads which are symmetrical to each other diplomatically and militarily and which seem to be preoccupied with one another to the extent that the United States and the

TABLE V-5

Summary of Results of Tables V-1 through V-4

	Means of maximum		Means of minimum		Agreement between obs. and proj. F/H ratios
	Obs.	Proj.	Obs.	Proj.	
U.S. toward U.S.S.R. 1965–67	7.50	6.84	5.02	4.32	92%
U.S.S.R. toward U.S. 1965–67	8.08	8.02	5.10	5.08	83%
Egypt toward Israel 1955–57	10.28	10.37	5.44	5.52	95%
Israel toward Egypt 1955–57	10.61	10.69	5.41	5.66	86%

Soviet Union are, on the one hand, and Egypt and Israel, are on the other, tend to behave symmetrically toward one another. They tend to behave in a tit-for-tat fashion at both ends of the scale. Their foreign policies toward one another may be described in terms of their interactions as follows: A will be as friendly and/or hostile toward B as B is toward A. This type of foreign policy is a *reactive* one based on high competition for influence and resources and on some level of distrust which requires continuous monitoring and speedy and active responsiveness. Such a foreign policy is a very sensitive one in that a mistake or a miscalculation can yield hostile and costly internation behavior. Our findings are supportive of the findings of many other scholars in international relations and foreign policy (Hermann 1969; McClelland 1968a; North 1968; Zinnes 1968; and others). We must hasten to add, however, that the economic model employed here and the rich data set we used can encourage us to make theoretical generalizations only about the behavior of those dyads which fit the constraints mentioned above. We are not, at this point, prepared to make very sweeping generalizations regarding all types of dyads. Furthermore, we must emphasize that our effort represents an attempt at making short-term projections of future foreign policy profiles and not an attempt at *explaining* why these projections are as good as we found them to be. Although we have suggested some explanatory variables, such as symmetry of capabilities and dyadic saliency, we feel that more comprehensive explanations are necessary.

Appendix
Measuring Events with a Thirteen-Point Scale

Measurement is an indispensable tool in social science research. Through the assignment of numerical values to the properties of objects being studied, the better-developed physical and biological sciences have achieved a high degree of precision and clarity of communication. The accumulation of scientific knowledge in international relations, however, has been somewhat inhibited by the reluctance of many scholars to apply quantitative techniques to their objects of study and by the difficulty of assigning numbers to human behaviors.

Despite the problems associated with the measurement of behavioral phenomena, a few international politics researchers have been seeking to develop better quantitative techniques to measure the increasing amounts of data available on international interactions. These scholars have applied innovative measurement techniques to various dimensions of internation behavior. As early as 1941, Klingberg examined psychometric techniques for their potential application to measuring the relations among international actors (Klingberg 1941). Using the judgments of experts in international affairs, he developed a scale measuring friendliness-hostility. Other scholars, while not developing any particular scales of their own, have illustrated the potential usefulness of assigning scale values, based on objective criteria, to tension levels between international actors (Holsti 1963). More recently, a number of individuals and groups have concentrated on the measurement of international events.

All of these researchers have attempted to measure changes of internation behavior with the aid of some yardstick. In the absence of an absolute yardstick in international relations, the specific techniques cited above have been designed to measure the particular internation

TABLE V-6

Paired Comparison Scale Values

13-point ordering	Paired comparison values
1	0.000
2	0.405
3	0.957
4	1.321
5	1.623
6	2.331
7	2.774
8	3.011
9	3.247
10	3.741
11	4.203
12	4.828
13	5.536

behavioral properties which interest the researchers. With such advances on the part of several researchers now available, we inquired into the similarity and redundancy in scaling instruments, and developed the 13-point interval scale (Azar 1970a; Azar et al. 1972b).

Using the following 13-point scale, we measured the amount of violence contained in each of the events included in COPDAB. The scale contains thirteen behaviors, ranging from most to least cooperative:

1. Nations A and B merge to form a new nation state.
2. Nations A and B establish their own regional organization.
3. Nation A extends economic aid to nation B.
4. Nations A and B establish a friendship agreement.
5. Nation A receives support for its internal and/or external policies.
6. Nations A and B communicate regarding issues of mutual concern.
7. Nation A experiences limited internal political difficulties.
8. Nation A makes a protest directed against nation B.
9. Nation A increases its military capabilities.
10. Nation A encounters domestic politico-military violence.
11. Nation A initiates subversion in nation B.
12. Nations A and B engage in limited war activities.
13. Nation A engages in an all-out war against nation B.

While the 13-point scale can differentiate events into classes, we determined the interval widths between these thirteen points through the technique of paired comparisons (Torgerson 1958). All possible distinct pairs of the thirteen markers (totaling seventy-eight pairs) were submitted in a random order to fifty-two students for rank-ordering. The resulting scale values are shown in Table V-6.

Furthermore, we tested the adequacy of the internal scale by correlating the scale widths resulting from the paired comparisons technique with results from the rank-ordering task. The Pearson product-moment correlations between the 13-point ordering and the paired-comparison scores equalled 0.98.

Part VI

Foreign Policy Research Materials

9

Methods and Data for the
Comparative Analysis of Foreign Policy

PATRICK J. McGOWAN and MICHAEL K. O'LEARY

While the preceding essays in this volume indicate that the comparative analysis of foreign policy is a legitimate field of study, the accumulation of reliable knowledge about foreign policy behavior has only recently begun. Much more empirical work is needed on a great variety of hypotheses. This article is intended to offer an opportunity for such research by providing the student with the necessary materials and methods.

As a primer in quantitative foreign policy research, the following discussion focuses upon many of the methodological issues illustrated in the previous selections. First, we discuss a framework for analysis which delineates the types of variables that might be employed to formulate hypotheses explaining foreign policy behavior. Next, a summary of the procedures relating to research design in the comparative study of foreign policy is presented. Finally, we provide a data set incorporating indicators for each of these variables and offer a series of instructions for data manipulation. By employing some of these simple statistical procedures, the student can confront his own theories with empirical data.

This chapter was originally published under the title *Comparative Foreign Policy Analysis Materials*, Learning Package 4 (copyright © 1971 by Markham Publishing Company), Learning Packages in International Relations, William D. Coplin. gen. ed. Copyright © 1972 by Syracuse University, International Relations Program. Reprinted by permission of the authors and publisher.

A Framework for Comparative Foreign Policy Analysis

A framework is a device for categorizing the possible causes or sources of observed patterns of foreign policy behavior. These causes of foreign policy are termed *source variables,* which are classified into ten distinct *clusters.* Eight source variable clusters are attributes of national societies and their foreign policy decision-makers. Two variable clusters include features of the external environment within which national societies and their policymakers conduct foreign affairs.

Foreign policy patterns represent outputs originating from decision-making processes within national societies. Within the comparative study of foreign policy, these patterns are thought of as dependent variables to be accounted for by comparative foreign policy theory based on the ten source variable clusters. Source variables are pictured as "determining" foreign policy behavior by influencing the policy formation process both directly and indirectly. The eight clusters that are attributes of the national society and its elites are seen as variables within the nation-state that have a direct bearing on the decision-making process. The two variable clusters that originate in the environment are inputs to the national society; we suggest that these clusters are indirect causes of observed foreign policy behavior. Finally, characteristics of the decision-making process itself are conceived of as intervening variables that may modify the impact of the ten types of source variables. (For further discussion of policy formation, see Snyder, Bruck, and Sapin 1962; Frankel 1959; and Hilsman 1971.)

Let us briefly specify the nature of each source variable category, and suggest how each might be used to construct research questions and hypotheses for analysis.

1. Individual source variables. Individual source variables are the characteristics of identifiable persons (for example, presidents, prime ministers, and dictators) who regularly make foreign policy decisions for national societies. Personalities, perceptions, beliefs, values, experiences, and social backgrounds are considered relevant characteristics. This category is distinct because it deals with the inherent attitudes and convictions that the decision-maker brings to his job. No individual variable is included in the data set which follows, but the reader can easily create one—experience—by determining how long the individual has been making foreign policy. President Nixon's experience as president began in early 1969, while President Tubman's (of Liberia) started in 1944. Is it possible that differences in this variable influence a decision-maker's policies? Are experience and cautious policy directly related?

2. *Regime source variables.* These are the aggregate characteristics of the country's foreign policy elite. Every state's foreign policy is formulated by a relatively small group of men and women. What is their average age and educational attainment? What proportion of this elite is civilian and what proportion is military? Most important, who are these elites, how did they get to be foreign-policy makers, and how do they retain their posts? These are important questions. At least one can be addressed with the materials presented here: that is, what is the difference between the foreign policies of civilian regimes and military regimes? This variable—character of regime—is included in the data set (variable 3).

3. *Establishment source variables.* Establishment source variables refer to the organizational features of the society's foreign policy and national security establishments. How many organizations are involved on a continuing basis in the creation and administration of foreign and defense policy? How large are these organizations and to what extent are they bureaucratized? What are their typical patterns of conflict and coalition? Which are most influential and on what issues? Both the observations and behavior of certain well-placed specialists in foreign policy indicate that these questions are very important (Kissinger 1969, pp. 11–50). For example, Kissinger argues that if a state lacks a highly organized policy establishment, its foreign policies will be erratic. This proposition is amenable to empirical testing. The data set contains a variable—average size of diplomatic mission (variable 6)—that is an indicator of the degree of bureaucratization of a country's foreign policy establishment.

4. *Political source variables.* Political source variables relate to attributes of the national political system, such as its level of development, its capabilities, its structure, the nature of its party system, and the effect of pressure groups and public and elite opinion on the process of

policymaking. With respect to capabilities, the data set contains figures that represent the military expenditure of each nation in the set (variable 5). This is a measure of the political system's military capability. Do countries with great military capabilities engage in conflict more frequently than do countries with low capabilities? The hypothesis can be easily tested with data. The second political source variable in the data set is type of political system (variable 4). This variable indicates whether the system is an open system, with a participatory political style, or a closed system, in which parties, unions, and pressure groups are largely controlled by, and may even be eliminated by, the political elite.

5. Economic source variables. These variables comprise the characteristics of domestic economies, including their levels of development and technology, rates of growth, and patterns of specialization. The data set includes a measure of total economic transactions within a nation—gross national product (variable 8). This is an indicator of economic resources. What similarities and differences may be discerned in the foreign policy behavior of high resource and low resource countries?

6. Social source variables. Social source variables are aspects of the social structure, broadly defined, of national societies. This category includes such features as population size (variable 7 in the data set) and population growth rates, social stratification, and the degree of social integration, or conversely, the degree of civil strife in the society (variable 8 in the data set). A possible hypothesis for investigation is whether domestic conflict leads to foreign conflict as the political elite tries to project its internal problems to the outside world.

7. Cultural source variables. Here, we are concerned with the cultural systems of national societies. Cultural source variables may include degree of cultural pluralism and patterns of national identity. Are pluralistic societies more subject to intervention by foreign actors than integrated societies are? Also included in this category are features of the society's information processing system—that is, its development and use of mass media and the role of national ideology in public life. Each of the countries in the data set is classified as belonging to a sociocultural region, such as the Western, Latin American, or Afro-Asian communities (variable 10). Do countries with similar cultures follow similar foreign policies? Are all Communist states equally hostile to the United States?

8. External source variables. External source variables are the historical traces of the actor's past foreign policy behavior. Obviously, traditions of past foreign economic and political involvement are likely to influence current and future behavior. Thus, all of the past official actions of decision-makers and their agents—as manifested in treaties, diplomatic representation, memberships in international organizations, foreign trade, foreign investment, balance-of-payments performance, and so on—are included in this variable cluster. The data set contains information on the alliance bloc membership of each country, which is an indicator of a previous decision either to join or not to join an alliance (variable 11); these data enable one to compare the policies of allies of the United States, allies of the Soviet Union, and nonallied countries.

9. Direct demands and supports. This source variable cluster represents the actions directed by other international actors toward the society or societies under analysis, that is, the foreign policy inputs of other actors into the national society and their impact on its policy-making process. Ten measures of the foreign policy inputs of other societies into foreign societies are included in the data set, ranging from cooperative acts on the part of the United States to conflict acts received from inside and outside the actor's own region (variables 12–21). When a country receives conflict acts, does it tend to respond with conflictive or cooperative behavior? Obviously, the answer to this question has tremendous import for the creation of a peaceful world order.

10. Systemic context variables. Systemic context variables represent the sociopolitical and physical environment of the actor, such as its geographic position, its role within the international system, its status rank in the system, and characteristics of the international system itself (that is, its degrees of polarity, organization, and violence). The data set contains a variable that enumerates the neighboring countries of each state in the set (variable 22). Is there a relationship between the number of countries contiguous to any state and the state's foreign policy? If so, what is the nature of that relationship?

The framework provided by the source variables allows systematic thought about the causes of foreign policy behavior from a comparative perspective. It thus helps in the formation of hypotheses for research. The framework also indicates what one should include in a research design and what one should attempt to control (as in comparing the relationship between military expenditures and foreign conflict for countries of similar types, such as rich or poor). Finally, the framework is a device for sorting research findings and for classifying the propositions found in the literature.

Procedures for Comparative Foreign Policy Analysis

The materials in this section are designed to provide a basis on which the researcher can make a rudimentary, yet systematic, study of foreign policy from a comparative perspective. For this study, neither previous experience with quantitative data, knowledge of statistics, nor access to card-sorting equipment or electronic computers is necessary. Through sophisticated use of the available materials, through reliance on the references to more advanced work, and through use of the machine-readable set of data cards, any student can carry out sophisticated social science research.

Sampling

The list of 114 nations provided in the third section of this chapter constitutes what statisticians term a *universe* of all the independent nation-states as of 1966 for which it was possible to obtain the indicated foreign policy data.[1] One may want to study this entire universe or prefer to study a sample, or partial set, of the countries included. Depending on the research purpose, samples may be selected in several ways. It is possible to select a sample on a random basis in such a way that each nation has an equal chance of being chosen. Statisticians agree that in many cases, a truly random sample of only 5 or 10 percent of the total may provide a very accurate picture of the total. On the other hand, a sample may be chosen according to some very explicit *a priori*

[1] Some variables are available for years slightly earlier or later than 1966. In these cases the differences between the actual year and the base year of 1966 are unlikely to alter substantially any analytical results.

criterion. For example, the student may wish to study only Communist countries. In that case, the sample would consist of only those countries with Communist governments.

For the purposes of illustration in this chapter, we shall draw a sample using a combination of these two techniques. Because the sample should roughly represent the entire set of countries, it should be a random sample, but composed of a representative proportion of states from the major regions of the world. This is so because certain attributes of states, such as their geographic location, are extremely important in understanding their foreign policy performance. Sample states are selected from geographic regions at random. This technique, called a *stratified random sample*, is useful when researchers want a sample that is not only random, but accurately representative of one or more highly salient characteristics of a data set.

In this data set, the approximate proportioned distribution of countries by six major geographic areas (variable 1) is as follows: Western Hemisphere, three; Western Europe, two; Eastern Europe, one; Africa, four; Middle East, two; Asia, three. The stratified random sample of fifteen nations shown in Table VI–1 corresponds to this distribution.

TABLE VI–1

Random Sample of Fifteen States
(Stratified According to Geographic Location)

Western Hemisphere	Mexico
	Costa Rica
	Brazil
Western Europe	France
	Denmark
Eastern Europe	Poland
Africa	Ivory Coast
	Mali
	Nigeria
	Ghana
Middle East	Egypt
	Lebanon
Asia	India
	Pakistan
	Indonesia

In the subsequent discussion of analysis methods, various procedures are demonstrated using these states as examples. In some cases, the small numbers involved will permit the student to do the calculations. A note of caution: whenever one is dealing with such a small sample, a single score can easily cause substantial changes in the results of some calculation. Consequently, statistical results drawn on the basis of such small numbers are termed "unstable" although they are interesting for introducing some techniques of analysis. But the actual numbers must be treated with a good deal of suspicion. Throughout the discussion, the results of the various analyses are also presented for the entire universe of 114 nations in the data set.

Cases, Variables, and Scales

When social scientists speak of "cases," they refer to the entities they are studying. Our cases are nations. When they speak of "variables," they refer to some attribute which each case possesses but which is not necessarily the same for each case. This set of data contains 114 cases, with thirty-eight variables for each case. In the listing of data contained in the third section of this chapter (see p. 271), the first case is the United States, indicated by its identification number (variable 1) and its abbreviated name, USA. Reading across the first line in this listing of data, column heading 8 represents the number of the variable gross national product, abbreviated GNP. The score for the United States is $749.9 billion, while the score for the second case, Canada, is only $53.3 billion. Some of the variables do not vary as much as the GNP does. In fact, variable 3, civilian or military character of the regime, varies only between 0 (if the case has a civilian regime) and 1 (if the case has a military regime).

The GNP and the character of regime are two basic types of information presented in the data set. GNP is measured on an interval scale, which means that the variable GNP is given a score in some unit (in this case, United States dollars) for which it is sensible to speak of differences —or equal intervals—of amounts. Other examples of interval scales in the set are population and number of contiguous countries. Character of regime is an example of a nominal scale. The score for this variable is not, as is the case with interval data, a quantity of some sort that can be added or subtracted. Instead, it is merely the numerical "name" (from the Latin word *nomina*) of the category into which that particular case is classified on that particular variable.

Certain things can be done with interval data (because they can be arithmetically manipulated) that cannot be done with nominal data (which represent categories of cases). Nevertheless, both types of data have important uses.

The scores on the variables are estimated records of events that occurred in the mid-1960s. It is important to remember the word "estimate." Even in the most compulsive record-keeping countries, such as the United States, the population figure, to take an example, is an estimate as of a certain point in time, although in this case, the gap between the estimate and the reality is undoubtedly small and trivial. But for other cases and other variables, this gap is likely to be larger.

Another reason for remembering that these numbers are estimates is that the questions concern to what extent a given variable, or combination of variables, constitutes a "good" measure of some general phenomenon under study. Because these scores are estimates, they can never define the "real" measures of such concepts as international conflict, international support for the United States, or countless other subjects of interest. While it is a goal of scientific, systematic research to develop measures of concepts that will be as generally accepted by as many people as possible, there are no absolutely right or wrong ways of measuring concepts. Consider the concept of national wealth. How can the wealth of a nation be measured? GNP is an obvious variable with which to begin measurement. But consider the richest nations according to this measure. The top ten countries, ranked according to GNP in billions of dollars, are as follows:

Country	GNP	Country	GNP
(1) USA	750	(6) Japan	97
(2) USSR	347	(7) China	80
(3) W. Germany	120	(8) Italy	61
(4) U.K.	105	(9) Canada	53
(5) France	101	(10) India	37

The straightforward measure of GNP includes as "rich" nations some countries, such as India, normally considered to be poor. The problem is that while more goods and services are available in India than, for example, in Sweden, there is an even greater demand for these goods and services from the huge population of India. This suggests that the measure of wealth should include not just one variable, but a combination of two variables—GNP, divided by total population (variable 7).

By combining these variables, an index of wealth is derived that takes account not only of total goods and services available but also of how many people they must be divided among. According to this measure of wealth, the list of ten richest countries, ranked according to per capita GNP (PGNP) in U.S. dollars, is as follows:

Country	PGNP		Country	PGNP
(1) USA	3,838		(6) Denmark	2,313
(2) Iceland	3,000		(7) Australia	2,083
(3) Canada	2,650		(8) France	2,052
(4) Sweden	2,625		(9) Norway	2,000
(5) Switzerland	2,500		(10) W. Germany	2,000

This list probably comes closer to satisfying most people's notion of wealth than the first one did. When we speak of "wealth" in the next few pages, we refer to this measure—per capita gross national product.

Univariate Analysis

When social scientists work with a single variable, they normally ask how it is distributed among the cases. A first step is to look at each variable by itself to see how it is distributed among the cases. The distribution can be expressed in many ways: by the *range,* which is the difference between the highest and lowest values found for that variable, or by some single measure of *central tendency,* such as the *mean.* Related to the mean is the concept of *variance.* Although not computed in the illustrative exercises, its importance can be seen from the following example. In the set of 114 countries, the average PGNP is $495. This figure could have been obtained if 50 percent of the cases had a PGNP of $496 and the other 50 percent had a PGNP of $494. A much more extreme variation in scores could have produced this same average, however. For example, half the scores might have been $195 and the other half $795. The statistician's measure of variance would be much higher in the latter distribution of cases than in the former.

Bivariate Analysis

Bivariate analysis investigates the relationship between variables. One question that is often asked is how states differ in their friendships with the United States. This involves once more the problem of measurement, since there are numerous ways of measuring friendship. Even with the limited data set given in the last section of this chapter, friendship could be measured by alliance membership (variable 11), by number of cooperative acts directed toward the United States (variable 25), or even, for those intrigued by Cold War strategies, by the number of conflict acts directed toward the Soviet Union (variable 27). For this illustration, the measure of voting agreement with the United States in the General Assembly of the United Nations (variable 33) is employed as an estimate of friendship.

Table VI–2 lists the sample of fifteen countries with their scores on

TABLE VI–2

Per Capita GNP and Voting Agreement with the United States
for Fifteen-Nation Sample

Country	PGNP	USUN	RGM
Mexi	$ 493.10	−0.15	0
Cost	419.92	−0.12	0
Braz	288.25	−0.13	1
Fran	2,052.63	0.12	0
Denm	2,313.95	0.06	0
Pola	993.75	−0.69	0
Ivor	260.20	−0.35	0
Mali	51.57	−0.68	0
Ngra	93.00	−0.48	1
Ghan	219.38	−0.49	1
UAR	168.34	−0.61	1
Leba	508.13	−0.40	0
Indi	74.95	−0.40	0
Paki	123.89	−0.29	1
Indo	84.11	−0.50	1

PGNP = Per capita gross national product, in U.S. dollars.
USUN = Voting agreement with the United States in the United Nations.
RGM = Character of regime (0 = civilian; 1 = military).

PGNP and voting agreement with the United States in the United Nations, abbreviated as USUN. To give a clear picture of the relationship between these two variables, fifteen points are plotted, one for each country, with respect to a horizontal and a vertical axis. In this case, the horizontal axis represents the range of scores on wealth, and the vertical axis represents the scores for voting agreement with the United States. Figure VI–1 shows the point for the first country on the list, Mexico, located to represent its wealth score of $493 and its U.S. agreement score of −0.15.

FIGURE VI-1

Plotting Mexico as a Data Point: An Illustration

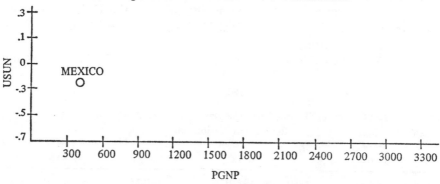

When the other points are plotted, a clear picture of the relationship between wealth and voting agreement with the United States emerges: in general, the richer a country is, the more often it votes with the United States, and the poorer a country is, the more often it opposes the United States in the United Nations. But scholars are generally interested in precision ("How much wealth leads to how much of an increase in voting support for the United States?") and also in communicating their findings to other scholars ("How can I summarize these results clearly and concisely so that others can appreciate them?"). Therefore, they want something more than a pattern of points. For this kind of analysis, the overwhelming practice among scholars is to summarize the results by drawing a regression line.

In its normal use by social scientists, a regression line is a straight line drawn as close to all points as possible. In somewhat more formal terms, it is a straight line drawn to minimize the total squared distance of all points from the line. The mathematics of selecting such a line and of demonstrating that a given line satisfies the requirements of a regression line are extremely complex. But the computing formula for drawing such a line for two variables is easy to follow, although somewhat tedious to apply for very many cases.

First, one must decide which variable is to be the dependent variable and which will be the independent variable. The dependent variable is the one whose values are said to depend on the values of the independent variable. The selection of dependent and independent variables is done in terms of a specific hypothesis and implies no ultimate conclusion about the "true" causation of one variable by another. One's immediate purposes determine the categorization of variables. In the present instance, we have no particular theory to guide us, but we can reasonably assume that a country can change its voting pattern in the United Nations much more easily than it can alter the wealth available to its citizens. Consequently, insofar as there is a systematic relationship between wealth and U.N. voting, it makes more sense to hypothesize that voting depends on wealth than that wealth depends on voting. Therefore, we will treat our foreign policy measure, voting, as the dependent variable and our source variable, wealth, as the independent variable.

The calculations for selecting a regression line for the sample of fifteen countries are shown in Table VI–3.

The steps in calculating the line are as follows:

1. Compute the mean (average) value of each of the two variables. For the per capita GNP of the sample, abbreviated PGNP (column 2 of Table VI–3), this mean is $543.01; for voting agreement, abbreviated USUN (column 5 of the table), the mean is −0.34.

2. Subtract the mean from each value of the independent variable (column 3 of Table VI–3) and do the same for the dependent variable (column 6 of Table VI–3).

3. Square each of the independent variable's difference-from-mean scores (column 4 of Table VI–3).

4. Multiply each difference-from-mean score for the independent variable by the equivalent figure for the dependent variable (column 3 times column 6 in Table VI–3, entered in column 7).

5. Find the sum of all the products (column 7) and divide it by the sum of the squared difference-from-mean scores of the independent variable (column 4). The result, represented by the letter b, is the slope of the regression line, or the amount of change in units of the dependent variable that are associated with a unit change in the independent variable. In this example, $b = 0.00023$.

6. Multiply b by the mean of the independent variable, and subtract that product from the mean of the dependent variable, to obtain the value a (see the calculation for a in Table VI–3). This value indicates where the regression line crosses the coordinate representing the independent variable, or the estimated hypothesized value of the dependent variable if the independent variable were equal to zero.

7. Finally, choose some arbitrary value for the independent variable

TABLE VI-3

Computations for Selecting a Regression Line for Fifteen-Nation Sample

Country (1)	PGNP (2)	PGNP − mean (3)	(PGNP − mean)² (4)	USUN (5)	USUN − mean (6)	(USUN − mean)(PGNP − mean) (7)
Mexi	$ 493.10	−49.91	2,491.01	−0.15	0.19	−9.52
Cost	419.92	−123.09	15,151.15	−0.12	0.22	−27.16
Braz	288.25	−254.76	64,902.66	−0.13	0.21	−53.67
Fran	2,052.63	1509.62	2,278,952.54	0.12	0.46	695.43
Denm	2,313.95	1770.94	3,136,228.48	0.06	0.40	709.55
Pola	993.75	450.74	203,166.55	−0.69	−0.35	−157.46
Ivor	260.20	−282.81	79,981.50	−0.35	−0.01	2.64
Mali	51.57	−491.44	241,513.27	−0.68	−0.34	166.76
Ngra	93.00	−450.01	202,509.00	−0.48	−0.14	62.70
Ghan	219.38	323.63	104,736.38	−0.49	−0.15	48.33
UAR	168.34	374.67	140,377.61	−0.61	−0.27	100.91
Leba	508.13	−34.88	1,216.61	−0.40	−0.06	2.07
Indi	74.95	−468.06	219,080.16	−0.40	−0.06	27.77
Paki	123.89	−419.12	175,661.57	−0.29	0.05	−21.24
Indo	84.11	−458.90	2,109.89	−0.50	−0.15	73.12
Sums	8,145.18	0.00	6,866,078.38	−5.11	0.00	1,620.24
Means	543.01			−0.34	0.00	

$$b = \frac{\Sigma(USUN - mean)(PGNP - mean)}{\Sigma(PGNP - mean)^2} = \frac{1,620.24}{6,866,078.38} = 0.00023$$

$$a = (mean\ of\ USUN) - b(mean\ of\ PGNP) = -0.34 - (0.00023)(543.01) = -0.465$$

$$USUN = a + b(PGNP)$$

$$USUN = -0.465 + (0.00023)(PGNP)$$

and substitute that value into the regression formula (dependent variable $= a + b$ [independent variable]) in order to obtain a second point with which to draw the regression line. If we choose 500 as an arbitrary value for PGNP and substitute it into the regression formula (USUN $= -0.465 + 0.00023 \times 500$), the regression line can be drawn from the point -0.46 on the vertical axis (which is the hypothetical value of USUN when PGNP is zero) and the second point, -0.35.

From these figures one can also easily calculate what is called a correlation coefficient, a somewhat more compressed summary of the relationship between the two variables. This particular correlation coefficient is called Pearson's r and is one of the most widely used of the many correlation coefficients available. Pearson's r summarizes the extent to which any two variables covary: it varies from $+1.00$ to -1.00. If, when one variable has a high value, the other also has a high value (which is true in our present study), Pearson's r will have a score close to $+1.00$ for those two variables, and the regression line will slope upward. If, when one variable has a high value, the other usually has a low value, Pearson's r will have a score close to -1.00, and the regression line will slope downward. If there is no systematic relationship between the scores of the two variables, Pearson's r will have a score close to 0.00, and the regression line will be horizontal.

Table VI–4 shows a sample calculation of Pearson's r correlation coefficient. It is computed as follows:

1. Compute the sums of the two variables (columns 2 and 4 in Table VI–4).
2. Square each value, and sum the squares (columns 3 and 5 in Table VI–4).
3. Multiply each value of the two variables together, and sum the product (column 6 in Table VI–4).
4. Pearson's r is then calculated by the rather complex fraction shown in Table VI–4. This calculation produces r; the usual procedure is to report r^2, which is called the amount of covariance between the two variables.

Thus far, interval measures have been employed in analysis. But there are also nominal, or categoric, variables in this data set. Since the numbers in these variables are merely codes for categories and not values that can be arithmetically manipulated, regression and correlation techniques

TABLE VI–4

Calculation of Pearson's r for Fifteen-Nation Sample

Country (1)	PGNP (2)	PGNP² (3)	USUN (4)	USUN² (5)	(PGNP) (USUN) (6)
Mexi	$ 493.10	243,149.86	−0.15	0.022	−73.96
Cost	419.92	176,332.17	−0.12	0.014	−50.39
Braz	288.25	83,086.72	−0.13	0.017	−37.47
Fran	2,052.63	4,213,296.40	0.12	0.014	246.32
Denm	2,313.95	5,354,347.09	0.06	0.004	138.84
Pola	993.75	987,461.16	−0.69	0.476	−685.69
Ivor	260.20	67,706.16	−0.35	0.122	−91.07
Mali	51.57	2,659.31	−0.68	0.462	−35.07
Ngra	93.00	8,649.63	−0.48	0.230	−44.64
Ghan	219.38	48,129.01	−0.49	0.240	−107.50
UAR	168.34	28,338.96	−0.61	0.372	−102.69
Leba	508.13	258,196.18	−0.40	0.160	−203.25
Indi	74.95	5,617.18	−0.40	0.160	−29.98
Paki	123.89	15,348.96	−0.29	0.084	−35.93
Indo	84.11	7,074.85	−0.50	0.250	−42.06
Sums	8,145.18	11,499,478.62	−5.11	2.630	−1,154.55
Means	543.01		−0.34		

$$r = \frac{\Sigma(PGNP)(USUN) - [\Sigma(PGNP)\Sigma(USUN)]/N}{\sqrt{\{\Sigma PGNP^2 - [(\Sigma PGNP)^2/N]\}\{\Sigma USUN^2 - [(\Sigma USUN)^2/N]\}}}$$

$$r = \frac{-1,154.55 - [(8145.18)(-5.11)/15]}{\sqrt{[11,499,478.62 - (8145.18)^2/15][2.630 - (-5.11)^2/15]}}$$

$$r = \frac{1620.24}{2508.13} = 0.646 \qquad r^2 = 0.417$$

N = number of cases.

cannot be used. Other types of analyses, however, can be performed to extract useful information from the data. In general, these types of analyses use a method of organizing data called contingency tables.

What a contingency table is can best be shown by an example. Suppose a researcher is concerned with examining the frequently-repeated charge that American foreign policy is strongly marked by a tendency to ally with military regimes and has selected ten countries from the data list and studied two variables—the characters of the regime and alliance membership. Assume that in our sample there are eight civilian regimes and two military regimes. Further assume that, of these ten countries, five are allied with the United States and five are not. Since alliance with the United States is the topic of study, two categories— alliance with Communist governments and nonalliance—can be combined into one category for this particular analysis. A contingency table is used to test the strength of association between the two variables. The logic of most statistical tests involved with contingency tables is to measure the extent to which there is deviation from random distribution between the two variables under study.

For example, suppose, in the hypothetical example, that there is, in fact, no systematic relationship between type of regime and alliance with the United States. If this is the case, what is the distribution of cells in a contingency table that compares the two variables? That is, how many instances can be found of the four possible types of combinations: civilian regimes allied with the United States, civilian regimes not allied with the United States, military regimes allied with the United States, and military regimes not allied with the United States? Consider one classification—civilian regimes allied with the United States. In the example there were eight (out of ten) instances of civilian regimes. That is the same as saying that civilian regimes constitute 0.8 of the sample. States allied with the United States are found to constitute 0.5 of the sample. The proportion in the cell for civilian regimes allied with the United States is found by multiplying the two $(0.8 \times 0.5 = 0.4)$. The total number of cases expected in that cell is that proportion multiplied by the total in the sample $(0.4 \times 10 = 4)$. The entire contingency cell distributions under conditions of random, unsystematic relationship between the two variables would be expected to look like that shown in Table VI–5.

If, however, there is some systematic relationship between military regimes and alliance with the United States, one would expect to find

TABLE VI–5

Contingency Table Showing No Relationship between
Regime Type and Alliance Posture

Alliance	Regime		Row totals
	Civilian	Military	
With the U.S.	4	1	5
Not with the U.S.	4	1	5
Column totals	8	2	

disproportionately larger numbers of countries in the Military Regime/ Allied with U.S. cell. In general, statistics concerned with analyzing nominal variables are ways of systematically measuring the extent to which the actual distribution of a given table deviates from the kind of random pattern illustrated in Table VI–5.

When researchers compute contingency-table statistics, they are usually concerned with two things: the likelihood that a given distribution is a random pattern, and the strength of the relationship between two variables.

Many statistics are used to test the strength of the relationship between two variables in a contingency table. The formula for calculating only one of them—a statistic called *lambda* (λ)—indicates in percentage terms how the distribution of cases (nations) on one variable is related to the distribution of cases on another variable. It ranges from 0, when there is no relationship, to 1, when there is a 100 percent relationship. In symbolic form, the instructions for computing lambda are:

$$\lambda = \frac{\Sigma f_i - F_d}{N - F_d}$$

where Σf_i is the sum of the largest number in each subcategory of the independent variable; F_d is the largest number found among the totals of the dependent variable; and N is the total number of cases.

Table VI–6 presents a calculation of lambda using the actual distributions for the sample of fifteen countries. Table VI–7 presents the same information for all states. Notice that in both cases, the value for lambda (0 and 0.06) suggests that there is virtually no relationship between character of the regime (the independent variable) and alliance pattern (the dependent variable).

TABLE VI–6

Relationship between Character of Regime and Alliance with the United States for Fifteen-Nation Sample

| Alliance | Regime | | Row totals |
	Civilian	Military	
With U.S.	4	2	6
Not with U.S.	5	4	9

$$\lambda = \frac{\Sigma f_i - F_d}{N - F_d} = \frac{(5+4) - 9}{15 - 9} = \frac{9 - 9}{6} = 0$$

TABLE VI–7

Relationship between Character of Regime and Alliance
with the United States for 113 Nations

Alliance	Regime		Row totals
	Civilian	Military	
With U.S.	32	21	52
Not with U.S.	43	18	61

$$\lambda = \frac{\Sigma f_i - F_d}{N - F_d} = \frac{(43 + 21) - 61}{113 - 61} = \frac{64 - 61}{52} = 0.06$$

Control of Third Variables

In the discussion thus far, only two variables have been dealt with, and in the case of nominal variables, each has been treated as possessing only two values. A third variable, however, can be introduced into the analysis.

Suppose, in these studies of regime type and alliance with the United States, and of level of development and voting agreement with the United States, one wanted to investigate those relationships only for the underdeveloped nations and wanted to ignore the developed states. In statistical jargon this is known as "controlling" for another variable— in this case development, or wealth. One way to do this is to take some measure of wealth—in this example, per capita gross national product— and then establish some value of that variable above which states will be termed "developed" and below which states will be termed "underdeveloped." This cutoff point may be more or less arbitrary, or it may be mathematically based on substantive research; but in either case, it must always be clearly stated and well defined.

In this example, we shall use the arbitrary cutoff point of $500, which is approximately the mean for the variable PGNP. All states above that level are termed developed, and all states at or below that level are termed underdeveloped. In effect, the interval variable, PGNP, has been transformed into a nominal variable. If one wished, of course, he could use this transformed variable in a contingency table with some other variable. To control for development, we perform exactly the same regression, correlation, and contingency-table calculations as before but consider only those countries which fall within the newly defined category of underdeveloped. The analysis could be performed separately on those now classified as developed, but in the sample there are only four countries—France, Poland, Lebanon, and Denmark—that meet the criterion of possessing a PGNP of more than $500. This is really too few to analyze statistically. The results of PGNP and voting agreement with the United States, considering only those countries within our sample that classify as underdeveloped, are as follows:

$$USUN = -0.44 + 0.00015 \times PGNP$$
$$r = 0.14$$
$$r^2 = 0.02$$

Table VI-8 presents the lambda calculations for the same states, using the relationship between the character of regime and alliance with the United States.

The results of regression and correlation of PGNP and voting agree-

TABLE VI-8

Relationship between Character of Regime and Alliance
with the United States for Underdeveloped
Subset of Fifteen-Nation Sample

Alliance	Regime		Row totals
	Civilian	Military	
With U.S.	2	2	4
Not with U.S.	3	4	7
$\lambda = 0$			

ment with the United States for the entire data set of developed and underdeveloped states are as follows:

Table VI–9 presents the lambda calculations for the same states, again using the relationship between character of regime and alliance with the United States. Note that in the case of the regression and correla-

States with PGNP less than or equal to $500

$$USUN = -0.37 + 0.00002 \times PGNP$$
$$r = 0.017$$
$$r^2 = 0.0003$$

States with PGNP greater than $500

$$USUN = -0.40 + 0.00026 \times PGNP$$
$$r = 0.61$$
$$r^2 = 0.37$$

tion analyses, the same variable is used (nominally scaled) as a control and (intervally scaled) as the independent variable.

These figures raise several questions of interpretation: How well does the fifteen-nation sample represent the whole data set for the various analyses? Does controlling for wealth make a difference in the tendency

TABLE VI-9

Relationship between Character of Regime and Alliance
with the United States for Subsets of 114-Nation Sample

Alliance	Regime		Row totals
	Civilian	Military	
	States with PGNP less than or equal to $500		
With U.S.	13	17	30
Not with U.S.	34	18	52
$\lambda = 0$			
	States with PGNP greater than $500		
With U.S.	18	4	22
Not with U.S.	9	0	9
$\lambda = 0$			

for certain regime types to be allied with the United States? Does it
make a difference with respect to U.N. voting support of the United
States?

This discussion represents only a rapid overview of a few ways the
student can extract information about the world of foreign policy and
international relations from the data provided. It should be quite clear
from the comments made throughout the foregoing discussion that the
suggested modes of analysis are only the beginning. Whether the
student is confined to completing the work by hand or has the use of an
electronic computer, there is a vast, unexplored realm represented by
these materials.

Data for the Comparative Study of Foreign Policy

This section consists of four parts:

1. A Country Code Key listing all of the countries, along with their
   number codes and abbreviated name designations.
2. A description of the data, including source and mode of operationalization.
3. A Codebook for the Data Listing describing the modes so that the
   reader can translate the numbers in the listing into information.
4. A Listing of Comparative Foreign Policy Data, organized in the
   manner described in the Codebook.

Country Code Key

Num	Name	Country	Num	Name	Country
002	USA	United States of America	290	POLA	Poland
			305	AUST	Austria
020	CANA	Canada	310	HUNG	Hungary
040	CUBA	Cuba	315	CZEC	Czechoslovakia
041	HAIT	Haiti	325	ITAL	Italy
042	DOMI	Dominican Republic	339	ALBA	Albania
051	JAMA	Jamaica	345	YUGO	Yugoslavia
052	TRIN	Trinidad and Tobago	350	GREE	Greece
			352	CYPR	Cyprus
070	MEXI	Mexico	355	BULG	Bulgaria
090	GUAT	Guatemala	360	RUMA	Rumania
091	HOND	Honduras	365	USSR	Union of Soviet Socialist Republics
092	EL S	El Salvador			
093	NICA	Nicaragua	375	FINL	Finland
094	COST	Costa Rica	380	SWED	Sweden
095	PANA	Panama	385	NORW	Norway
100	COLO	Colombia	390	DENM	Denmark
101	VENE	Venezuela	395	ICEL	Iceland
130	ECUA	Ecuador	432	MALI	Mali
135	PERU	Peru	433	SENE	Senegal
140	BRAZ	Brazil	434	DAHO	Dahomey
145	BOLI	Bolivia	435	MAUR	Mauritania
150	PARA	Paraguay	436	NIGE	Niger
155	CHIL	Chile	437	IVOR	Ivory Coast
160	ARGE	Argentina	438	GUIN	Guinea
165	URUG	Uruguay	439	UPPE	Upper Volta
200	UK	United Kingdom	450	LIBE	Liberia
205	IREL	Ireland	451	SIER	Sierra Leone
210	NETH	Netherlands	452	GHAN	Ghana
211	BELG	Belgium	461	TOGO	Togo
212	LUXE	Luxembourg	471	CAME	Cameroon
220	FRAN	France	475	NGRA	Nigeria
225	SWIT	Switzerland	481	GABO	Gabon
230	SPAI	Spain	482	CENT	Central African Republic
235	PORT	Portugal			
255	W GR	West Germany	483	CHAD	Chad
265	E GR	East Germany	484	CONB	Congo (Brazzaville)
			490	CONK	Congo (Kinshasa)

Num	Name	Country	Num	Name	Country
500	UGAN	Uganda	670	SAUD	Saudi Arabia
501	KENY	Kenya	678	YEME	Yemen
510	TANZ	Tanzania	700	AFGH	Afghanistan
516	BURU	Burundi	710	CPR	Chinese People's
517	RWAN	Rwanda			Republic
520	SOMA	Somalia	713	TAIW	Republic of China
530	ETHI	Ethiopia	732	S KR	Republic of Korea
560	S AF	South Africa	740	JAPA	Japan
580	MLGY	Malagasy	750	INDI	India
600	MORO	Morocco	770	PAKI	Pakistan
615	ALGE	Algeria	775	BURM	Burma
616	TUNI	Tunisia	780	CEYL	Ceylon
620	LIBY	Libya	790	NEPA	Nepal
625	SUDA	Sudan	800	THAI	Thailand
630	IRAN	Iran	811	CAMB	Cambodia
640	TURK	Turkey	812	LAOS	Laos
645	IRAQ	Iraq	817	S VN	Republic of Vietnam
651	UAR	United Arab	820	MALA	Malaysia
		Republic	840	PHIL	Philippines
652	SYRI	Syria	850	INDO	Indonesia
660	LEBA	Lebanon	900	ASTL	Australia
663	JORD	Jordan	920	NEWZ	New Zealand
666	ISRA	Israel			

Description of the Data

VARIABLE

1 Country Code Number

Number used as world region indicator:
000–099	North and Central America
100–199	South America
200–399	Europe
400–599	Africa
600–699	Middle East
700–899	Asia
900–999	Oceania

Source: Russett, Singer, and Small 1968.

2 Country Name

Source: Clark, O'Leary, and Wittkopf 1971.

VARIABLE

3   Character of Regime
Nominal Scaling Code:
    0   Civilian
    1   Military
    9   Unclassified
Sources: Council on Foreign Relations 1968; Putnam 1967.

4   Type of Political System
Nominal Scaling Code:
    0   Open
    1   Closed
Source: Rosenau and Hoggard 1974.

5   Military Expenditure
    Data in millions of U.S. dollars (for 1968). The number 99999
    indicates data not available.
    Source: United States Arms Control and Disarmament Agency
    1970.

6   Average Size of Diplomatic Mission
    Data in number of diplomatic employees.
    Source: Alger and Brams 1967.

7   Population
    Data in thousands of people (for 1966).
    Source: Statistical Office of the United Nations 1968.

8   Gross National Product
    Data in millions of U.S. dollars (for 1966).
    Source: United States Arms Control and Disarmament Agency
    1970.

9   Level of Civil Strife
    Figures are frequencies of internal unrest weighted for their
    severity, magnitude, and scope (for 1961–65). The number 999.
    indicates data not available.
    Source: Gurr 1969.

VARIABLE

10   Sociocultural Classification

Nominal Scaling Code:
  1   Afro-Asia
  2   Western community
  3   Latin America
  4   Semideveloped Latins
  5   Eastern Europe
  9   Unclassifiable
Source: Russett 1967.

11   Alliance Bloc Membership

Nominal Scaling Code:
  1   Western bloc
  2   Communist bloc
  3   Neutral bloc
  9   Unclassified
Source: Burton 1965.

12–21   Number of Cooperative and Conflict Acts Received

Variables coded from the World Event/Interaction Survey (WEIS) of the University of Southern California. The data were aggregated over the period of January 1966 to August 1969.

22   Number of Contiguous Countries

Data in number of countries.
Source: Council on Foreign Relations 1968.

23–32   Number of Cooperative and Conflict Acts Sent

Variables coded from the World Event/Interaction Survey (WEIS). The data were aggregated over the period of January 1966 to August 1969.

33–35   Voting Agreement

Data represent relative voting agreement during the 1963 United Nations General Assembly. The figures are percentages: a positive number indicates the percentage of votes agreeing with the country in question (the United States, the Soviet Union, or

VARIABLE

India) above an average, or expected agreement, figure. A negative number indicates the percentage of agreeing votes below the expected figure. The number 99. indicates data not available.
Source: Brams and O'Leary 1970, 1971.

36 Degree of Support for the United Nations

Figures are percentages based on voting in the 1963 United Nations General Assembly. They represent relative voting support for resolutions strengthening the United Nations. The positive sign represents support above an average expected level; the negative sign indicates support below an average expected level. The number 9999. indicates data not available.
Source: Clark, O'Leary, and Wittkopf 1971.

37 Level of Trade

Data represent combined exports and imports in millions of U.S. dollars. The number 9999 indicates data not available.
Source: Statistical Office of the United Nations 1967.

38 Degree of Support for International Law

Data represent an index based on the number and manner of introduction of cases before the Permanent Court of International Justice and the International Court of Justice. The index ranges from 0.0 (no participation) to 3.0 (meaningful, active participation).
Source: Rochester 1971.

Codebook for the Data Listing

Card One

Column	Variable	Variable Number
1–3	Country code number	1
4–7	Country name	2
8	*1* (first card designator)	
9	Character of regime	3
10	Type of political system	4
11–15	Military expenditure	5
16–17	Average size of diplomatic mission	6
18–23	Population	7
24–29	Gross national product	8
30–33	Level of civil strife	9
35	Sociocultural classification	10
36	Alliance bloc membership	11
38–41	No. of cooperative acts received, total	12
42–45	No. of conflict acts received, total	13
46–49	No. of cooperative acts received from U.S.	14
50–53	No. of conflict acts received from U.S.	15
54–57	No. of cooperative acts received from U.S.S.R.	16
58–61	No. of conflict acts received from U.S.S.R.	17
62–65	No. of cooperative acts received from region	18
66–69	No. of conflict acts received from region	19
70–73	No. of cooperative acts received from outside region	20
74–77	No. of conflict acts received from outside region	21
79–80	No. of contiguous countries	22

Card Two

Column	Variable	Variable Number
1–3	Country code number	1
4–7	Country name	2
8	2 (second card designator)	
10–13	No. of cooperative acts sent, total	23
14–17	No. of conflict acts sent, total	24
18–21	No. of cooperative acts sent to U.S.	25
22–25	No. of conflict acts sent to U.S.	26
26–29	No. of cooperative acts sent to U.S.S.R.	27
30–33	No. of conflict acts sent to U.S.S.R.	28
34–37	No. of cooperative acts sent to region	29
38–41	No. of conflict acts sent to region	30
42–45	No. of cooperative acts sent outside region	31
46–49	No. of conflict acts sent outside region	32
51–54	Voting agreement with U.S.	33
55–58	Voting agreement with U.S.S.R.	34
59–62	Voting agreement with India	35
64–68	Degree of support for U.N.	36
70–74	Level of trade	37
76–78	Degree of support for international law	38

```
  1    2 34  5 6    7       8      9 11    1 2  1 3 1 4 1 5 1 6 1 7 1 8 1 9 2 0 2 1 2 2
                               01

002USA 100  8080596928196920749900010.2 21 1719 1553  0   0  175 247 105 6516 14 1488  2  2
020CANA 100 1783 7 20050  533001  3.1  21  109   28  30   5   10   9  30   6  79  22   2
040CUBA 101  300 5  7833  35001   5.2  42   57   31  13  11   13   1  15  12  42  19   3  2
041HAIT 111    7 2  4485    334   7.8  91    4    6   2   1    0   0   2   3   2   3   1  2
042DMOI 110   30 4  3754  10122   1.9  31   15    3  10   2    0   0  10   2   5   1   1  2
051JAMA 100    5 6  1839    946   1.5  91    6    1   1   0    0   0   3   1   4   0   1  1
052TRIN 100    3 4  1000  672999   .7  21    7    0   2   0    1   0  25   3   7   0   3
070MEXI 100  184 4 44145  21768   4.7  31   32    4  21   3    0   0   0   7   4   1   3
090GUAT 110   16 3  4575 137514.5 31    10    21   5   0        18   4   1   4
091HOND 110    9 3  2363    545   8.3  31   11   20   3   1    0   0   5  17   3   3  3
092EL S 110   10 4  3037    837   5.4  31    8   20   5   1    0   0   6   2   0   1  2
093NICA 110   10 4  1715    600   9.4  31    6    0   4   0    0   0   6   7   2   1  2
094COST 100 9999 4  1486    624   2.7  31    8    3   4   3    0   0   5   0   7   0  2
095PANA 110    1 3  1287    698   9.5  31    7    8   5   1    0   0   8   2   4   0  4
100COLO 100   98 4 18596  427016.9 31   23    1   6   1    2   0   9   7  15   0  4
101VENE 110  194 4  8921  793520.3 31   16    7   4   1    1   0  11   4   7   1  2
130ECUA 110   26 4  5326  123810.1 31    8    2   6   0    0   0   5   0  35   3  5
135PERU 110  132 4 12012  499612.3 31   46    0  20   9    6   0   8   1  51   2 10
140BRAZ 110  651 5 83175  23975   7.4  31   56    1  21   1    0   0  14  10   5   1  5
145BOLI 110   17 3  3748  66115.2 31    13    4   5   2    0   0   8   3   3   6  3
150PARA 110   10 3  2094    460   5.0  31    4    0   5   0    0   0   4  10  12   0  5
155CHIL 100  127 4  8750   6139   4.9  41   16    9   5   3    1   1   5   3  15   0  3
160ARGE 110  380 5 22691 1932013.2 21   20   14   8   0    1   0  79  10   6   4  5
165URUG 100   23 3  2749   1455   6.2  41    7    2   4   3   38   0   2  53 350 277  2
200UK  100 554515 54744 105300   5.9  21  429  330  69  11    0  30  79   5   1   1  2
205IREL 100   27 3  2884   2900   2.3  21    3    6   0   0    1   0   2   2  15  12  2
210NETH 100  906 5 12455  20800   0.0  21   20   14   5   0        1   5   2
```

1 2 34	5	6	7	8	9	11	01	12	13	14	15	16	17	18	19	20	21	22
211BELGI100	602	4	9528	18100	10.5	2	1	24	8	5	0	3	0	6	1	18	7	4
212LUXE100	8	2	335	700	999.	2	1	5	0	0	0	0	0	4	0	1	0	3
220FRAN100	61181	2	49400	101400	12.1	2	1	320	126	64	18	36	10	84	29	236	97	6
225SWIT100	365	3	5999	15000	1.2	2	3	26	5	7	0	2	1	1	0	25	5	4
230SPAI111	913	5	31871	24600	5.2	4	1	58	23	19	1	5	0	12	13	46	10	2
235PORT101	359	3	9335	4100	9.3	4	1	25	23	5	1	0	0	10	1	15	22	1
255W GR100	5278	8	57485	119600	4.6	2	1	307	163	83	7	32	51	116	75	191	88	7
265E GR101	14501	0	15988	27200	5.5	5	2	81	71	3	16	17	0	35	33	46	38	3
290POLA101	359	7	31698	31500	3.3	5	2	67	28	11	10	12	0	18	6	49	22	3
305AUST100	150	5	7290	10000	3.1	2	3	27	7	4	0	7	5	18	6	9	1	6
310HUNG101	340	6	10179	11700	2.8	5	2	34	10	7	1	9	0	21	4	13	6	5
315CZEC101	1360	7	14240	24300	5.3	5	2	186	148	10	9	83	77	123	91	63	57	4
325ITAL100	2245	6	51962	61400	12.3	2	1	66	23	12	3	8	1	25	8	41	15	2
339ALBA101	76	4	1914	700	0.0	5	2	21	6	2	0	2	3	6	2	15	4	6
345YUGO101	456	5	19735	9000	3.3	5	3	114	27	22	4	7	3	47	10	67	17	4
350GREE111	367	5	8614	67000	11.6	2	1	64	48	13	11	1	1	33	13	31	35	1
352CYPR101	6	5	603	44000	999.	2	3	30	10	3	0	0	0	26	5	4	5	4
355BULG101	300	5	8257	7500	3.9	5	2	18	15	2	4	3	0	9	7	9	8	4
360RUMA101	700	9	19143	17200	0.0	5	2	101	24	16	2	12	8	38	12	63	12	4
365USSR101	55000	2	1233105	347000	3.6	5	2	876	616	225	129	2	0	175	105	701	511	12
375FINL100	156	3	4639	8600	2.1	2	3	23	2	3	0	12	2	14	2	9	9	3
380SWED100	977	4	7808	21300	0.0	2	3	28	10	4	5	5	1	8	1	20	6	2
385NORW100	322	4	3753	7600	0.0	2	1	12	7	2	2	7	1	3	1	9	2	3
390DENM100	345	4	4797	11100	0.0	2	1	17	7	1	1	1	1	2	5	15	0	1
395ICEL100	9999	2	196	600	999.	2	1	4	0	0	0	0	0	3	0	1	0	0
432MALI101	5	3	4654	240	8.3	1	3	4	0	4	0	0	0	1	0	3	0	7
433SENE101	15	3	3580	716	5.1	1	3	6	0	0	0	0	0	0	0	6	0	5

1	5	6	7	8	9	11	12	13	14	15	16	17	18	19	20	21	22
434DAHO111	4	2	2410	170	7.8	13	4	0	1	0	0	0	0	0	4	0	4
435MAUR101	8	2	1070	145	999*	13	3	0	3	1	0	0	0	0	3	1	4
436NIGE101	3	2	3433	270	5.8	13	4	2	2	0	2	0	0	2	4	0	7
437IVOR101	17	3	3920	1020	1.8	13	8	16	2	0	0	0	3	0	5	0	5
438GUIN111	14	4	3608	290	9.5	13	21	0	0	6	2	0	7	0	4	6	6
439UPPE111	5	3	4955	250	0.6	13	3	2	2	0	0	0	1	0	3	0	6
450LIBE100	3	2	1090	226	6.6	13	6	9	0	0	0	1	0	0	0	2	3
451SIER110	3	4	2403	370	6.5	13	3	10	3	0	0	0	0	1	3	8	2
452GHAN111	44	5	7945	1743	7.9	13	36	58	13	2	4	0	5	1	1	0	3
461TOGO101	3	3	1680	190	4.1	13	4	0	0	0	0	0	2	0	1	0	3
471CAME101	19	4	5350	720	13.1	13	95	5	1	0	0	0	0	5	6	15	6
475NGRA111	91	6	58600	5450	13.8	13	2	3	12	3	8	0	9	3	4	0	5
481GABO101	3	2	468	150	999*	13	3	29	1	0	0	0	29	0	7	0	8
482CENT111	3	2	1437	183	1.3	13	7	2	0	0	0	0	1	4	3	1	5
483CHAD101	8	3	3361	250	7.2	13	8	25	2	0	0	0	3	0	7	25	5
484CONB101	6	2	850	140	999*	13	35	30	0	0	1	0	1	0	2	2	8
490CONK111	44	5	15986	1300	48.7	13	10	9	8	4	5	0	2	1	4	2	5
500UGAN100	16	3	7740	910	15.6	13	28	17	1	0	0	0	6	0	0	4	5
501KENY100	15	3	9643	2260	15.0	13	6	2	3	1	0	0	6	0	4	0	5
510TANZ100	13	3	11833	860	6.2	13	12	6	2	1	2	0	2	2	19	0	7
516BURU111	9999	2	3274	1920	10.9	13	42		0	2	0	0	1	1	14	3	3
517RWAN101	9999	2	3204	1830	28.2	13	24		2	0	0	0	5	2	41	8	4
520SOMA100	8	4	2580	155	7.9	13	1	5	4	0	3	0	0	0	19	15	2
530ETHI111	41	3	23000	1484	13.2	13	26	9	12	0	2	0		3	14	2	3
560S AF100	356	9	18298	11960	10.0	91	24	17	3	4	0	0	12		44	3	6
580MLGY190	13	5	6200	665	999*	19	1	2	0	0	0	0	18	3		7	1
600MORO100	76	4	13725	2475	6.7	13	26	6	7	0	2	0		3	14	3	3
615ALGE111	100	4	12150	2662	19.5	13	62	10	11	1	13	0		3	44	2	6

Code	5	6	7	8	9	01/11	12	13	14	15	16	17	18	19	20	21	22
616TUNI1100	14	4	4460	9391	1.8	13	23	4	6	0	1	0	4	3	19	1	2
620LIBY101	37	4	1677	1300	6.3	13	9	0	4	0	0	0	1	0	8	0	5
625SUDA101	74	0	13940	1457	20.2	13	19	7	2	3	1	1	9	0	10	7	8
630IRAN101	530	7	25283	6423	8.4	11	66	9	17	1	8	2	16	7	50	2	5
640TURK110	573	7	31910	9400	5.0	11	65	11	14	0	5	0	10	0	55	11	6
645IRAQ111	280	5	8338	2235	20.5	13	60	27	2	8	11	1	26	16	34	11	6
651UAR 111	666	8	30147	5075	3.9	13	263	231	34	17	58	0	103	199	160	32	3
652SYRI111	137	5	5400	1101	17.8	13	96	106	2	1	16	1	50	95	46	11	4
660LEBA100	45	2	2460	1250	5.8	13	25	21	3	0	2	0	9	20	16	1	2
663JORD101	105	4	2059	520	8.1	11	143	238	28	2	6	1	70	230	73	8	4
666ISRA100	672	5	2629	3822	14.0	21	239	728	65	0	8	41	45	569	194	159	4
670SAUD101	383	5	6870	1670	1.1	13	45	29	6	1	0	1	34	27	11	2	8
678YEME111	14	3	5000	5152	3.6	13	29	20	4	7	6	0	15	8	14	12	2
700AFGH101	16	4	15397	1355	2.0	13	10	0	3	0	2	8	3	0	7	0	4
710CPR 111	7500	10	710000	80000	5.7	92	209	317	36	14	25	138	45	71	173	272	11
713TAIW111	425	6	12791	3138	0.0	11	30	8	19	0	0	0	5	6	25	2	1
732S KR101	235	6	29086	3822	10.2	11	76	62	46	4	1	9	11	54	65	8	1
740JAPA100	1146	9	98865	97480	5.9	21	118	32	48	8	21	2	16	13	102	19	6
750INDI100	1603	7	7498680	37375	11.0	13	185	70	63	6	28	0	36	54	149	16	4
770PAKI111	518	4	4105004	13014	6.3	11	136	21	30	2	19	0	54	18	82	3	4
775BURM111	107	3	311491	1740	13.9	13	25	18	2	0	1	0	14	18	11	0	1
780CEYL100	13	3	11491	1750	8.2	13	19	0	6	0	2	0	1	0	18	0	3
790NEPA101	53	3	10294	772	10.3	13	12	3	3	0	0	1	3	3	9	3	3
800THAI101	157	7	31508	4654	10.3	11	61	21	31	0	3	1	17	18	44	12	3
811CAMB101	65	4	6320	875	3.8	13	60	20	33	9	2	0	11	8	49	2	5
812LAOS101	34	4	2700	1899	99.8	13	36	28	10	1	0	1	12	6	24	21	3
817S VN111	613	5	16543	20863	2.8	11	207	89	113	7	5	0	39	68	168	21	2
820MALA100	108	5	9725	3056	4.5	11	80	10	4	0	0	0	53	9	27	1	2

```
 1   2 34     5 6       7       8    9 11    1    1    1    1    1    1    1    1    2    2   2
                                       01    2    3    4    5    6    7    8    9    0    1   2

840PHIL100   116 6 33477    5728 8.3 31     60   15   26    3    1    0   27   12   33    3   1
850INDO111   313 7107000    900033.7 13     77   42   15   -4    3    2   36    4   41   38   1
900ASTL100   968 8 11541  25100 2.6 21      55    4   28    0    1    0    2    0   53    4   1
920NEWZ100    86 8   2676   5500 0.0 21     11    1    4    0    0    0    2    0    9    1   1
```

```
 1    2        2    2    2    2    2    2    2    3    3    3     3    3    3       3       3   3
               3    4    5    6    7    8    9    0    1    2     3    4    5       6       7   8

002USA 2 2477 605    0    0  166  105   75   152402  590   .62-.70-.40  -.176  55458 2.7
020CANA2  186 150   11   33    6    8   26   12  124   24   .22-.66-.17   .081  18867 0.0
040CUBA2   71  69    9    1    1    0   16   36   55   33 -.69 .61 .04  -.713   1451 0.0
041HAIT2    6   6    4    1    0    0    2    1    4    5 -.31-.21 .16   .104     72 0.0
042DOMI2    9   7    0    0    1    0    6    4    3    3  99. 99. 99.   .261    298 0.0
051JAMA2    2   0    0    0    0    0    0    0    2    0 -.12-.21 .24  9999.    550 0.0
052TRIN2    2   2    0    2    0    0    0    0    2    0 -.35-.25 .19  9999.    882 0.0
070MEXI2   26   4    1    2    0    0   16    3   10    1 -.15-.26 .22   .184   2878 0.0
090GUAT2    4   4    2    1    0    0    3    2    1    2 -.15-.42 .11   .317    435 1.0
091HOND2    2   1    0    1    0    0    2    0    0    0  99. 99. 99.   .312    294 3.0
092EL S2    2   2    2    2    0    0    2    2    0    0  .11-.54 .21   .299    409 0.0
093NICA2    3   3    1    3    0    0    1    1    2    0  .15-.46 .11   .233    319 1.5
094COST2    7   4    2    4    0    0    4    1    3    0 -.12-.30 .23   .347    317 0.0
095PANA2    7   8    2    6    1    2    4    3    3    1 -.18-.30 .05  -.124    304 0.0
100COLO2   30   7    2    1    0    0    9    0   21    7 -.20-.31 .10  -.010   1182 2.0
101VENE2   18  10    3    0    1    0    5    3   13    7 -.16-.27 .13   .184   3901 0.0
130ECUA2   10   8    1    5    0    2    0    0   10    8 -.09-.36 .17   .226    296 0.0
```

2	23	24	25	26	27	28	29	30	31	32	33	34	35	36	37	38
135PERU2	19	10	8	7	1	2	9	0	10	10	-.16	-.37	.04	-.124	1581	2.0
140BRAZ2	42	20	6	3	15	0	3	0	39	20	-.13	-.03	.06	.030	3237	2.0
145BOLI2	25	2	0	1	0	0	0	0	15	2	-.21	-.27	.28	.286	264	0.0
150PARA2	5	2	3	2	0	0	2	0	3	1	-.12	-.54	.17	-.108	99	0.0
155CHIL2	29	11	5	4	0	0	5	3	24	8	-.15	-.26	.31	.287	1633	1.0
160ARGE2	18	17	3	2	0	2	3	5	15	12	-.13	-.39	.10	.184	2717	0.0
165URUG2	9	5	0	2	1	0	3	6	6	5	-.27	-.12	.29	-.299	350	0.0
200UK 2	550	170	5	2	12	0	54	31	496	139	-.37	-.77	-.42	-.176	30239	2.4
205IREL2	7	4	5	0	5	1	1	3	6	1	-.10	-.49	-.03	.081	1725	0.7
210NETH2	25	22	0	5	2	1	10	6	21	16	-.27	-.66	-.15	.247	14768	2.7
211BELG2	46	28	5	5	1	1	4	2	36	26	-.31	-.07	-.26	.030	7002	2.4
212LUXE2	5	0	0	0	0	0	1	0	1	0	-.33	-.69	-.18	.249	7001	0.0
220FRAN2	409	113	46	26	38	11	62	27	347	86	-.12	-.60	-.63	-.639	22732	2.4
225SWIT2	29	4	7	1	1	1	3	1	26	3	99.99	99.99	99.99	9999.	7217	0.0
230SPAI2	54	40	17	12	3	2	12	22	40	18	-.03	-.64	-.21	-.030	4826	1.8
235PORT2	39	33	2	2	0	1	9	6	30	27	-.15	-.81	-.63	-.500	1643	3.0
255W GR2	434	88	63	15	24	28	101	23	333	65	99.99	99.99	99.99	9999.	38870	0.0
265E GR2	99	93	8	8	9	1	33	47	66	46	-.69	-.63	.02	-.742	6476	1.1
290POLA2	90	77	11	22	14	1	12	9	78	68	-.04	-.05	-.07	.030	4766	0.7
305AUST2	35	3	2	13	14	5	14	2	21	1	-.69	-.61	.02	-.742	4012	1.7
310HUNG2	46	26	4	11	10	27	21	7	25	19	-.69	-.63	.02	-.742	3162	1.0
315CZEC2	202	84	13	15	58	27	97	39	105	45	-.28	-.57	-.14	-.742	5474	2.5
325ITAL2	90	33	13	6	7	8	28	16	62	17	-.67	-.50	.21	-.133	16603	1.0
339ALBA2	18	24	0	5	0	12	6	15	12	9	-.56	-.14	-.37	-.334	158	1.5
345YUGO2	148	41	23	6	8	9	49	20	99	21	-.20	-.53	-.13	-.030	2795	1.1
350GREE2	72	37	14	8	0	1	27	10	45	27	-.27	-.23	.31	-.099	1629	2.3
352CYPR2	33	7	1	0	0	1	20	3	13	4	-.27	-.23	.31	-.280	232	0.0

1 2	2 3	2 4	2 5	2 6	2 7	2 8	2 9	3 0	3 1	3 2	3 3	3 4	3 5	3 6	3 7	3 8
355BULG2	28	20	4	5	5	0	11	7	17	13	.69	.62	.02	-.734	2779	1.5
360RUMA2	121	31	.10	2	11	10	45	17	76	14	.65	.56	.06	-.691	2399	0.0
365USSR2	974	620	117	221		0	171	116	803	504	.70	.63	.01	-.783	16754	0.0
375FINL2	20	1	2	1	10	0	10	0	9	1	-.03	-.51	.09	.124	3232	0.5
380SWED2	59	13	16	5	8	1	17	4	42	9	-.02	-.51	.03	.030	8840	1.5
385NORW2	17	8	3	4	2	1	9	5	8	4	-.06	-.49	.03	.030	3966	1.5
390DENM2	33	10	5	3	1	0	13	1	20	5	-.11	-.51	.07	.059	5456	3.0
395ICEL2	3		1	0	0	0	1	0	2	0	.68	.54	.15	-.285	300	0.0
432MALI2	10	3	0	0	0	0	0	0	9	3	-.40	-.10	.16	.045	49	0.0
433SENE2	14	1	4	2	0	0	0	0	14	1	-.54	-.11	.29	.359	310	0.0
434DAHO2	4		0	0	0	0	0	0	4	1	-.39	-.13	.35	.093	45	0.0
435MAUR2	9	3	1	2	0	0	2	3	9	1	-.39	-.06	.26	.302	62	0.0
436NIGF2	5	2	2	0	0	0	4	2	2	2	-.35	-.11	.29	.236	80	0.0
437IVOR2	21	0	2	6	1	0	2	0	3	0	-.50	-.03	.24	-.017	567	0.0
438GUIN2	11	4	3	0	0	0	2	3	17	11	-.51	-.18	.28	-.267	111	0.0
439UPPE2	3	3	0	0	0	0	1	2	1	0	-.20	-.12	.27	.290	54	0.0
450LIRE2	40	1	2	0	2	0	6	7	9	1	-.50	-.27	.31	.262	265	0.0
451SIER2	2		0	0	0	0	2	1	2	2	-.49	.06	.28	.099	183	0.0
452GHAN2	1	20	8	0	0	0	0	0	34	13	-.43	-.15	.39	.263	596	0.0
461TOGO2	85	1	0	0	3	0	30	35	0	0	-.38	-.23	.31	.339	82	3.0
471CAME2	2	0	1	9	0	5	1	2	1	0	-.48	-.16	.29	.133	291	0.0
475NGRA2	85	67	3	0	0	0	2	2	55	32	-.40	-.17	.36	.273	1510	0.0
481GABO2	2	2	1	0	0	0	2	2	1	0	-.37	-.15	.30	.336	166	0.0
482CENT2	2	3	0	0	0	0	0	1	3	1	-.39	-.08	.24	.350	66	0.0
483CHAD2	5	4	1	0	0	0	4	5	2	2	-.48	-.12	.37	.277	56	0.0
484CONB2	2	6	0	2	0	1	0	0	36	5	-.37	-.14	.32	.194	113	0.0
490CONK2	40	26	3		2	0	4	5	36	21			.24		739	0.0

12	23	24	25	26	27	28	29	30	31	32	33	34	35	36	37	38
500UGAN2	13	5	1	0	0	0	5	1	8	4	-.64	.03	.28	9999.	307	0.0
501KENY2	22	20	2	2	1	3	9	2	13	18	99.	99.	99.	9999.	488	0.0
510TANZ2	27	12	3	3	1	1	6	3	21	9	-.54	-.12	.41	.191	440	0.0
516BURU2	9	2	1	1	0	0	2	0	7	2	-.69	.07	.26	9999.	9999.	0.0
517RWAN2	4	0	0	0	0	0	2	0	2	0	-.32	-.25	.24	9999.	9999.	0.0
520SOMA2	14	8	3	1	1	0	3	2	12	6	-.56	-.02	.36	.069	75	0.0
530ETHI2	39	6	6	0	2	0	3	1	36	5	-.54	-.03	.27	-.100	264	0.0
560S AF2	37	38	2	4	0	0	8	2	29	36	-.15	-.96	.67	-.366	3984	0.0
580MLGY2	3	0	0	0	0	2	0	0	3	0	-.26	-.26	.25	-.307	240	0.0
600MORO2	26	4	5	0	1	0	12	1	14	3	.57	.09	.27	-.052	906	0.0
615ALGE2	63	47	4	3	5	1	16	5	47	42	-.61	.12	.20	9999.	1430	0.0
616TUNI2	25	13	6	2	0	1	4	7	21	6	-.47	-.00	.32	-.066	389	0.0
620LIBY2	11	2	2	1	0	1	2	1	9	1	-.44	-.12	.28	-.286	1400	0.0
625SUDA2	21	12	1	2	0	0	10	1	11	1	-.45	-.03	.24	-.140	422	0.0
630IRAN2	56	4	1	0	3	0	12	3	44	28	.17	-.26	.19	.318	9999.	1.5
640TURK2	73	28	1	0	4	2	6	0	67	21	.21	-.55	.08	.236	1216	2.0
645IRAQ2	75	32	9	0	7	1	32	11	43	114	-.66	.06	.29	-.176	1428	0.0
651UAR 2	311	258	33	60	31	1	73	144	238	50	-.61	.01	.28	-.176	1674	1.5
652SYRI2	114	138	4	23	14	0	36	88	78	12	-.56	.07	.33	-.161	460	0.0
660LEBA2	21	25	2	5	1	0	7	13	14	30	-.40	-.11	.24	-.077	636	1.5
663JORD2	175	192	15	6	2	2	46	162	129	112	-.50	-.12	.19	-.166	223	0.0
666ISRA2	409	422	35	11	8	15	50	310	359	8	-.16	-.27	.15	-.184	1288	3.0
670SAUD2	56	19	6	2	2	2	31	11	25	15	.63	-.18	.10	-.084	9999.	0.0
678YEME2	26	20	3	0	0	1	9	5	17	0	-.66	.14	.29	-.132	9999.	0.0
700AFGH2	8	0	3	10	1	0	3	1	5	415	-.50	.04	.31	-.081	9999.	0.0
710CPR 2	238	486	14	136	9	127	35	71	203	6	99.	99.	99.	99.	9999.	0.0
713TAIW2	20	10	5	1	0	0	4	4	16	6	-.01	-.39	.11	-.239	1159	0.0

1	2	23	24	25	26	27	28	29	30	31	32	33	34	35	36	37	38
	732S KR2	88	74	34	8	0	0	5	62	83	12	99.	99.	99.	9999.	966	0.0
	740JAPA2	162	33	33	16	19	3	17	6	145	27	-.10	-.51	-.05	.184	19301	0.0
	750INDI2	180	95	31	27	20	6	32	46	148	49	-.40	-.01	.62	.287	4429	1.0
	770PAKI2	115	25	15	3	8	0	36	16	79	9	-.29	-.19	.32	.331	1501	0.0
	775BURM2	17	4	1	0	0	0	9	4	8	0	-.58	-.17	.13	.176	350	0.0
	780CEYL2	16	4	1	1	2	0	3	0	13	4	-.43	-.00	.31	.073	783	0.0
	790NEPA2	7	1	2	1	0	0	1	0	6	1	-.50	-.21	.26	—	9999.	0.0
	800THAI2	82	23	20	2	0	2	22	9	60	14	-.16	-.23	.32	.051	1860	1.0
	811CAMB2	94	91	26	58	1	0	13	24	81	67	-.48	-.04	.27	.285	178	3.0
	812LAOS2	44	20	7	2	0	0	4	16	40	4	-.48	-.20	.32	.159	44	0.0
	817S VN2	201	64	59	21	0	1	31	21	170	43	99.	99.	99.	9999.	393	0.0
	820MALA2	65	15	5	1	4	0	41	14	24	1	-.18	-.23	.31	.287	2431	0.0
	840PHIL2	100	19	19	6	0	1	38	3	62	16	-.18	-.27	.18	.099	1795	0.0
	850INDO2	104	28	12	4	3	1	47	6	57	22	-.50	-.12	.41	9999.	1262	0.0
	900ASTL2	74	14	18	1	1	0	19	3	55	11	-.26	-.68	.27	.073	6271	0.0
	920NEWZ2	29	7	6	1	0	1	13	1	16	6	-.22	-.58	.25	.124	2179	0.0

Bibliography

Alcock, N. Z. 1972. *The War Disease*. Oakville, Ont.: Canadian Peace Research Institute.

Alger, C. F. 1968. "Interaction in a committee of the United Nations General Assembly," pp. 51–84 in J. D. Singer, ed., *Quantitative International Politics*. New York: Free Press.

Alger, C. F., and S. J. Brams. 1967. "Patterns of representation in national capitals and intergovernmental organizations." *World Politics* 19 (July) :646–63.

Alker, H. R., Jr. 1969. "Dimensions of conflict in the General Assembly," pp. 142–69 in J. E. Mueller, ed., *Approaches to Measurement in International Relations*. New York: Appleton-Century-Crofts.

Alker, H. R., Jr., and B. M. Russett. 1965. *World Politics in the General Assembly*. New Haven, Conn.: Yale Univ. Press.

Alker, H. R., Jr., and R. C. Snyder. 1970. "A review of the Stanford studies in international conflict and integration." Stanford Center for International Studies, Stanford University (mimeo).

Allison, G. T. 1971. *Essence of Decision*. Boston: Little, Brown.

Almond, G. A. 1960. "A functional approach to comparative politics," pp. 3–64 in G. A. Almond and J. S. Coleman, eds., *The Politics of the Developing Areas*. Princeton: Princeton Univ. Press.

———. 1958. "Comparative study of foreign policy," pp. 1–8 in R. C. Macridis, ed., *Foreign Policy in World Politics*. Englewood Cliffs, N.J.: Prentice-Hall.

———. 1956. "Comparative political systems." *J. of Politics* 18 (August) :391–409.

———. 1950. *The American People and Foreign Policy*. New York: Harcourt, Brace.

Almond, G. A., and G. B. Powell, Jr. 1966. *Comparative Politics: A Developmental Approach*. Boston: Little, Brown.

Almond, G. A., and S. Verba. 1963. *The Civic Culture*. Princeton: Princeton Univ. Press.

Andrade, E. N. da C. 1957. *An Approach to Modern Physics*. Garden City, N.Y.: Anchor.

Angell, R. C.; V. S. Dunham; and J. D. Singer. 1964. "Social values and foreign policy attitudes of Soviet and American elites." *J. of Conflict Resolution* 8 (December) :329–491.

Anscombe, G. L. M. 1957. *Intention.* Oxford: Basil Blackwell.

Apter, D. E. 1965. *The Politics of Modernization.* Chicago: Univ. of Chicago Press.

Aron, R. 1966. *Peace and War.* Garden City, N.Y.: Doubleday.

Ashby, W. R. 1952. *Introduction to Cybernetics.* New York: Barnes and Noble.

Axline, W. A. N.d. "Common markets, free trade areas, and the comparative study of foreign policy" (mimeo).

Azar, E. E. 1973. "An early warning system of internation violence." Paper presented at the Conference on Forecasting in International Relations, Peace Research Society (International), Cambridge, Mass.

————. 1972. "Conflict escalation and conflict reduction in an international crisis: Suez, 1956." *J. of Conflict Resolution* 16 (June):183–201.

————. 1970a. "Analysis of international events." *Peace Research Reviews* 4 (November):1–106.

————. 1970b. "Profiling and predicting patterns of inter-nation interactions: a signal accounting model." Paper presented at the Annual Meeting of the American Political Science Association, Los Angeles.

Azar, E. E., and J. D. Ben-Dak, eds. 1974. *Theory and Practice of Events Research.* New York: Gordon and Breach, forthcoming.

Azar, E. E.; J. Bennett; and T. Sloan. 1973. "Steps toward forecasting models of international interaction." Paper presented at the North American Peace Science Conference, Peace Science Society (International), Cambridge, Mass.

Azar, E. E.; R. A. Brody; and C. A. McClelland, eds. 1972. *International Events Interaction Analysis: Some Research Considerations.* Beverly Hills: Sage.

Azar, E. E.; S. H. Cohen; T. O. Jukam; and J. M. McCormick. 1972a. "Making and measuring the international event as a unit of analysis," pp. 59–77 in E. E. Azar, R. A. Brody, and C. A. McClelland, *International Events Interaction Analysis.* Beverly Hills: Sage.

————. 1972b. "The problem of source coverage in the use of international events data." *International Studies Quarterly* 16 (September):373–88.

Bales, R. 1968. "Interaction process analysis," pp. 465–70 in D. Sills, ed., *The International Encyclopedia of the Social Sciences,* vol. 7. New York: MacMillan and Free Press.

————. 1950. *Interaction Process Analysis: A Method for the Study of Small Groups.* Reading, Mass.: Addison-Wesley.

Banks, A. S., and R. B. Textor. 1963. *A Cross-Polity Survey.* Cambridge: M.I.T. Press.

Barber, J. D. 1973. *The Presidential Character.* Englewood Cliffs, N.J.: Prentice-Hall.

Bauer, R. A. 1966. "Detection and anticipation of impact: the nature of the task," pp. 1–67 in R. A. Bauer, ed., *Social Indicators.* Cambridge: M.I.T. Press.

Bell, D. 1970. "Twelve modes of prediction—a preliminary sorting of approaches in the social sciences," pp. 378–408 in D. V. Edwards, ed., *International Political Analysis.* New York: Holt, Rinehart and Winston.

Bestuzhev-Lada, I. 1969. "Forecasting—an approach to the problems of the future." *International Social Science Journal* 21:526–34.

Blake, D. H. 1969. "The identification of foreign policy output." Paper presented at the Annual Meeting of the Midwest Political Science Association, Ann Arbor.

Blalock, H. M., Jr. 1972. *Social Statistics.* New York: McGraw-Hill.

———. 1971. *Causal Models in the Social Sciences.* New York: Aldine-Atherton.

———. 1969. *Theory Construction.* Englewood Cliffs, N.J.: Prentice-Hall.

———. 1964. *Causal Inferences in Non-experimental Research.* Chapel Hill: Univ. of North Carolina Press.

Blong, C. K. 1973*a.* "A comparative study of the foreign policy behavior of political systems exhibiting high versus low levels of external penetration." Ph.D. dissertation, University of Maryland.

———. 1973*b.* "Foreign policy behavior in penetrated political systems." Paper presented at the Annual Meeting of the International Studies Association, New York.

Bobrow, D. B. 1973. "Criteria for valid forecasting." Paper presented at the Conference on Forecasting in International Relations, Peace Research Society (International), Cambridge, Mass.

———. 1972*a. International Relations: New Approaches.* New York: Free Press.

———. 1972*b.* "The relevance potential of different products." *World Politics* 24 (supplement):204–28.

———. 1971. "Data banks, foreign affairs, and feasible change." Paper presented at the Conference on Data Banks for International Studies, Washington, D.C.

Brady, L. P. 1973. "The impact of situational variables on foreign policy." Paper presented at the Annual Meeting of the Midwest Political Science Association, Chicago.

Braithwaite, R. B. 1968. *Scientific Explanation.* London: Cambridge Univ. Press.

Brams, S. J., and M. K. O'Leary. 1971. "PROVOTE: A computer program for the probabilistic analysis of voting bodies." *Behavioral Science* 16 (May–June):261–63.

———. 1970. "An axiomatic model of voting bodies." *American Political Science Review* 64 (June):449–70.

Brecher, M. 1972. *The Foreign Policy System of Israel.* New Haven: Yale Univ. Press.

Brecht, A. 1959. *Political Theory.* Princeton: Princeton Univ. Press.

Bridgeman, P. W. 1927. *The Logic of Modern Physics.* New York: MacMillan.

Brody, R. A.; A. Benham; and J. S. Milstein. 1967. "Hostile international communication, arms production, and perceptions of threat." Peace Research Society (International) *Papers* 7:15–40.

Brown, R. 1963. *Explanation in Social Science.* Chicago: Aldine.

Brzezinski, Z., and S. P. Huntington. 1964. *Political Power: USA/USSR.* New York: Viking.

Buck, P. W., and M. Travis, Jr., eds. 1957. *Control of Foreign Relations in Modern Nations.* New York: Norton.

Burgess, P. M. 1970*a.* "The comparative analysis of policy environments: a report on the CAPE project." Behavioral Sciences Laboratory, Ohio State University (mimeo).

———. 1970*b.* "Nation-typing for foreign policy analysis: a partitioning procedure for constructing typologies," pp. 3–66 in E. H. Fedder, ed., *Methodological Concerns in International Studies.* St. Louis: Center for International Studies, University of Missouri–St. Louis.

Burgess, P. M., and R. W. Lawton. 1972. *Indicators of International Behavior: An Assessment of Events Data Research.* Beverly Hills: Sage.

Burns, A. L. 1968. *Of Powers and Their Politics.* Englewood Cliffs, N.J.: Prentice-Hall.

Burrowes, R. 1972. "Theory sí, data no!" a decade of cross-national research." *World Politics* 25 (October) :120–44.

Burrowes, R.; D. Muzzio; and B. Spector. 1974. "Mirror, mirror on the wall . . . : a source comparison study of internation events data," in J. N. Rosenau, ed., *Comparing Foreign Policies.* Beverly Hills: Sage, forthcoming.

———. 1971. "Sources of Middle East international event data." *Middle East Association Bulletin* 5 (May) :54:71.

Burrowes, R., and B. Spector. 1973. "The strength and direction of relationships between domestic and external conflict and cooperation," pp. 294–321 in J. Wilkenfeld, ed., *Conflict Behavior and Linkage Politics.* New York: David McKay.

———. 1970. "Conflict and cooperation within and among nations: enumerative profiles of Syria, Jordan, and the United Arab Republic, January 1965 to May 1967." Paper presented at the Annual Meeting of the International Studies Association, Pittsburgh.

Burton, J. W. 1965. *International Relations: A General Theory*. Cambridge, Eng.: Birkenhead.

Butwell, R., ed. 1969. *Foreign Policy and the Developing Nation*. Lexington: Univ. of Kentucky Press.

Calhoun, H. L. 1972. "Exploratory applications to scaled event data." Paper presented at the Annual Meeting of the International Studies Association, Dallas.

Campbell, A.; W. Miller; D. Stokes; and P. Converse. 1960. *The American Voter*. New York: Wiley.

Campbell, D. T., and J. C. Stanley. 1966. *Experimental and Quasi-experimental Designs for Research*. New York: Rand McNally.

Carnap, R. 1966. *Philosophical Foundations of Physics*. New York: Basic Books.

Chapman, J. W. 1971. "Political forecasting and strategic planning." *International Studies Quarterly* 15 (September):317–57.

Chittick, W. O. 1974. *The Analysis of Foreign Policy Outputs*. Columbus, Ohio: Merrill, forthcoming.

Choucri, N. 1974. "Forecasting in international relations: problems and prospects." *International Interactions* 1, forthcoming.

———. 1973. "Applications of econometric analysis to forecasting in international relations." Paper presented at the Conference on Forecasting in International Relations, Peace Research Society (International), Cambridge, Mass.

Choucri, N., with the collaboration of R. C. North. 1972. "In search of peace systems: Scandinavia and the Netherlands, 1870–1970," pp. 239–74 in B. M. Russett, ed., *Peace, War, and Numbers*. Beverly Hills: Sage.

Choucri, N., and T. Robinson, eds. 1974. *Forecasting in International Relations*. San Francisco: Freeman, forthcoming.

Clark, J. F.; M. K. O'Leary; and E. R. Wittkopf. 1971. "National attributes associated with support for the United Nations." *International Organization* 25 (Winter):1–25.

Claude, I. L., Jr. 1971. *Swords into Plowshares*. New York: Random House.

Cobb, R. W., and C. Elder. 1970. *International Community: A Regional and Global Study*. New York: Holt, Rinehart and Winston.

Cohen, B. C. 1963. *The Press and Foreign Policy*. Princeton: Princeton Univ. Press.

———. 1961. "Foreign policymakers and the news," pp. 220–28 in J. N. Rosenau, ed., *International Politics and Foreign Policy*. New York: Free Press.

Collingwood, R. G. 1946. *The Idea of History*. New York: Oxford Univ. Press.

Collins, J. N. 1973. "Foreign conflict behavior and domestic disorder in Africa," pp. 251–93 in J. Wilkenfeld, ed., *Conflict Behavior and Linkage Politics.* New York: David McKay.

Commission on the Year 2000 of the American Academy of Arts and Sciences. 1967. "Working session II: the nature and limitations of forecasting." *Daedalus* 96 (Summer) :936–47.

Coplin, W. D., and C. W. Kegley, Jr., eds. 1971. *A Multi-Method Introduction to International Politics.* Chicago: Markham.

Coplin, W. D., and M. K. O'Leary. 1972. *Everyman's PRINCE.* Belmont, Calif.: Duxbury.

Cornelius, W. G. 1961. "The 'Latin-American bloc' in the United Nations." *J. of Inter-American Studies* 3 (July) :419–35.

Corson, W. 1970. "Measuring conflict and cooperation intensity in East-West relations: a manual and codebook." University of Michigan (mimeo) .

———. 1969. "Measuring conflict and cooperation intensity in international relations." Paper presented at the Michigan State University International Events Data Conference, East Lansing.

Couch, A. 1969. "Psychological determinants of interpersonal behavior." Ph.D. dissertation, Harvard University.

Council on Foreign Relations. 1968. *Political Handbook and Atlas of the World.* New York: Harper and Row.

Dahl, R. A. 1968. "The evaluation of political systems," pp. 47–57 in C. L. Taylor, ed., *Aggregate Data Analysis.* The Hague: Mouton.

———. 1950. *Congress and Foreign Policy.* New York: Harcourt, Brace.

———, ed. 1966. *Political Oppositions in Western Democracies.* New Haven: Yale Univ. Press.

de Rivera, J. H. 1968. *The Psychological Dimension of Foreign Policy.* Columbus, Ohio: Merrill.

Deutsch, K. W. 1969. "The point of no return in the progression toward war," pp. 60–61 in D. G. Pruitt and R. C. Snyder, eds., *Theory and Research on the Causes of War.* Englewood Cliffs, N. J.: Prentice-Hall

———. 1966. "The future of world politics." *Political Quarterly* 37 (January–March) :9–32.

———. 1963. *The Nerves of Government.* New York: Free Press.

———. 1957. "Mass communications and the loss of freedom in decision-making." *J. of Conflict Resolution* 1 (June) :200–211.

Deutsch, K. W., and L. J. Edinger. 1959. *Germany Rejoins the Powers.* Stanford: Stanford Univ. Press.

Deutsch, K. W.; R. Kann; M. Lee; M. Lichterman; R. Lindgren; F. Loewenheim; and R. van Wagenen. 1957. *Political Community in the North Atlantic Area.* Princeton: Princeton Univ. Press.

Deutsch, K. W., and J. D. Singer. 1964. "Multipolar power systems and international stability." *World Politics* 16 (April) :390–406.

Deutsch, M., and R. M. Krauss. 1965. *Theories in Social Psychology.* New York: Basic Books.

Donagan, A. 1966. "The Popper-Hempel theory reconsidered," pp. 127–59 in W. H. Dray, ed., *Philosophical Analysis and History.* New York: Harper and Row.

Dowse, R. E. 1969. *Modernization in Ghana and the U.S.S.R.* London: Routledge and Kegan Paul.

————. 1966. "A functionalist's logic." *World Politics* 18 (July) :607–22.

Dray, W. H. 1959. " 'Explaining what' in history," pp. 403–8 in P. Gardiner, ed., *Theories in History.* New York: Free Press.

Duverger, M. 1964. *An Introduction to the Social Sciences.* Trans. by M. Anderson. New York: Praeger.

East, M. A. 1972. "Status discrepancy and violence in the international system," pp. 299–319 in J. N. Rosenau, V. Davis, and M. A. East, eds., *The Analysis of International Politics.* New York: Free Press.

————. 1969. "Stratification and international politics." Ph.D. dissertation, Princeton University.

East, M. A., and P. M. Gregg. 1967. "Factors influencing cooperation and conflict in the international system." *International Studies Quarterly* 11 (September) :244–69.

Eckstein, H. 1964. "A perspective on comparative politics, past and present," pp. 3–32 in H. Eckstein and D. E. Apter, eds., *Comparative Politics.* New York: Free Press.

Effros, W. G. 1970. *Quotations Vietnam: 1945–1970.* New York: Random House.

Eggan, F. 1954. "Social anthropology and the method of controlled comparison." *American Anthropologist* 56 (October) :743–63.

Eldridge, A. F. N.d. "Foreign policy and discrimination: the politics of indigenization." Duke University (mimeo).

Eley, J. W. 1973. "Events data and foreign policy theory: an analysis of American foreign policy toward internal wars, 1945–1970." Paper presented at the Annual Meeting of the International Studies Association, New York.

Eley, J. W., and J. H. Peterson. N.d. "Societal attributes and foreign policy behavior in Latin America, 1963–1969." Western Kentucky University (mimeo).

Elliot, F., and M. Summerskill. 1957. *A Dictionary of Politics*. Baltimore: Penguin.

Evans-Pritchard, E. E. 1963. *The Comparative Method in Social Anthropology*. London: Athlone.

Ezekiel, M., and K. A. Fox. 1959. *Methods of Correlation and Regression Analysis*. New York: Wiley.

Farrell, R. B., ed. 1966. *Approaches to Comparative and International Politics*. Evanston, Ill.: Northwestern Univ. Press.

Feierabend, I. K., and R. Feierabend. 1966a. "Aggressive behavior within polities, 1948–1962." *Journal of Conflict Resolution* 10 (March):41–64.

———. 1966b. "The relationship of systemic frustration, political coercion, international tension, and political stability." Paper presented at the annual meeting of the American Psychological Association.

Festinger, L. and D. Katz, eds. 1953. *Research Methods in the Behavioral Sciences*. New York: Dryden.

Fisher, S. N., ed. 1963. *The Military in the Middle East*. Columbus: Ohio State University Press.

Frankel, J. 1959. *The Making of Foreign Policy*. New York: Oxford Univ. Press.

Freeman, L. C. 1965. *Introductory Applied Statistics*. New York: Wiley.

Friedrich, C. J. 1938. *Foreign Policy in the Making*. New York: Norton.

Froman, L. A., Jr. 1967. "An analysis of public policies in cities." *Journal of Politics*, (February); pp. 94–108.

Fulbright, J. W. 1966. *The Arrogance of Power*. New York: Vintage.

Furniss, E. S., Jr. 1954. *The Office of Premier in French Policymaking*. Princeton: Foreign Policy Analysis Project, Princeton University.

Gallie, W. B. 1959. "Explanations in history and the genetic sciences," pp. 386–402 in P. Gardiner, ed., *Theories of History*. New York: Free Press.

Galtung, J. 1964. "A structural theory of aggression." *J. of Peace Research* 1:95–119.

Gamson, W. A., and A. Modigliani. 1971. *Untangling the Cold War*. Boston: Little, Brown.

George, A. L. 1972. "The case for multiple advocacy in making foreign policy." *American Political Science Review* 66 (September):751–85.

———. 1960. "Prediction of political action by means of propaganda analysis." *Public Opinion Quarterly* 20 (November):334–45.

George, A. L., and J. George. 1956. *Woodrow Wilson and Colonel House*. New York: Day.

George, A. L.; D. K. Hall; and W. E. Simons. 1971. *The Limits of Coercive Diplomacy*. Boston: Little, Brown.

Glazer, B. G., and A. L. Strauss. 1967. *The Discovery of Grounded Theory*. Chicago: Aldine.

Good, R. C. 1962. "State-building as a determinant of foreign policy in the new states," pp. 3–12 in L. W. Martin, ed., *Neutralism and Nonalignment*. New York: Praeger.

Goodenough, W. E. 1970. *Description and Comparison in Cultural Anthropology*. Chicago: Aldine.

Goodman, R.; J. Hart; and R. Rosecrance. 1972. "Testing international theory: methods and data in a situational analysis of international politics." Paper 2, Situational Analysis Project, Cornell University.

Graham, G. J., Jr. 1971. *Methodological Foundations for Political Analysis*. Waltham, Mass.: Xerox Publishings.

Greeno, J. G. 1970. "Evaluation of statistical hypotheses using information transmitted." *Philosophy of Science* 37 (June) :279–93.

Greenstein, F. I. 1969. *Personality and Politics*. Chicago: Markham.

Gregg, R. W., and C. W. Kegley, Jr., eds. 1971. *After Vietnam: The Future of American Foreign Policy*. New York: Anchor Books.

Gross, F. 1954. *Foreign Policy Analysis*. New York: Philosophical Library.

Grosser, A. 1972. *L'explication politique: une introduction a l'analyse comparative*. Paris: Libraire Armand Colin.

Gurr, T. R. 1969. "A comparative study of civil strife," pp. 572–632 in H. D. Graham and T. R. Gurr, eds., *The History of Violence in America*. New York: Bantam.

———. 1968. "A causal model of civil strife." *American Political Science Review* 62 (December) : 1104–24.

Haas, M. 1962. "Comparative analysis." *Western Political Quarterly* 15 (June): 294–303.

Halle, L. J. 1952. *Civilization and Foreign Policy*. New York: Harper and Brothers.

Halper, T. 1971. *Foreign Policy Crises: Appearance and Reality in Decision Making*. Columbus, Ohio: Merrill.

Halperin, M. 1972. "The decision to deploy the ABM." *World Politics* 25 (October) :62–95.

Halpern, A. M., ed. 1965. *Policies Toward China: Views from Six Continents*. New York: McGraw-Hill.

Handelman, J. R.; J. A. Vasquez; M. K. O'Leary; and W. D. Coplin. 1973. "Color it Morgenthau: a data-based assessment of quantitative international relations research." Paper presented at the Annual Meeting of the International Studies Association, New York.

Hannah, H. 1968. "Some dimensions of international settlement procedures and outcomes." Dimensionality of Nations Project Research Report 11, University of Hawaii.

Hanrieder, W. F., ed. 1971a. *Comparative Foreign Policy*. New York: David McKay.

———. 1971b. *Foreign Policies and the International System*. Morristown, N.J.: General Learning.

———. 1967a. "Compatability and consensus: a proposal for the conceptual linkage of external and internal dimensions of foreign policy." *American Political Science Review* 59 (September) :971–82.

———. 1967b. *West German Foreign Policy, 1949–1963*. Stanford: Stanford Univ. Press.

Hanson, N. R. 1958. *Patterns of Discovery*. London: Cambridge Univ. Press.

Hartz, L. 1964. *The Founding of New Societies*. New York: Harcourt, Brace.

Heider, F. 1958. *The Psychology of Interpersonal Relations*. New York: Wiley.

Hempel, C. G. 1966. *Philosophy of Natural Science*. Englewood Cliffs, N.J.: Prentice Hall.

———. 1965. *Aspects of Scientific Explanation*. New York: Free Press.

———. 1952. *Fundamentals of Concept Formation in Empirical Science*. Chicago: Univ. of Chicago Press.

Hempel, C. G., and P. Oppenheim. 1948. "The logic of explanation." *Philosophy of Science* 15 (April) :135–75.

Hermann, C. F. 1973. "Bureaucratic politics and foreign policy: a theoretical framework using events data." Paper presented at the Annual Meeting of the International Studies Association, New York.

———. 1972. "Policy classification: a key to the comparative study of foreign policy," pp. 58–79 in J. N. Rosenau, V. Davis, and M. A. East, eds., *The Analysis of International Politics*. New York: Free Press.

———. 1971. "What is a foreign policy event?" pp. 295–321 in W. F. Hanrieder, ed., *Comparative Foreign Policy*. New York: David McKay.

———. 1969. *Crises in Foreign Policy: A Simulation Analysis*. Indianapolis: Bobbs-Merrill.

Hermann, C. F., and M. A. East. 1974. "Do nation-types account for foreign policy behavior?" in J. N. Rosenau, ed., *Comparing Foreign Policies*. Beverly Hills: Sage, forthcoming.

Hermann, C. F., and M. G. Hermann. 1963. *Validation Studies of Inter-Nation Simulation*. China Lake, Calif.: U.S. Naval Test Station.

Hermann, C. F.; S. A. Salmore; and M. A. East. 1971. "Code manual for an analytic deck of comparative foreign policy events." Ohio State University (mimeo).

Hermann, C. F., and K. N. Waltz, eds. 1970. *Basic Courses in Foreign Policy: An Anthology of Syllabi.* Beverly Hills: Sage.

Hermann, M. G. 1972. "How leaders process information and the effects on foreign policy." Paper presented at the Annual Meeting of the American Political Science Association, Washington, D.C.

Hill, G. A., and F. Ebrahimi. 1970. "Multi-channel time series analysis: an introduction to analysis for international relations event prediction." World Event/Interaction Survey Support Study 3, University of Southern California.

Hilsman, R. 1971. *The Politics of Policy Making in Defense and Foreign Affairs.* New York: Harper & Row.

———. 1967. *To Move a Nation.* Garden City, N.Y.: Doubleday.

Hitlin, R. B. 1972. "Doctoral dissertations in political science, 1972." *PS* 5 (Fall) :513–74.

Hoffmann, S. 1968. *Gulliver's Troubles, or the Setting of American Foreign Policy.* New York: McGraw-Hill.

———. 1965. *The State of War.* New York: Praeger.

Hoggard, G. D. 1970. "Differential source coverage and the analysis of international interaction data." University of Southern California (mimeo).

———. 1969. "Indicators of international interaction." University of Southern California. (mimeo).

Holsti, K. J. 1972. *International Politics.* Englewood Cliffs, N.J.: Prentice-Hall.

———. 1963. "The value of international tension measurement." *J. of Conflict Resolution* 7 (September) :608–17.

Holsti, O. R. 1969. "The 1914 crisis," pp. 226–48 in J. E. Mueller, ed., *Approaches to Measurement in International Relations.* New York: Appleton-Century-Crofts.

———. 1968. "Content analysis in political research," pp. 111–53 in D. B. Bobrow and J. L. Schwartz, eds., *Computers and the Policy-Making Community.* Englewood Cliffs, N.J.: Prentice-Hall.

Holsti, O. R.; R. A. Brody; and R. C. North. 1969a. "The management of international crisis: affect and action in American-Soviet relations," pp. 62–79 in D. G. Pruitt and R. C. Snyder, eds., *Theory and Research on the Causes of War.* Englewood Cliffs, N.J.: Prentice-Hall.

———. 1969b. "Measuring affect and action in international reaction models: empirical materials from the 1962 Cuban crisis," pp. 679–96 in J. N. Rosenau, ed., *International Politics and Foreign Policy.* New York: Free Press.

Holsti, O. R.; R. C. North; and R. A. Brody. 1968. "Perception and action in the 1914 crisis," pp. 123–58 in J. D. Singer, ed., *Quantitative International Politics*. New York: Free Press.

Holt, R. T., and J. E. Turner, eds. 1970. *The Methodology of Comparative Research*. New York: Free Press.

———. 1966. *The Political Bases of Economic Development: An Exploration in Comparative Analysis*. Princeton, N.J.: Van Nostrand.

Hoopes, T. 1969. *The Limits of Intervention*. New York: David McKay.

Hovet, T., Jr. 1960. *Bloc Politics in the United Nations*. Cambridge: Harvard Univ. Press.

Huntington, S. P. 1965. "Political development and political decay." *World Politics* 17 (April) :386–430.

Isaak, A. C. 1969. *Scope and Methods of Political Science*. Homewood, Ill.: Dorsey.

Jacob, H. and K. N. Vines, eds. 1965. *Politics in the American States: A Comparative Analysis*. Boston: Little, Brown.

Jacobson, H. K., and W. Zimmerman, eds. 1969. *The Shaping of Foreign Policy*. New York: Atherton.

Janowitz, M. 1964. *The Military in the Political Development of New Nations: An Essay in Comparative Analysis*. Chicago: Univ. of Chicago Press.

Jeffrey, R. C. 1969. "Statistical explanation vs. statistical inference," pp. 104–13 in N. Rescher, ed., *Essays in Honor of Carl Hempel*. Dordrecht, Holland: Reidel.

Johnson, C. 1966. *Revolutionary Change*. Boston: Little, Brown.

Johnson, J. J., ed. 1962. *The Role of the Military in Underdeveloped Countries*. Princeton: Princeton Univ. Press.

Johnston, J. 1972. *Econometric Methods*. New York: McGraw-Hill.

Jones, R. E. 1970. *Analyzing Foreign Policy: An Introduction to Some Conceptual Problems*. London: Routledge and Kegan-Paul.

Jones, S., and J. D. Singer. 1972. *Beyond Conjecture in International Politics*. Itasca, Ill.: Peacock.

Kalleberg, A. L. 1966. "The logic of comparison: a methodological note on the comparative study of political systems." *World Politics* 19 (October) :69–83.

Kaplan, A. 1964. *The Conduct of Inquiry*. San Francisco: Chandler.

Kay, D. A. 1970. *The New Nations in the United Nations*. New York: Columbia Univ. Press.

Kegley, C. W., Jr. 1973. *A General Empirical Typology of Foreign Policy Behavior*. Beverly Hills: Sage.

————. 1971. "Toward the construction of an empirically grounded typology of foreign policy output behavior." Ph.D. dissertation, Syracuse University.

Kegley, C. W., Jr.; S. A. Salmore; and D. Rosen. 1974. "Convergences in the analysis of the structure of interstate behavior," pp. 309–39 in P. J. McGowan, ed., *Sage Yearbook of Foreign Policy Studies, II*. Beverly Hills: Sage.

Kent, G. 1972. "Plan for designing the future." *Bulletin of Peace Proposals* 3:280–85.

Keohane, R. O. 1967. "The study of political influence in the General Assembly." *International Organization* 21 (Spring):221–37.

Keohane, R. O., and J. S. Nye, Jr., eds. 1972. *Transnational Relations and World Politics*. Cambridge: Harvard Univ. Press.

Kerlinger, F. N. 1964. *Foundations of Behavioral Research*. New York: Holt, Rinehart, and Winston.

Kissinger, H. A. 1969. *American Foreign Policy*. New York: Norton.

————. 1966. "Domestic structure and foreign policy." *Daedalus* 95 (Spring): 503–29.

Klingberg, F. L. 1941. "Studies in measurement of the relations among sovereign states." *Psychometrika* 6 (December):355–62.

Kluckholm, C. 1953. "Universal categories of culture," pp. 507–23 in A. L. Kroeber, ed., *Anthropology Today*. Chicago: Univ. of Chicago Press.

Kolko, G. A. 1969. *The Roots of American Foreign Policy*. Boston: Beacon.

Knorr, K., and J. N. Rosenau, eds. 1969. *Contending Approaches to International Politics*. Princeton: Princeton Univ. Press.

Kuhn, T. S. 1970a. "Logic of discovery or psychology of research?" pp. 1–23 in I. Lakatos and A. Musgrave, eds., *Criticism and the Growth of Knowledge*. Cambridge: Cambridge Univ. Press.

————. 1962, 1970b. *The Structure of Scientific Revolutions*. Chicago: Univ. of Chicago Press.

Land, K. G. 1969. "Principles of path analysis," pp. 3–37 in E. F. Borgatta, ed., *Sociological Methodology 1969*. San Francisco: Jossey-Bass.

Lanphier, V. 1972. "Foreign relations indicator project." Paper presented at the Annual Meeting of the International Studies Association, Dallas.

LaPalombara, J., ed. 1963. *Bureaucracy and Political Development*. Princeton: Princeton Univ. Press.

LaPalombara, J., and M. Weiner, eds. 1966. *Political Parties and Political Development*. Princeton: Princeton Univ. Press.

Lasswell, H. D. 1968. "The future of the comparative method." *Comparative Politics* 1 (October):3–18.

Lasswell, H. D. 1956. *The Decision Process: Seven Categories of Functional Analysis.* College Park, Md.: Bureau of Government Research.

———. 1942. "The politically significant content of the press: coding procedures." *Journalism Quarterly* 19 (March) :12–23.

Lawley, D., and A. Maxwell. 1963. *Factor Analysis as a Statistical Method.* London: Butterworth.

Lazarsfeld, P. F., and A. H. Barton. 1951. "Qualitative measurement in the social sciences: classification, typologies, and indices," pp. 155–92 in D. Lerner and H. D. Lasswell, eds., *The Policy Sciences.* Stanford: Stanford Univ. Press.

Leary, T. 1957. *Interpersonal Diagnosis of Personality.* New York: Ronald.

Leng, R. J., and J. D. Singer. 1970. "Toward a multi-theoretical typology of international behavior." Paper presented at the Michigan State University International Events Data Conference, East Lansing.

Levi, W. 1969. "The relative irrelevance of moral norms in international politics," pp. 191–98 in J. N. Rosenau, ed., *International Politics and Foreign Policy.* New York: Free Press.

Lewis, O. 1961. "Comparisons in cultural anthropology," pp. 50–85 in F. W. Moore, ed., *Readings in Cross-Cultural Methodology.* New York: HRAF Press.

Lijphart, A. 1971. "Comparative politics and the comparative method." *American Political Science Review* 65 (September) :682–93.

Lindblom, C. E. 1959. "The science of 'muddling through.'" *Public Administration Review* 19 (Spring) :79–88.

Lipson, L. 1957. "The comparative method in political studies." *Political Quarterly* 28 (October–December) :372–82.

Liska, G. 1968. *Alliances and the Third World.* Baltimore: Johns Hopkins Press.

———. 1967. *Imperial America: The International Politics of Primacy.* Baltimore: Johns Hopkins Press.

London, K. 1949. *How Foreign Policy Is Made.* New York: Van Nostrand.

Lovell, J. P. 1970. *Foreign Policy in Perspective: Strategy, Adaptation, Decision Making.* New York: Holt, Rinehart and Winston.

McClelland, C. A. 1972. "The beginning, duration, and abatement of international crises: comparisons in two conflict arenas," pp. 83–105 in C. F. Hermann, ed., *International Crises.* New York: Free Press.

———. 1969. "International interaction analysis in the predictive mode." World Event/Interaction Survey Technical Report 3, University of Southern California.

———. 1968a. "Access to Berlin: the quantity and variety of events, 1948–1963," pp. 159–86 in J. D. Singer, ed., *Quantitative International Politics.* New York: Free Press.

———. 1968*b*. "Interaction analysis and foreign policy futures." University of Southern California (mimeo).

———. 1968*c*. "International interaction analysis: basic research and some practical applications." World Event/Interaction Survey Technical Report 2. University of Southern California.

———. 1966. *Theory and the International System.* New York: MacMillan.

———. 1961. "The acute international crisis." *World Politics* 14 (October):182–204.

McClelland, C. A., and A. Ancoli. 1970. "An interaction survey of the Middle East." University of Southern California (mimeo).

McClelland, C. A., and G. D. Hoggard. 1969. "Conflict patterns in the interactions among nations," pp. 711–23 in J. N. Rosenau, ed., *International Politics and Foreign Policy.* New York: Free Press.

McClelland, C. A.; R. G. Tomlinson; R. G. Sherwin; G. A. Hill; H. L. Calhoun; P. H. Fenn; and J. D. Martin. 1971. *The Management and Analysis of International Event Data: A Computerized System for Monitoring and Projecting Event Flows.* Los Angeles: University of Southern California.

McGowan, P. J. 1974. "A Bayesian approach to the problem of events data validity in comparative and international political research," in J. N. Rosenau, ed., *Comparing Foreign Policies.* Beverly Hills: Sage, forthcoming.

———. 1973*a*. "Culture and foreign policy behavior in Black Africa: an exploratory, comparative study." Paper presented at the Annual Meeting of the American Political Science Association, New Orleans.

———. 1973*b*. "Dimensions of African foreign policy behavior: in search of dependence." Paper presented at the Annual Meeting of the Canadian Association of African Studies, Ottawa.

———, ed. 1973*c*. *Sage International Yearbook of Foreign Policy Studies.* Beverly Hills: Sage.

———. 1970*a*. "A formal theory of foreign policy behavior as adaptive behavior." Paper presented at the Annual Meeting of the American Political Science Association, Los Angeles.

———. 1970*b*. "A manual and codebook for the coding of foreign policy acts." Syracuse University (mimeo).

———. 1970*c*. "Theoretical approaches to the comparative study of foreign policy." Ph.D. dissertation, Northwestern University.

———. 1970*d*. "The unit-of-analysis problem in the comparative study of foreign policy." Paper presented at the Michigan State University International Events Data Conference, East Lansing.

———. 1969. "The pattern of African diplomacy." *J. of Asian and African Studies* 4 (July):202–21.

McGowan, P. J. 1968. "Africa and nonalignment." *International Studies Quarterly* 12 (September) : 262–95.

McGowan, P. J., and H. B. Shapiro 1973. *The Comparative Study of Foreign Policy: A Survey of Scientific Findings.* Beverly Hills: Sage.

McKay, V., ed. 1966. *African Diplomacy: Studies in the Determinants of Foreign Policy.* New York: Praeger.

Macridis, R. C., ed. 1958, 1962, 1972. *Foreign Policy in World Politics.* Englewood Cliffs, N.J.: Prentice-Hall.

————, ed. 1968. *Modern European Governments: Cases in Comparative Foreign Policy Making.* Englewood Cliffs, N.J.: Prentice-Hall.

Marsh, R. M. 1967. *Comparative Sociology.* New York: Harcourt, Brace and World.

————. 1964. "The bearing of comparative analysis on sociological theory." *Social Forces* 43 (December) :188–96.

Marshall, C. B. 1954. *The Limits of Foreign Policy.* New York: Henry Holt.

Mayer, L. C. 1972. *Comparative Political Inquiry: A Methodological Survey.* Homewood, Ill.: Dorsey.

Mead, G. H. 1938. *The Philosophy of the Act.* Chicago: Univ. of Chicago Press.

Meehan, E. J. 1969. *Value Judgement and Social Science.* Homewood, Ill.: Dorsey.

————. 1968. *Explanation in Social Science: A System Paradigm.* Homewood, Ill.: Dorsey.

————. 1965. *The Theory and Method of Political Analysis.* Homewood, Ill.: Dorsey.

Merritt, R. L. 1970. *Systematic Approaches to Comparative Politics.* Chicago: Rand McNally.

Merritt, R. L., and S. Rokkan, eds. 1966. *Comparing Nations.* New Haven: Yale Univ. Press.

Merton, R. K. 1957. *Social Theory and Social Structure.* Glencoe, Ill.: Free Press.

Mill, J. S. 1843. *A System of Logic.* London: Longmans.

Millikan, M. F. 1969. "Inquiry and policy: the relation of knowledge to action," pp. 277–84 in E. T. Crawford and A. D. Biderman, eds., *Social Scientists and International Affairs.* New York: Wiley.

Milstein, J. S. 1972. "American and Soviet influence, balance of power, and Arab-Israeli violence," pp. 139–66 in B. M. Russett, ed., *Peace, War, and Numbers.* Beverly Hills: Sage.

Modelski, G. 1954, 1962. *A Theoretical Analysis of the Formation of Foreign Policy.* London: University of London.

Moore, D. W. 1970. "Governmental and societal influences on foreign policy: a partial examination of Rosenau's adaptation model." Ph.D. dissertation, Ohio State University.

Moore, J. A., and R. A. Young. 1969. "Some preliminary short-term predictions of international interaction." World Event/Interaction Survey Working Paper 1, University of Southern California.

Morgenthau, H. J. 1967. *Politics Among Nations*. New York: Knopf.

Moses, L. E.; R. A. Brody; O. R. Holsti; J. B. Kadane; and J. S. Milstein. 1967. "Scaling data on internation action." *Science* 156 (May 26):1054–59.

Munger, F., ed. 1966. *American State Politics: Readings for Comparative Analysis*. New York: Crowell.

Munton, D. 1973. "Waiting for Kepler: event data and relational model explanations of Canadian foreign policy." Paper presented at the Annual Meeting of the International Studies Association, New York.

Nadel, S. F. 1952. "Witchcraft in four African societies: an essay in comparison. *American Anthropologist* 54:18–29.

———. 1951. *The Foundations of Social Anthropology*. London: Cohen and West.

Nagel, E. 1965. "Types of causal explanations in science," pp. 11–32 in D. Lerner, ed., *Cause and Effect*. New York: Free Press.

———. 1961. *The Structure of Science: Problems in the Logic of Scientific Explanation*. New York: Harcourt, Brace, and World.

Namenwirth, J. Z., and T. L. Brewer. 1966. "Elite editorial comment on European and Atlantic communities in four countries," pp. 401–27 in P. J. Stone, ed., *The General Inquirer*. Cambridge: M.I.T. Press.

Naroll, R. 1968. "Some thoughts on comparative method in cultural anthropology," pp. 236–77 in H. M. Blalock, Jr., and A. B. Blalock, eds., *Methodology in Social Research*. New York: McGraw-Hill.

———. 1962. *Data Quality Control*. New York: Free Press.

Ness, G. D. 1969. "Foreign policy and social change," pp. 41–66 in R. Butwell, ed., *Foreign Policy and the Developing Nations*. Lexington: Univ. of Kentucky Press.

Neumann, S. 1959. "The comparative study of politics." *Comparative Studies in Society and History* 1 (January):105–12.

———. 1957. "Comparative politics: a half-century appraisal." *J. of Politics* 19 (May):369–90.

Neustadt, R. 1970. *Alliance Politics*. New York: Columbia Univ. Press.

Newcomb, T. M. 1950. *Social Psychology*. New York: Dryden.

Newcombe, A. 1974. "Initiatives and responses in foreign policy," in E. E. Azar and J. Ben-Dak, eds., *Theory and Practice of Events Research.* New York: Gordon and Breach, forthcoming.

Newcombe, A., and J. Wert. 1972. *An Inter-Nation Tensiometer for the Prediction of War.* Oakville, Ontario: Canadian Peace Research Institute.

Newcombe, H., and A. Newcombe. 1969. *Peace Research Around the World.* Oakville, Ontario: Canadian Peace Research Institute.

North, R. C. 1968. "The behavior of nation-states: problems of conflict and integration," pp. 303–56 in M. A. Kaplan, ed., *New Approaches to International Relations.* New York: St. Martin's.

North, R. C.; R. A. Brody; and O. R. Holsti. 1964. "Some empirical data on the conflict spiral." Peace Research Society (International) *Papers* 1: 1–14.

North, R. C., and N. Choucri. 1968. "Background conditions to the outbreak of the First World War." Peace Research Society (International) *Papers* 9:125–37.

North, R. C.; O. R. Holsti; M. G. Zaninovich; and D. A. Zinnes, eds. 1963. *Content Analysis.* Evanston, Ill.: Northwestern Univ. Press.

Oakeshott, M. 1933. *Experience and Its Modes.* London: Cambridge Univ. Press.

O'Leary, M. K. 1969. "Linkages between domestic and international politics in underdeveloped nations," pp. 324–46 in J. N. Rosenau, ed., *Linkage Politics.* New York: Free Press.

Organski, A. F. K. 1968. *World Politics.* New York: Knopf.

———. 1965. *The Stages of Political Development.* New York: Knopf.

Osgood, C.; G. Suci; and P. Tannenbaum. 1957. *Measurement of Meaning.* Urbana: Univ. of Illinois Press.

Osgood, J.; N. Choucri; and W. Mitchell. 1974. "Action and perception in the Sino-Indian border conflict," in E. E. Azar and J. Ben-Dak, eds., *Theory and Practice of Events Research.* New York: Gordon and Breach, forthcoming.

Paige, G. D. 1968. *The Korean Decision.* New York: Free Press.

Palmer, R. E. 1969. *Hermaneutics.* Evanston, Ill.: Northwestern Univ. Press.

Parsons, T. 1951. *The Social System.* New York: Free Press.

Parsons, T., and E. A. Shils, eds. 1962. *Toward a General Theory of Action.* New York: Harper.

Payne, J. 1970. *The American Threat.* Chicago: Markham.

Phillips, W. R. 1973a. "The conflict environment of nations: a study of conflict inputs to nations in 1963," pp. 124–47 in J. Wilkenfeld, ed., *Conflict Behavior and Linkage Politics.* New York: David McKay.

———. 1973b. "Theoretical underpinnings of the events data movement."

Paper presented at the Annual Meeting of the International Studies Association, New York.

———. 1972. "Two views of foreign policy interaction: substantially the same or different?" Paper presented at the Annual Meeting of the International Studies Association/Midwest Section and Peace Research Society (International), Toronto.

Phillips, W. R., and R. C. Crain. 1972. "Dynamic foreign policy interactions: reciprocity and uncertainty in foreign policy." Paper presented at the Annual Meeting of the American Political Science Association, Washington, D.C.

Plano, J. C., and R. E. Riggs. 1967. *Forging World Order*. London: MacMillan.

Popper, K. R. 1959. *The Logic of Scientific Discovery*. New York: Basic Books.

Powell, C. A.; D. Andrus; W. Fowler; and K. Knight. 1974. "Determinants of foreign policy behavior: a causal modeling approach," in J. N. Rosenau, ed., *Comparing Foreign Policies*. Beverly Hills: Sage.

Price, D. 1968. "Micro- and macro-politics: notes on research strategy," pp. 102–40 in O. Garceau, ed., *Political Research and Political Theory*. Cambridge: Harvard Univ. Press.

Przeworski, A., and H. Teune. 1970. *The Logic of Comparative Social Inquiry*. New York: Wiley-Interscience.

———. 1966. "Equivalence in cross-national research." *Public Opinion Quarterly* 30 (Winter):551–68.

Putnam, R. 1967. "Towards explaining military intervention in Latin American Politics." *World Politics* 20 (October):83–110.

Radcliffe-Brown, A. R. 1957. *A Natural Science of Society*. Glencoe, Ill.: Free Press.

Rapoport, J. 1971. *Small States and Territories: Status and Problems*. New York: UNITAR Studies.

Redfield, R. 1941. *The Folk Culture of Yucatan*. Chicago: Univ. of Chicago Press.

Rescher, N., ed. 1967. *The Logic of Decision and Action*. Pittsburgh: Univ. of Pittsburgh Press.

Richardson, J. L. 1966. *Germany and the Atlantic Alliance: The Interaction of Strategy and Politics*. Cambridge: Harvard Univ. Press.

Richardson, L. F. 1960. *Arms and Insecurity*. Pittsburgh: Boxwood.

Richman, A. 1969. "The impact of international events on American public opinion." Purdue University (mimeo).

Rieselbach, L. N. 1960. "Quantitative techniques of studying voting behavior in the UN General Assembly." *International Organization* 14 (Spring): 291–306.

Riker, W. 1957. "Events and situations." *J. of Philosophy* 54 (January):57–70.

Robinson, T. W. 1969. "National interests," pp. 182–90 in J. N. Rosenau, ed., *International Politics and Foreign Policy*. New York: Free Press.

Rochester, J. M. 1971. *Learning Package 3: Dyadic Disputes Before the Permanent Court of International Justice, the International Court of Justice, the League of Nations, and the United Nations: Analytical and Empirical Materials*. Chicago: Markham.

Rosecrance, R. 1973. *International Relations: Peace or War?* New York: McGraw-Hill.

Rosenau, J. N., ed. 1974. *Comparing Foreign Policies*. Beverly Hills: Sage, forthcoming.

———. 1972. "Adaptive politics in an interdependent world." *Orbis* 16 (Spring):153–73.

———. 1971. *The Scientific Study of Foreign Policy*. New York: Free Press.

———. 1970. *The Adaptation of National Societies: A Theory of Political System Behavior and Transformation*. New York: McCaleb-Seiler.

———. 1969a. "The actions of states: theories and approaches," pp. 166–74 in J. N. Rosenau, ed., *International Politics and Foreign Policy*. New York: Free Press.

———, ed. 1969b. *Linkage Politics: Essays on the Convergence of National and International Systems*. New York: Free Press.

———. 1968a. "Comparative foreign policy: fad, fantasy, or field?" *International Studies Quarterly* 12 (September):296–329.

———. 1968b. "Moral fervor, systematic analysis, and scientific consciousness in foreign policy research," pp. 197–236 in A. Ranney, ed., *Political Science and Public Policy*. Chicago: Markham.

———. 1968c. "Private preferences and political responsibilities: the relative potency of individual and role variables in the behavior of U.S. Senators," pp. 17–50 in J. D. Singer, ed., *Quantitative International Politics: Insights and Evidence*. New York: Free Press.

———. 1967a. *Of Boundaries and Bridges: A Report on a Conference on the Interdependencies of National and International Political Systems*. Research Monograph 27, Center of International Studies, Princeton University.

———. 1967b. "Compatibility, consensus and an emerging political science of adaptation." *American Political Science Review* 61 (December):983–88.

———. 1967c. "Foreign policy as an issue area," pp. 11–50 in J. N. Rosenau, *Domestic Sources of Foreign Policy*. New York: Free Press.

————. 1967d. "The premises and promises of decision-making analysis," pp. 189–211 in J. C. Charlesworth, ed., *Contemporary Political Analysis*. New York: Free Press.

————. 1967e. "Review." *J. of Asian Studies* 26 (February):287–88.

————. 1966. "Pre-theories and theories of foreign policy," pp. 27–92 in R. B. Farrell, ed., *Approaches to Comparative and International Politics*. Evanston, Ill.: Northwestern Univ. Press.

————. 1963. *Calculated Control as a Unifying Concept in the Study of International Politics and Foreign Policy*. Research Monograph 15, Center of International Studies, Princeton University.

Rosenau, J. N.; P. M. Burgess; and C. F. Hermann. 1973. "The adaptation of foreign policy research: a case study of an anti-case study project." *International Studies Quarterly* 17 (March):119–44.

Rosenau, J. N., and G. D. Hoggard. 1974. "Foreign policy behavior in dyadic relationships: testing a pre-theoretical extension," in J. N. Rosenau, ed., *Comparing Foreign Policies*. Beverly Hills: Sage, forthcoming.

Rosenau, J. N., and G. R. Ramsey, Jr. 1973. "External vs. internal sources of foreign policy behavior: testing the stability of an intriguing set of findings." Paper presented at the World Congress of the International Political Science Association, Montreal.

Rothstein, R. L. 1972. *Planning, Prediction, and Policymaking in Foreign Affairs*. Boston: Little, Brown.

————. 1968. *Alliances and Small Powers*. New York: Columbia Univ. Press.

Rowe, E. T. 1969. "Changing patterns in the voting success of member states in the United Nations General Assembly: 1945–1966." *International Organization* 23 (Spring):231–53.

Rudner, R. S. 1966. *Philosophy of Social Science*. Englewood Cliffs, N.J.: Prentice-Hall.

Rummel, R. J. 1972a. *The Dimensions of Nations*. Beverly Hills: Sage.

————. 1972b. "U.S. foreign relations: conflict, cooperation, and attribute distances," pp. 71–113 in B. M. Russett, ed., *Peace, War, and Numbers*. Beverly Hills: Sage.

————. 1970. *Applied Factor Analysis*. Evanston, Ill.: Northwestern Univ. Press.

————. 1969a. "Field theory and indicators of international behavior." Dimensionality of Nations Project Research Report 29, University of Hawaii.

————. 1969b. "Forecasting international relations: a proposed investigation of three-mode factor analysis." *Technological Forecasting* 1:197–216.

————. 1969c. "Some empirical findings on nations and their behavior." *World Politics* 21 (January): 226–41.

Rummel, R. J. 1968. "The relationship between national attributes and foreign conflict behavior," pp. 187–214 in J. D. Singer, ed. *Quantitative International Palitics*. New York: Free Press.

————. 1967a. "Some attributes and behavior patterns of nations." *J. of Peace Research* 2:109–206.

————. 1967b. "Understanding factor analysis." *J. of Conflict Resolution* 11 (December):444–80.

————. 1966. "Dimensions of conflict behavior within nations." *J. of Conflict Resolution* 10 (March):65–73.

————. 1963. "Dimensions of conflict behavior within and between nations." *General Systems*, 8:1–50.

Russett, B. M. 1972. "A macroscopic view of international politics," pp. 109–24 in J. N. Rosenau, V. Davis, and M. A. East, eds., *The Analysis of International Politics*. New York: Free Press.

————. 1968. "Delineating international regions," pp. 317–52 in J. D. Singer, ed., *Quantitative International Politics*. New York: Free Press.

————. 1967. *International Regions and the International System*. Chicago: Rand McNally.

————. 1966. "Discovering voting groups in the United Nations." *American Political Science Review* 60 (June):327–99.

Russett, B. M.; H. R. Alker, Jr.; K. W. Deutsch; and H. D. Lasswell. 1964. *World Handbook of Political and Social Indicators*. New Haven: Yale Univ. Press.

Russett, B. M.; J. D. Singer; and M. Small. 1968. "National political units in the twentieth century: a standardized list." *American Political Science Review* 62 (September):932–59.

Salmon, W. C. 1971. *Statistical Explanation and Statistical Relevance*. Pittsburgh: Univ. of Pittsburgh Press.

————. 1970. "Statistical explanation," pp. 173–231 in R. G. Colodny, ed., *Nature and Function of Scientific Theories*. Pittsburgh: Univ. of Pittsburgh Press.

————. 1966. *The Foundations of Scientific Inference*. Pittsburgh: Univ. of Pittsburgh Press.

Salmore, B., and S. Salmore. 1972. "Structure and change in regimes—their effect on foreign policy." Paper presented at the Annual Meeting of the American Political Science Association, Washington, D.C.

Salmore, S. A. 1972. "Foreign policy and national attributes: a multivariate analysis." Ph.D. dissertation, Princeton University.

Salmore, S. A., and C. F. Hermann. 1969. "The effects of size, development and accountability on foreign policy." Peace Research Society (International) *Papers* 14:15–30.

Salmore, S. A., and D. Munton, 1974. "Classifying foreign policy behavior: an empirically based typology," in J. N. Rosenau, ed., *Comparing Foreign Policies*. Beverly Hills: Sage, forthcoming.

Samuelson, P. A. 1965. "Some notions on causality and teleology in economics," pp. 99–143 in D. Lerner, ed., *Cause and Effect*. New York: Free Press.

Sartori, G. 1970. "Concept misformation in comparative politics." *American Political Science Review* 64 (December) :1033–53.

Sawyer, J. 1967. "Dimensions of nations: size, wealth, and politics." *Amer. J. of Sociology* 73 (September) :145–72.

Scheffler, I. 1963. *The Anatomy of Inquiry*. Cambridge: Harvard Univ. Press.

Schleicher, C. P. 1973. *Participant's Manual for Real-Nation Gaming*. Columbus, Ohio: Merrill.

Schon, D. 1967. "Forecasting and technological forecasting." *Daedalus* 196 (Summer) :759–69.

Schou, A., and A. O. Brundtland, eds. 1971. *Small States in International Relations*. New York: Wiley.

Schrag, C. O. 1967. "Phenomenology, ontology, and history in the philosophy of Heidegger," pp. 277–94 in J. Kockelmans, ed., *Phenomenology*. Garden City. N.Y.: Doubleday.

Schuetz, A. 1951. "Choosing among projects of action." *Philosophy and Phenomenological Research* 12 (December) :161–84.

Scott, A. M. 1965. *The Revolution in Statecraft: Informal Access*. New York: Random House.

Scott, W. A. 1965. "Psychological and social correlates of international images," pp. 71–103 in H. C. Kelman, ed., *International Behavior: A Social-Psychological Analysis*. New York: Holt, Rinehart, Winston.

Segall, M. H.; D. T. Campbell; and M. J. Herskovits. 1966. *The Influence of Culture on Visual Perception*. Indianapolis, Ind.: Bobbs-Merrill.

Sewell, W. H., Jr. 1967. "Marc Bloch and the logic of comparative history." *History and Theory* 6:208–18.

Sigler, J. H. 1972. "Reliability problems in the measurement of international events in the elite press," in J. H. Sigler, J. O. Field, and M. L. Adelman, *Applications of Events Data Analysis*. Beverly Hills: Sage.

Sigler, J. H.; J. O. Field; and M. A. Adelman. 1972. *Applications of Events Data Analysis: Cases, Issues, and Programs in International Interaction*. Beverly Hills: Sage.

Simon, H. A. 1969. *The Sciences of the Artificial*. Cambridge: M.I.T. Press.

Simon, H. A. 1957. *Administrative Behavior.* New York: MacMillan.

Simon, J. L. 1969. *Basic Research Methods in Social Science.* New York: Random House.

Singer, J. D. 1972. *The Scientific Study of Politics: An Approach to Foreign Policy Analysis.* Morristown, N.J.: General Learning.

———. 1969a. "The behavioral science approach to international politics," pp. 65–69 in J. N. Rosenau, ed., *International Politics and Foreign Policy.* New York: Free Press.

———. 1969b. "The level-of-analysis problem in international relations," pp. 20–29 in J. N. Rosenau, ed., *International Politics and Foreign Policy.* New York: Free Press.

———, ed. 1968. *Quantitative International Politics.* New York: Free Press.

———. 1965. "Data-making in international relations." *Behavioral Science* 10 (January) : 68–80.

Singer, M. R. 1972. *Weak States in a World of Powers.* New York: Free Press.

Sjoberg, B. 1955. "The comparative method in the social sciences." *Philosophy of Science* 22 (April) : 106–17.

Smelser, N. J. 1967. "Notes on the methodology of comparative analysis of economic activity." *Social Science Information* 6 (April–June) : 7–21.

Smoker, P. 1969. "A time series analysis of Sino-Indian relations." *J. of Conflict Resolution* 8 (June) :172–91.

———. 1966. "Integration and escalation: a study of the three world arms races." Northwestern University (mimeo) .

Snyder, R. C.; H. W. Bruck; and B. M. Sapin. 1962. *Foreign Policy Decision Making.* New York: Free Press.

———. 1954. *Decision-Making as an Approach to the Study of International Politics.* Foreign Policy Analysis Project, Princeton University.

Sondermann, F. A. 1961. "The linkage between foreign policy and international politics," pp. 8–17 in J. N. Rosenau, ed., *International Politics and Foreign Policy.* New York: Free Press.

Sorokin, P. 1956. *Fads and Foibles.* Chicago: Henry Regnery.

Soroos, M. S. 1973. "Some methods of futures research." Paper presented at the Annual Meeting of the Peace Science Society (International) /Southern Section, Lake Cumberland, Ky.

Southall, A. 1965. "A critique of the typology of states and political systems," pp. 106–33 in M. Banton, ed., *Political Systems and the Distribution of Power.* London: Tavistock.

Sprout, H., and M. Sprout. 1969. "Environmental factors in the study of international politics," pp. 41–56 in J. N. Rosenau, ed., *International Politics and Foreign Policy*. New York: Free Press.

——. 1968. "The dilemma of rising demands and insufficient resources." *World Politics* 20 (July):660–93.

——. 1965. *The Ecological Perspective on Human Affairs*. Princeton: Princeton Univ. Press.

——. 1961. "Explanation and prediction in international politics," pp. 60–72 in J. N. Rosenau, ed., *International Politics and Foreign Policy*. New York: Free Press.

Stassen, G. H. 1972. "Individual preference versus role-constraint in policy-making: Senatorial response to Secretaries Acheson and Dulles." *World Politics* 25 (October):96–119.

Statistical Office of the United Nations. 1968. *Statistical Yearbook 1967*. New York: United Nations.

Stinchcombe, A. L. 1968. *Constructing Social Theories*. New York: Harcourt, Brace and World.

Suchman, E. A. 1964. "The comparative method in social research." *Rural Sociology* 29 (June):123–37.

Sveics, V. V. 1970. *Small Nation Survival: Political Defense in Unequal Conflicts*. Jericho, N.Y.: Exposition.

Tanter, R. 1972. "Explanation, prediction, and forecasting in international politics," pp. 41–57 in J. N. Rosenau, V. Davis, and M. A. East, eds., *The Analysis of International Politics*. New York: Free Press.

——. 1966. "Dimensions of conflict behavior within and between nations, 1958–1960." *J. of Conflict Resolution* 10 (March):41–64.

Taylor, C. L., ed. 1968. *Aggregate Data Analysis*. The Hague: Mouton.

Taylor, C. L., and M. C. Hudson. 1972. *World Handbook of Political and Social Indicators*. New Haven: Yale Univ. Press.

Thiam, D. 1965. *The Foreign Policy of African States: Ideological Bases, Present Realities, Future Prospects*. New York: Praeger.

Thorson, S. J. 1974. "National political adaptation in a world environment: toward a systems theory of dynamic political processes," in J. N. Rosenau, ed., *Comparing Foreign Policies*. Beverly Hills: Sage, forthcoming.

Toch, H. 1969. *Violent Men*. Chicago: Aldine.

Torgerson, W. S. 1958, 1967. *The Theory and Methods of Scaling*. New York. Wiley.

Toulmin, S. 1953. *The Philosophy of Science*. New York: Harper.

Tucker, R. C. 1967. "On the comparative study of communism." *World Politics* 19 (January):242–57.

Tufte, E. R. 1969. "Improving data analysis in political science." *World Politics* 21 (July):641–54.

United States Arms Control and Disarmament Agency. 1970. *World Military Expenditures 1970*. Washington, D.C.: U.S. Government Printing Office.

Useem, J., and A. D. Crimshaw. 1966. "Comparative sociology." *Items* 20 (December):46–51.

Van Dyke, V. 1960. *Political Science: A Philosophical Analysis*. Stanford: Stanford Univ. Press.

Verba, S. 1967. "Some dilemmas in comparative research." *World Politics* 20 (October):111–27.

Vital, D. 1971. *The Survival of Small States: Studies in Small Power/Great Power Conflict*. London: Oxford Univ. Press.

———. 1967. *The Inequality of States: A Study of the Small Power in International Relations*. Oxford: Clarendon.

Wallace, W. 1971. *The Logic of Science in Sociology*. Chicago: Aldin-Atherton.

Walsh, W. H. 1942. "The intelligibility of history." *Philosophy* 17 (April):133–35.

Waltz, K. N. 1967. *Foreign Policy and Democratic Politics*. Boston: Little, Brown.

———. 1954. *Man, the State, and War*. New York: Columbia Univ. Press.

Webb, E. J.; D. T. Campbell; R. D. Schwartz; and L. Sechrest. 1966. *Unobtrusive Measures: Nonreactive Research in the Social Sciences*. Chicago: Rand McNally.

Weede, E. 1970. "Conflict behavior of nation-states." *J. of Peace Research* 7:229–35.

Weinstein, F. B. 1972. "The uses of foreign policy in Indonesia: an approach to the analysis of foreign policy in the less developed countries." *World Politics* 24 (April):356–81.

Wilcox, W. 1971. "Forecasting models and foreign policy," pp. 385–402 in W. F. Hanrieder, ed., *Comparative Foreign Policy*. New York: David McKay.

Wilkenfeld, J., ed. 1973a. *Conflict Behavior and Linkage Politics*. New York: David McKay.

———. 1973b. "Domestic and foreign conflict," pp. 107–23 in J. Wilkenfeld, ed., *Conflict Behavior and Linkage Politics*. New York: David McKay.

———. 1972. "Models for the analysis of foreign conflict behavior of nations," pp. 275–98 in B. M. Russett, ed., *Peace, War, and Numbers*. Beverly Hills: Sage.

————. 1969. "Some further findings regarding the domestic and foreign conflict behavior of nations." *J. of Peace Research* 6:147–56.

————. 1968. "Domestic and foreign conflict behavior of nations." *J. of Peace Research* 5:56–69.

Wilkinson, D. O. 1969. *Comparative Foreign Relations: Framework and Methods.* Belmont, Calif.: Dickenson.

Winch, P. 1958. *The Idea of a Social Science and Its Relation to Philosophy.* London: Routledge and Kegan Paul.

Winch, R. F., and D. T. Campbell. 1969. "Proof? No. Evidence? Yes. The significance of tests of significance." *American Sociologist* 4 (May) :140–43.

Winham, G. R. 1970. "Developing theories of foreign policymaking: a case study of foreign aid." *J. of Politics* 32 (February) :41–70.

Wittkopf, E. R. 1973*a*. "Foreign aid and United Nations votes: a comparative study." *American Political Science Review* 67 (September) :868–88.

————. 1973*b*. "Putting politics back into Easton: the General Assembly and the Federal budget." Paper presented at the Inter-University Comparative Foreign Policy Project Conference on the Future of Foreign Policy Studies, Ojai, Calif.

Wolfers, A. 1969. "The pole of power and the pole of indifference," pp. 175–81 in J. N. Rosenau, ed., *International Politics and Foreign Policy.* New York: Free Press.

————. 1941. *Britain and France Between Two Wars.* New York: Norton.

Wolf-Phillips, L. 1964. "Metapolitics: reflections on a 'methodological revolution.' " *Political Studies* 12:352–69.

Wright, G. H. von. 1971. *Explanation and Understanding.* Ithaca, N.Y.: Cornell Univ. Press.

Wright, Q. 1965. "The escalation of international conflict." *J. of Conflict Resolution* 9 (December) :434–49.

Young, O. R. 1972. "The perils of Odysseus: on constructing theories of international relations." *World Politics* 24 (Supplement) :179–203.

Young, R. A. 1974. "A classification of nations according to foreign policy output," in E. E. Azar and J. Ben-Dak, eds., *Theory and Practice of Events Research.* New York: Gordon and Breach, forthcoming.

————. 1970. "Prediction and forecasting in international relations: some theoretical isues." World Event/Interaction Survey Technical Report 5, University of Southern California.

Zelditch, M., Jr. 1971. "Intelligible comparison," pp. 267–307 in I. Vallier, ed., *Comparative Methods in Sociology.* Berkeley: Univ. of California Press.

Zetterberg, H. L. 1964. *On Theory and Verification in Sociology: A Much Revised Edition*. Totowa, N.J.: Bedminster.

Zinnes, D. A. 1972. "Some evidence relevant to the man-milieu hypothesis," pp. 209–52 in J. N. Rosenau, V. Davis, and M. A. East, eds., *The Analysis of International Politics*. New York: Free Press.

————. 1968. "The expression and perception of hostility in pre-war crises: 1914," pp. 85–122 in J. D. Singer, ed., *Quantitative International Politics*. New York: Free Press.

————. 1966. "A comparison of hostile behavior of decision-makers in simulate and historical data." *World Politics* 18 (April):457–502.

Zinnes, D. A.; J. L. Zinnes; and R. D. McClure. 1972. "Hostility in diplomatic communication: a study of the 1914 crisis," pp. 139–62 in C. F. Herman, ed., *International Crises*. New York: Free Press.

Contributors

Edward E. Azar was born in Beshamoon, Lebanon, in 1938. After earning his B.A. degree from the American University of Beirut (1960), Professor Azar received his M.A. degree from the University of the Pacific (1965) and his Ph.D. in political science from Stanford University (1968). Professor Azar has been a leader of the events data movement and one of the most prolific contributors to its growing literature. As an assistant professor at Michigan State University, he sponsored three conferences on issues in the collection and analysis of international events data, and continues to play an active role in the events research movement in his current positions as associate professor of political science at the University of North Carolina at Chapel Hill and director of the Studies of Conflict and Peace program. His publications in this area include "Analysis of International Events," which appeared as a special issue of *Peace Research Reviews* (November 1970), and *Theory and Practice of Events Research* (forthcoming), of which he is co-editor. He is editor-in-chief of the new quarterly *International Interactions* and has written *Probes for Peace* (1973) as well as a number of articles, including "The Problems of Source Coverage in the Use of International Events Data" and "Conflict Escalation and Conflict Reduction in an International Crisis: Suez, 1956."

Richard A. Brody was born in New York City in 1930. He received his undergraduate education at San Francisco State University (1958), and earned his M.A. (1959) and Ph.D. (1963) degrees in political science at Northwestern University. Dr. Brody was a fellow at the Center for Advanced Study in the Behavioral Sciences during 1967–68, and is currently professor of international relations at Stanford University. A co-author of *Simulation in International Relations* (1963), his many articles and monographs include "Some Systemic Effects of the Spread of Nuclear Weapons," "Public Opinion and the War in Vietnam," "Cognition and Behavior," and "Modeling Opinion Responsiveness to Daily News." Professor Brody has also been a leading participant in the Studies in International Conflict and Integration program at Stanford University.

Philip M. Burgess is professor of political science and director of the Behavioral Sciences Laboratory at Ohio State University. In addition, he is an associate of the University's Mershon Center and of the OSU-Battelle Academy for Contemporary Problems. He was born in 1939 in Lebanon, Indiana, and holds a B.A. from Knox College (1961) and a Ph.D. from the American University (1964). Among his publications are a number of articles and monographs, including "Alliances and the Theory of Public Goods: A Simulation of Coalition Processes" and *Elite Images and Foreign Policy Outcomes: A Study of Norway*. Dr. Burgess is past president of the International Studies Association's Midwest Division.

Maurice A. East was born 1941 in Trinidad, Colorado. After receiving his B.A. from Colgate (1963), he earned his M.A. (1966) and Ph.D. (1969) degrees from Princeton University. Dr. East is presently associate professor at the Patterson School of Diplomacy and International Commerce at the University of Kentucky. A frequent contributor to scholarly journals, his publications include "Factors Influencing Cooperation and Conflict in the International System," and "Status Discrepancy and Violence in the International System." Professor East has co-edited *The Analysis of International Politics* and is co-editor of the *Sage Professional Papers, International Studies Series*.

Charles F. Hermann was born 1938 in Monmouth, Illinois. Currently professor of international politics at Ohio State University, he serves there as associate director of the Mershon Center. Dr. Hermann collaborates with Maurice East on the Comparative Research on the Events of Nations (CREON) project. He received his A.B. from DePauw University (1960), and his M.A. (1963) and Ph.D. (1965) degrees from Northwestern University. His publications include *Crises in Foreign Policy; International Crises: Insights from Behavioral Research;* "Some Consequences of Crisis Which Limit the Viability of Organizations"; "International Crisis as a Situational Variable"; "Policy Classification: A Key to the Comparative Study of Foreign Policy"; "What is a Foreign Policy Event?"; and "The Comparative Study of Foreign Policy."

Charles W. Kegley, Jr., was born in Evanston, Illinois, in 1944. He received his undergraduate education at The American University, Washington, D.C. (1966), and earned his Ph.D. (1971) under the International Relations Program at Syracuse University. He was on the faculty of the School of Foreign Service, Georgetown University, prior to coming to the University of South Carolina, where he is currently associate professor and chairman of the International Studies Program. Kegley has co-edited *A Multi-Method Introduction to International Politics* (1971) and *After Vietnam: The Future of American Foreign Policy* (1971). Some of his recent articles and monographs include "A General Empirical Typology of Foreign Policy Behavior," "The Case-for-Analysis Problem in the Comparative Study of Foreign Policy," "Convergences in the Measurement of Foreign Policy Behavior," "A Circumplex Model of International Interactions," "The Transformation of Inter-Bloc Relations," and "The Dimensionality of Regional Integration."

Raymond W. Lawton is a research associate at the Behavioral Sciences Laboratory at Ohio State University. He was born in 1946 in Boston, and holds a B.A. from SUNY, Oswego (1969), and M.A. (1971) and Ph.D. (1974) degrees in political science from Ohio State University. He is co-author of "The Study of International Events Behavior" and serves on the staff of *Leads and Lags*, a periodic newsletter of the Foreign Policy and International Events Section of the International Studies Association.

Patrick J. McGowan was born in 1939 in Brooklyn, New York. He earned his B.A. from the University of the South (1961), his M.A. from the School of Advanced International Studies of Johns Hopkins University (1966), and his Ph.D. from Northwestern University (1971). Professor McGowan is currently an associate professor at the University of Southern California. He is editor-in-chief of the *Sage International Yearbook of Foreign Policy Studies* and co-author of *American Foreign Policy* (1973) and *The Comparative Study of Foreign Policy: A Survey of Scientific Findings*. His articles include "The Pattern of African Diplomacy: A Quantitative Comparison" and "Africa and Non-Alignment."

Michael Kent O'Leary was born in 1935 in Fresno, California. Currently professor of political science at Syracuse University, he is a member of the International Relations Program there. He holds an A.B. from the University of Southern California (1957), and an M.A. (1961) and Ph.D. (1965) from Princeton University. Dr. O'Leary has written extensively in the field of comparative foreign policy. His publications include *Congress in Crisis* (1966), *The Politics of Foreign Aid* (1967), and editorship of *European Views of America*. Professor O'Leary is author of many articles, among them, "Linkages between Domestic and International Politics in Underdeveloped Nations," "The Third World and American Politics," and "An Axiomatic Model of Voting Bodies." In collaboration with William D. Coplin he also has developed "PRINCE: A Programmed International Computer Environment," which is a computer-assisted instructional simulation. This simulation is described in *Everyman's PRINCE.*

Gregory A. Raymond was born in Irvington, New Jersey, in 1947. He received his undergraduate education at Park College, Kansas City, Missouri (1968), and his graduate training in international relations at the University of South Carolina. He presently is a faculty member of the political science department at Boise State University, Idaho. Some of his recent articles include "Armed Neutrality and the Nuclear Option: A Simulation Analysis" and "Spain and NATO." He is currently working on a quantitative indicator system for analyzing the formation and decay of international legal norms.

Robert M. Rood was born in Southampton, New York, in 1943. He received his A.B. from St. Lawrence University in 1966 and his Ph.D. in political science from Syracuse University in 1973. He is currently assistant professor in the Department of Government and International Studies of the University of South Carolina. He is also a research associate of the Institute of International Studies at the University of South Carolina. His research has focused on alliance formation and international conflict. His recent publications and papers include "Explaining War and Conflict: A Review of Contemporary Quantitative Studies," "Alliance Behavior in Balance of Power Systems," and "Flexibility in Balance of Power Alliance Systems and International War."

James N. Rosenau was born in 1924 in Philadelphia. Now professor of political science at the University of Southern California, Professor Rosenau received his B.A. from Bard College (1948), his M.A. from the School of Advanced International Studies of Johns Hopkins University (1949), and his Ph.D. from Princeton University (1957). Dr. Rosenau has been one of the most prolific contributors to the political science literature; a partial list of some of the major books he has authored or edited include *Domestic Sources of Foreign Policy, Contending Approaches to International Politics, Linkage Politics, International Politics and Foreign Policy, Public Opinion and Foreign Policy, The Analysis of*

International Politics, Comparing Foreign Policy, National Leadership and Foreign Policy, The Scientific Study of Foreign Policy, and *International Aspects of Civil Strife.* He has contributed to many scholarly journals and has led and facilitated the growth of the comparative study of foreign policy as a field of inquiry.

Richard A. Skinner was born in Savannah, Georgia in 1949. He received his B.A. degree from Georgia Southern College (1971) and his graduate training in international relations from the University of South Carolina, where he is now a research associate. His work includes "The Case-for-Analysis Problem in the Comparative Study of Foreign Policy" and "A Multidimensional Analysis of the Middle East Conflict System." He is currently conducting research with quasi-experimental designs for assessing policy impacts.

Eugene R. Wittkopf, assistant professor of political science at the University of Florida, was born 1943 in Algona, Iowa. He earned his B.A. degree from Valparaiso University (1965), his M.P.A. from Syracuse University (1966), and his Ph.D. from the International Relations Program of Syracuse University (1971). His publications include "The Concentration and Concordance of Foreign Aid Allocations: A Transaction-Flow Analysis," "Containment Versus Underdevelopment in the Distribution of United States Foreign Aid," "National Attributes Associated with Dimensions of Support for the United Nations," and "Foreign Aid and United Nations Votes."

Index